Equality, Participation and Inclusi

D0197756

- What are the experiences of children and young people?
- How can we think about the challenges they face?
- What systems and practices can support them?
- How can we develop greater equality, participation and inclusion across diverse settings?

This second edition of *Equality, Participation and Inclusion 1: Diverse perspectives* is the first of two Readers aimed at people with an interest in issues of equality, participation and inclusion for children and young people. This first Reader focuses in particular on the diverse perspectives held by different practitioners and stakeholders.

Comprising readings taken from the latest research in journal articles, newly commissioned chapters, as well as several chapters from the first edition that retain particular relevance, this fully updated second edition has broadened its focus to consider a greater diversity of perspectives. Whilst exploring how we think about the experiences of children and young people across a range of contexts it maintains a subtle, underlying emphasis upon education and the experiences of disabled people.

Drawing on the writing of academics, practitioners, children and young people, and people who have experienced exclusion, this book is a rich resource for students and practitioners who are interested in thinking about how inequality and exclusion are experienced, and how they can be challenged. Much of the material reflects on lived experiences and life stories, and will be of particular interest to those working in education, health, youth and community work, youth justice and social services, as well as to families and advocates.

Jonathan Rix is Senior Lecturer in inclusion, curriculum and learning at The Open University, UK.

Melanie Nind is Professor of Education at Southampton University, UK.

Kieron Sheehy is Senior Lecturer at the Centre for Childhood Development at The Open University, UK.

Katy Simmons is a Lecturer in inclusive and special education in the Centre for Curriculum and Teaching Studies at The Open University, UK.

Christopher Walsh is a Senior Lecturer in educational ICT and professional development at The Open University, UK.

Equality, Participation and Inclusion 1
Diverse perspectives

This Reader, and the companion volume *Equality, Participation and Inclusion 2: Diverse contexts*, form part of the Open University module *Equality, Participation and Inclusion* (E214). This is a 60-point module, which can be studied on its own or as part of an Open University undergraduate qualification.

Details of this and other Open University modules and qualifications can be obtained from the Student Registration and Enquiry Service, The Open University, PO Box 197, Milton Keynes MK7 6BJ, United Kingdom: tel. +44 (0)845 300 6090, e-mail general-enquiries@open.ac.uk

Alternatively, you may visit the Open University website at http://www.open.ac.uk where you can learn more about the wide range of modules and qualifications offered at all levels by The Open University.

Equality, Participation and Inclusion 1

Diverse perspectives
Second edition

Edited by
Jonathan Rix, Melanie Nind,
Kieron Sheehy, Katy Simmons
and Christopher Walsh

Routledge
Taylor & Francis Group

LONDON AND NEW YORK

The Open University

LEEDS TRINITY UNIVERSITY

This second edition published 2010
by Routledge
2 Park Square, Milton Park, Abingdon, Oxon OX14 4RN

Simultaneously published in the USA and Canada
by Routledge
270 Madison Avenue, New York, NY 10016

Routledge is an imprint of the Taylor & Francis Group, an informa business

Published in association with The Open University, Walton Hall, Milton Keynes,
MK7 6AA, UK.

Typeset in Bembo by Glyph International
Printed and bound in Great Britain by
CPI Antony Rowe, Chippenham, Wiltshire

British Library Cataloguing in Publication Data
A catalogue record for this book is available from the British Library

Library of Congress Cataloging in Publication Data
Equality, participation and inclusion 1 : diverse perspectives /
edited by Jonathan Rix...[et al.]. – 2nd ed.
     p. cm.
1. Inclusive education. 2. Special education. 3. Multicultural education.
I. Rix, Jonathan.
LC1200.E78 2010
371.9'046–dc22   2010018660

ISBN13: 978-0-415-58423-4 (hbk)
ISBN13: 978-0-415-58422-7 (pbk)
ISBN13: 978-0-203-83978-2 (ebk)

Contents

Acknowledgements

We wish to thank those who have written chapters for this Reader or who have given their permission for us to edit and reprint writing from other publications. Special thanks to Bharti Mistry and Christine Hardwick for their invaluable support in preparing these materials for publication. Grateful acknowledgement is made to the following sources for permission to reproduce material in this book. Every attempt has been made to contact the copyright holders of all articles reproduced in this book. If any requirements for the reproduction of these works remains unfulfilled, please contact the publisher. Those chapters not listed were specially commissioned.

Cooper, M. (1997) 'Mabel Cooper's life story', *Forgotten Lives: Exploring the History of Learning Disability*, ed. D. Atkinson, M. Jackson and J. Walmsley, Kidderminster: BILD. Reproduced with permission of BILD

Giangreco, M. F. (1996) "The stairs didn't go anywhere!": A self-advocate's reflections on specialized services and their impact on people with disabilities (an interview with Norman Kunc)', Physical Disabilities: Education and Related Services (*Journal of the Council for Exceptional Children, Division for Physical and Health Disabilities*) 14(2),1–12. Credit line: "EXCEPTIONAL CHILDREN by Giangreco, M. F. Copyright 1996 by COUNCIL FOR EXCEPTIONAL CHILDREN (VA). Reproduced with permission of COUNCIL FOR EXCEPTIONAL CHILDREN (VA) in the format Other book via Copyright Clearance Center."

Taylor & Francis Ltd for permission to reprint extracts from Heidi Safia Mirza, 'Race', gender and educational desire, in *Race Ethnicity and Education* Vol. 9, No. 2, July 2006, pp. 137–158. Reprinted by permission of the publisher (Taylor & Francis Ltd, http://www.tandf.co.uk/journals) and of the author.

Taylor & Francis Ltd for permission to reprint extracts from Taylor, Yvette, 'Brushed behind the bike shed: working-class lesbians' experiences of school', *British Journal of Sociology of Education*, 2007, 28:3,349 – 362. Reprinted by permission of the publisher (Taylor & Francis Ltd, http://www.tandf.co.uk/journals).

Taylor & Francis Books UK for permission to reprint McIntyre, D. (2000) 'Has classroom teaching served its day?', from *Routledge International Companion to Education*, edited by Robert L. Moon, M. Ben-Peretz and S. Brown, London: Routledge, pp 83–108. Copyright © 2000 Routledge. Reproduced by permission of Taylor & Francis Books UK.

Wiley Blackwell for permission to reprint Barton, L. (1995) 'The politics of education for all', *Support for Learning* 10(4), 156–60. Reproduced by permission of Wiley Blackwell Publishing Ltd.

Koninklijke Brill NV for permission to reprint Michael Freeman, Why It Remains Important to Take Children's Rights Seriously, *International Journal of Children's Rights*, 2007, 15: 1, pp 5–23. http://brill.publisher. ingentaconnect.com/content/mnp/chil/2007/ 00000015/00000001/art00002# Reprinted with permission of Koninklijke Brill NV and the author.

Children, Youth and Environments for permission to reprint "Youth Participation in the UK:Bureaucratic Disaster or Triumph of Child Rights?" *Children, Youth and Environments*, 2006, 16(2): 180-190.

Disability Awareness in Action UK (DAA) for kind permission to reprint Light, R. Social model or unsociable muddle?, www.daa.org.uk (accessed 19.7.02).

The Women's Press / Quartet Books for permission to reprint Crow, L. (1996) 'Including all of our lives: renewing the social model of disability', *Encounters with Strangers: Feminism and Disability*, ed. J. Morris. London: The Women's Press Ltd.

Taylor and Francis Ltd for permission to reprint extracts from Connors, Clare and Stalker, Kirsten 'Children's experiences of disability: pointers to a social model of childhood disability', *Disability and Society* (2007) 22:1, 19–33. Reprinted by permission of the publisher (Taylor & Francis Ltd, http://www.tandf.co.uk/journals) and the authors.

Swain, J. and French, S. (2000) 'Towards an affirmation model of disability', *Disability and Society* 15(4), 569-82. Reprinted by permission of the publisher (Taylor & Francis Ltd, http://www.tandf.co.uk/journals).

Taylor & Francis Ltd for permission to reprint extracts from Dorries, B. and Haller, B. (2001) 'The news of inclusive education: a narrative analysis', *Disability and Society* 16(6), 871–91. Reprinted by permission of the publisher (Taylor & Francis Ltd, http://www.tandf.co.uk/journals).

Taylor & Francis Ltd for permission to reprint extracts from Nancy Rice 'Guardians of tradition: presentations of inclusion in three introductory special education textbooks', *International Journal of Inclusive Education* (2005) Vol. 9, No. 4, October–December 2005, pp. 405–429. Reprinted by permission of the publisher (Taylor & Francis Ltd, http://www.tandf.co.uk/journals).

John Wiley & Sons Inc, and Wiley Blackwell for permission to reprint extracts from Culley L., 'Transcending transculturalism? Race, ethnicity and health-care' – *Nursing Inquiry* (2006) 13, 2 : 144–153. Reprinted with permission of Wiley Blackwell and the author.

Symposium Journals and the author for kind permission to reprint extracts from Linda J. Graham 'Countering the Attention Deficit Hyperactivity Disorder Epidemic: a question of ethics?' *Contemporary Issues in Early Childhood*, Volume 8, Number 2, 2007. www.symposium- journals.co.uk. http://dx.doi.org/10.2304/ciec.2007.8.2.166

Taylor & Francis Ltd for permission to reprint extracts from Pat Sikes, Hazel Lawson and Maureen Parker, 'Voices on: teachers and teaching assistants talk about inclusion – *International Journal of Inclusive Education*, 11, 3, 2007, pp. 355–370. Reprinted by permission of the publisher (Taylor & Francis Ltd, http://www.tandf.co.uk/journals) and the authors.

Taylor & Francis Ltd for permission to reprint extracts from Bentley, Judy K. 'Lessons from the 1%: children with labels of severe disabilities and their peers as architects of inclusive education', *International Journal of Inclusive Education*, (2008)12:5, 543–561. Reprinted by permission of the publisher (Taylor & Francis Ltd, http://www.tandf.co.uk/journals).

Emerald Group Publishing Limited for permission to reprint extracts from Virginia Morrow, 'Children's "social capital": implications for health and well-being', *Health Education*, 2004, 104: 4, pp. 211–225. Reprinted with permission of the publisher and the author. © Emerald Group Publishing Limited all rights reserved.

Scottish Executive for permission to reprint extracts from 'My Turn To Talk? The Participation of Looked After and Accommodated Children in Decision-Making Concerning Their Care' (Scottish Executive), http://www.scotland.gov.uk/Publications/2006/05/SpR–MTTT 1.23

Taylor & Francis Ltd for permission to reprint extracts from Deal, Mark, 'Aversive disablism: subtle prejudice toward disabled people', *Disability and Society*, 2007, 22:1, 93–107, Reprinted by permission of the publisher (Taylor & Francis Ltd, http://www.tandf.co.uk/journals).

Disclaimer

Every effort has been made to contact all the copyright holders of material included in the book. If any material has been included without permission, the publishers offer their apologies. We would welcome correspondence from those individuals/companies whom we have been unable to trace and will be happy to make acknowledgement in any future edition of the book.

Chapter 1

Introduction

Another point of view

Jonathan Rix, Christopher Walsh, John Parry
and Rajni Kumrai

A different approach

This is the introduction to the second edition of two books aimed at people with an interest in issues of equality, participation and inclusion for children and young people. The first editions were rooted in inclusive education and had a primary focus upon the experiences of disabled people in educational contexts. The second edition has broadened its focus to consider a greater diversity of perspectives and contexts, whilst maintaining those emphases from the first edition. This shift reflects a belief we tried to capture in the opening image of the last introduction:

> What are we looking at? There is a nearly empty mug of coffee on the desk. If you were to look and notice it, you would probably think, 'That's a nearly empty mug of coffee on the desk'. If you were to move your head a few millimetres and look again you would probably think the same thing.
>
> But what if you were painting a picture of that mug? Maybe, you'd think about the light reflecting off its surface … after all, it is shiny. And what if you were allowed to drink only one cup of coffee a day? Maybe, you'd look at that mug and have a pang of disappointment that it was nearly empty, ignoring its 'mug' nature altogether. And how about if you couldn't see with your eyes but used your fingers instead? Would you know how much coffee was in it just from its outside?
>
> However simple something seems, it will always appear different if you approach it from a different angle.

What are the experiences of children and young people? How do we think about the challenges they face? Who are they and how should we support them? Who should be responsible for supporting them? What systems and practices do we need to create greater equality, participation and inclusion across diverse settings?

Each of us approaches these questions from different angles and using different lenses, aware (perhaps after a reminder) that underlying every challenge and every solution are numerous variables which we cannot always know and predict, but have to be ready to acknowledge. After all, a mug of coffee isn't just a mug of coffee:

> Who made the mug? Who dug up the clay? Who shipped the clay? How much did they pay those mug makers? Where did the coffee come from? Why do people in the UK drink instant coffee anyway?

And, of course, each attempt we make to answer the questions we ask, leads to more challenges, contradictions and unknowns; opening up the opportunity for further enquiries.

This ongoing process of exploration is at the heart of our development both as the individuals we perceive ourselves to be and the cultures in which our perceptions are formed. Like the coffee cup and the coffee contained within it, we are a result of numerous social interactions across time and history. Our practices and developing nature in turn feed the contexts in which we are. The view we take, the questions we ask, are both created from and create the contexts in which they arise:

> A person develops through *participation in* an activity, *changing* to be involved in the situation at hand in ways that contribute both to the ongoing event and to the person's preparation for involvement in similar events. The focus is on people's active transformation of understanding and engagement in dynamic activities.
>
> (Rogoff 2003: 254)

How do we see children?

The way we view children could in many ways be seen as hypocritical. Why do we place them in buildings that are generally poorly accessible, with varying quantities and qualities of facilities, and group them according to ability and age (often sex as well)? Why do we formally and informally identify/label and/or withdraw some who do not achieve targets or are perceived to be inherently different according to relative physical, behavioural, emotional, cultural and cognitive parameters? Why do we offer access to narrowly defined knowledge, which focuses on the majority culture's traditional definitions of what is important to learn? Why do we present our information in one language, structuring learning within middle class norms of behaviour, and then require diverse groups of children and young people to demonstrate their understandings within a variety of highly standardised and time constrained parameters, whilst informing them that their futures depend on their results?

Adults are not viewed developmentally in terms of ages and stages, so why do we try to squeeze children into developmental pathways? We tell each other through government sponsored programmes, university constructed courses and media soundbites that children are some contained part of humanity which exists from around about ages 0–18. There comes a moment when this development ceases and a fully fledged adult emerges, capable, responsible and with meaningful rights. Yet, when we stop, when we think, when we question, we know that this is just not true. Some children are incredibly capable and responsible – if we give them the chance – from a very early age; some adults are not.

Can we start from here?

Although many settings are more attuned to issues of equality, participation and inclusion than they were in the past, change is still needed to ensure that all contexts are more equitable in their treatment of children and young people. There is a long list of concerns. We still witness many settings that only enable access for people who can walk; issues of intellectual access are rarely considered; services for groups identified as being in a minority are typically added on rather than being at the heart of the mainstream; many practitioners find themselves within structures that only pay lip-service to joined-up working and inclusion; there is no systematic awareness-raising about children's rights amongst children or adults; children are rarely influential at strategic planning levels; practitioners are inhibited by a steady flow of new policy requirements; many practitioners find it hard to work in integrated ways that link or join up services to collaborate professionally; huge amounts have been spent on information recording systems which ironically take practitioners away from front-line work; the numbers of looked after children has been on the rise, with those in care more likely to end up arrested, pregnant, unemployed or homeless; exclusionary action is taken far more often against individuals from minority ethnic groups than those from the ethnic majority; numbers of segregated educational places have remained steady; many subjects within schools still involve streaming and setting; people with English as an Additional Language must still sit exams in English to gain any meaningful qualification; boys are more likely to get additional educational needs support than girls; children have no voice in defining and developing their schools and their learning; and the list does not stop there ...

These inequitable settings across the UK are not going to be changed completely or quickly. This is neither surprising nor something that we should demand. What they should change to and how they should change is open to debate. There is not a perfect system awaiting us on the shelf. What there is, instead, is a whole raft of best practice principles and processes from which we can choose. Applied research shows us many ways forward that can break down barriers to access, learning and services to increase the chances of participation and inclusion for diverse groups of children and young people. These best practice principles and processes are not going to lead us to one model of inclusion and equity, however. They will allow settings and contexts to respond to the differing circumstances in which they operate in the manner most suitable to the people within them and served by them. This has been recognised for some time:

> It is possible, indeed highly likely, that there is no single best structural solution for any given set of principles of good practice. There may be instead a range of possible solutions that represent various adaptations of principles of good practice to particular conditions.
>
> (Elmore 1995: 370)

Our chances of achieving structures and procedures that are responsive to individuals means we must not be wedded to any aspects of the system as it presently stands. We must be prepared to adapt to the circumstances, in a way that takes account of its ongoing impact on those affected. To develop in this way requires a great deal of flexibility. Our systems need to be capable of adapting and continuing to be adaptive without diminishing their cohesiveness or accountability. This is a tall order, but one that we can move towards.

Nearly everything about the construction of our current social system is based on separation and segregation. It is not a system which is as well suited to the delivery of equality, participation and inclusion. It is not going to be changed completely or overnight, but change is necessary. Importantly, we can influence changes to the system by drawing on the whole raft of best practices and processes which are currently being delivered across services, professions and contexts. These successful practices often require teamwork and the building up and maintaining of relationships and trust. This kind of work allows systems to be flexible without diminishing their organisational coherence or accountability and without retreating to tick-box criteria and top-down targets. It requires us to consider and understand the perspectives of those who are affected by and who affect the system's structures and processes.

This book is an opportunity to explore some of those perspectives. It brings together the voices and ideas of some of those who have been or are currently excluded from and frequently disabled by the education system and wider social structures. It incorporates the work of activists and researchers, theorists and practitioners. It presents personal experiences and reflections alongside socio-cultural analysis. It considers the development of ideas and beliefs and their application in the past, present and future; and it presents warnings and possibilities to guide and motivate both our thinking and the policies and actions we undertake in the delivery of services to children and young people in the coming years.

A collection of perspectives

This book is divided into five sections. In the opening section, *Looking back: A personal experience*, four writers (Mabel Cooper, Micheal Giangreco, Heidi Mirza and Yvette Taylor) look back at the systems and processes used in their education. We see how some aspects of the system supported a positive vision of the writers' individual identities, but more typically supported the negative. It is quite clear how systems highlighted their differences to some aspirational norm, and how informal networks within and beyond those systems could exacerbate or counteract the dislocation and limited sense of worth and possibility which the authors felt.

The second section, *Looking forwards: The development of new thinking*, is premised upon the need for a vision to drive change. The first two chapters (Donald McIntyre and Len Barton) mark a point in history, looking at the pitfalls of the education system and why it needs to change. The next two chapters (Michael Freeman, and Emily Middleton) help us to consider the importance of children's rights and the participation of children and young people across social settings. These chapters remind us that we need to accept all individuals having control of their own lives, having a say in the running of organisations that represent them and affecting the processes of the institutions that dominate much of what happens to them and around them.

The first four chapters in section three *Looking from within: Barriers and opportunities*, present their authors' perspectives as disabled people, or seek to represent the views of disabled people. The authors (Richard Light, Liz Crow, Clare Connors, Kirsten Stalker, John Swain and Sally French) explore the ways and means by which we describe our society and the practices and people within it, examining in particular the development of the social model of disability, its future and its possible evolution. The last four chapters in this section (Bruce Dorries, Beth Haller, Nancy Rice, Lorraine Culley and Linda Graham) examine how the ways in which we think about and describe difference can create barriers and opportunities for children and young people.

The fourth section, *Looking from within: The experience of inclusion*, has a specific focus upon the experiences of individuals within classrooms (Joy Jarvis, Indra Sinka Alessandra Iantaffi, Pat Sikes, Hazel Lawson and Maureen Parker). The chapters force us to question how we should best come to understand individuals' attitudes towards differing models and ideas, and remind us that often the responses we hear may not be the ones which sit comfortably with our own notions of what is and what isn't inclusive. The section concludes however with a chapter (Judy Bentley) which reaffirms our need to trust the children and young people within our schools and respect those who are frequently seen as the hardest to include.

In the final section, *Looking around us: A broader experience* we consider children's experiences in the wider community and with professionals (Virginia Morrow and Children in Scotland) and conclude with two chapters (Mark Deal, Jonathan Rix and Kieron Sheehy) which encourage us to examine our hidden assumptions and ways of seeing that may lead us to constrain other people. They provide us with ways to recognise that the development of the individual and the collective is an ongoing, interdependent relationship across time and contexts, and that the perspectives we bring to bear are paramount.

In editing this second edition we had to make some tough choices. It contains fourteen new chapters. Gone, for example, from this second edition are parental perspectives and the role of ICT. We did not remove these chapters because we felt they were no longer relevant, but because we wanted to include a more diverse range of issues and voices. This book is about *perspectives*. It is about learning from each other. It is telling us that if we wish to develop equality, participation and inclusion we must take time to explore our own views, to search out the views of others and to make sure that we listen to and act upon the issues presented. This collection reminds us that we all have multiple social voices. Our roles in the social context change across time and within different situations. This is a primary consideration when we are evaluating ourselves and when we are trying to understand and empathise with the people who share our systems, processes and day-to-day lives.

References

Elmore, R. (1995) 'Teaching, learning, and school organisation: principles of practice and the regularities of schooling', *Educational Administration Quarterly*, 31(3), 355–74.

Rogoff, B. (2003) *The Cultural Nature of Child Development*, New York: Oxford University Press.

Part 1

Looking back

A personal experience

Chapter 2

Mabel Cooper's life story

Mabel Cooper

This is Mabel Cooper's autobiography, constructed from tape recorded interviews. Her life reflects the changing policies and practices since the 1950s. As a child she lived first in a children's home and later in a long-stay hospital. Many years later she left hospital for a life in the community, where she became involved in self-advocacy. The telling of her story is a major landmark in Mabel's life. She hopes that it will inspire other people with learning difficulties to find ways of telling their own life stories.

Family

I didn't know at that time that I had anybody. A lady called Mary Mason, she was a nurse in St Lawrence's hospital, she helped me find my auntie. Auntie Edith. Then I went visiting her. She's still alive and I still go and see her sometimes.

I've got five cousins as well which I searched for when my auntie was taken ill. Auntie Edith gave me the number for them. One lives in Zimbabwe, in southern Africa, one lives in Croydon and the others all live in Bedford. I go and visit them from time to time.

It was a long time ago when I found my auntie. I was in the hospital then. She told me my mother had died. She was my auntie's sister. I don't know my father. My auntie doesn't know him. She said they were married.

My Gran lived in Croydon. My auntie moved and went to Bedford. My mother lived outside Bedford.

Childhood

When I was little I lived in another place like St Lawrence's, but it was just for children. This was in Bedford. It used to be run by nuns. And that had bars up at the windows as well, because they used to call them places madhouses. It was in Bedford. They haven't got it any more, they've vanished it.

I moved to St Lawrence's when I was seven, because they only took children what went to school in this home. And I never went to school, so I had to move. In them days they give you a test. You went to London or somewhere because they'd give you a test before they make you go anywhere. It used to be a big place, all full of offices and what-have-you. Because they said you should be able to read when you're seven or eight. I couldn't read, I hadn't been to school. That was 1952, I was seven years old.

The Hospital

First impressions

When I first went in there, even just getting out of the car you could hear the racket. You think you're going to a madhouse. When you first went there you could hear people screaming and shouting outside. It was very noisy but I think you do get used to them after a little while because it's like everywhere that's big. If there's a lot of people you get a lot of noise, and they had like big dormitories, didn't they? And the children were just as noisy, in the children's home, and they were all the same sort of people.

I went to St Lawrence's in 1952. I went to A2, that was the admissions ward. They didn't used to have many in there, they used to just take the new ones what came in. You were only there for about a week or two weeks. And they moved you on to another ward where there was all children. I stayed there till I was 15 and then I went to another ward where I was with adults.

There was bars on the windows when I first went to St Lawrence's, it was just like a prison. Of course it was called a nuthouse in them days, so it used to have bars on it. You couldn't open the windows. Well, you could, but not far enough to get out of them. You didn't have toys, no toys whatsoever. You couldn't have toys because they would just get broken and thrown through the bars in the window, and get caught in them.

It was big. There were lots and lots of wards. On the female side it was A to H. On the male side it was A to D. They all had about 75 people in. And then there was little houses on the grounds and they had about 50 people in.

School/work

There used to be children, there used to be two wards of children. One for little boys and one for girls. There was no school there, they only let you use your hands by making baskets and doing all that sort of thing. That's all you did. In them days they said you wasn't able enough to learn so you didn't go to school you went to like a big ward and they had tables. You just went there and made the baskets or what-have-you. Because in them days they said you wasn't capable enough to learn to do anything else, so that's what you did.

So in St Lawrence's they never went to school. They went and made baskets. If you didn't do that you went to one of the work places or in the laundry, or stayed in the ward and did nothing. As you got older you could stay doing baskets or you could go down the laundry or the workshops in the grounds. I made a friend of Eva and she did one of the workshops where I worked. I worked on the baskets. A lot of them used to stay on the ward, or go round and sit round on the field and didn't do anything. Because really, who wants to work in an old laundry? Not many people did that.

Some of them went out to work, where you'd go and try somewhere. Some of the people I used to be friends with did that. Gloria done it, my

Figure 1.1 St Lawrence's Hospital.

friend Gloria, because she was in hospital. She went to Purley Hospital and worked. She went out before me, she went out a long time before me. She stayed out, she never came back. If anything went wrong when they were out they used to go and pick them up, and bring them back.

Clothes

The worst thing was, I couldn't wear my own clothes, you had to wear other people's. Because you never, you never got your own because the beds were too close together, so you didn't have a locker or anything, you just went to this big cupboard and helped yourself. There might be six piles of dresses in this big cupboard. They had all the clothes in and you'd just go and help yourself to the clothes you want. I didn't like it, that you wasn't even allowed to wear your own clothes in them days.

Of course they had their own shoes, you couldn't wear your own shoes in them days, you had to wear their shoes and they were horrible. They made them there, in the hospital. You never went out for anything because they did everything in the hospital. The clothes were made in the hospital, in the sewing rooms.

They did everything there, they made their own bread and everything; they had a bakery. They had a farm. They used to have cows and sheep there.

Separation of men and women

On the male side you see they're different. The male side was different to the female side, there was more on the female side than there was on the male. There was a lot more on the female side. You couldn't mix with the men. You could go to a dance but you'd have men one side, women the other. You could dance with them, but they had to go back men one side, women the other side. Even in the dance hall there was two loads of staff in the middle, one full of women and one full of men, and you just danced around the staff in the middle.

The female staff were on one side, on one row and male on the other, and you just danced around them. You could go over and dance, and they had to go back to one side and I went back on the other.

Money

In them days you didn't have proper money. If they give you any money it's green, it's like little green coins. You can't use it outside, you can't buy anything outside, you could only use it in their canteen. You could just go down and spend it in the canteen. It was only for sweets.

Running away/hiding

If I got upset I'd just run away, for a couple of hours. You couldn't go out, so if I got upset I would just go off, and I would come back when I was ready. I wouldn't stay out the night or anything like that but I would come back when I was ready, and then I'd be all right. I would go round the field because their field is quite big at the back. And you could just sit there, there were seats and you could just sit and be on your own. And I'd come back when I was ready.

Life on the ward

Loads of people used to live in St Lawrence's. There were loads of them there. In a ward there was about 75, men or women – you couldn't get men with women. I was in a ward with 75 other women, and the beds were that small, they were that close to one another. Of course they had some in the grounds as well, and they had fifty in those places.

Because there was too many in the hospital they did no cooking in the ward kitchen. If you think, 75 in one ward, they couldn't do cooking in the wards. They had a kitchen there but they did no cooking. They couldn't teach you to do anything because there wasn't enough time for the nurses. They used to go off at half one and another lot used to come on and used to stay till nine, and then they would go off and a night nurse would come on. During the day there would be three different lots of staff.

The ward was blocked off, there was doors. You weren't allowed to sit on your beds. The beds were that close to one another, so you couldn't have anything private. I didn't have anything of my own, because they would get pinched, the other patients would pinch them.

Of course you wasn't allowed to stand on the corridors or do anything like that. If you didn't go into one of the workshops, or the laundry, or the basket making, or digging up gardens then you sat on the ward. Sometimes I did that, because it's all I knew. If that's all you know it's very difficult not to do anything else.

In the hospital you used to have to be in by eight, because of the night nurses at 9 o'clock. You had to be in bed by nine. If you wasn't in at 8 o'clock you'd have to go in one of the other wards and ask them to come and open the doors, especially if they haven't got a night nurse in one of the wards. In two of the wards they didn't have night nurses so if you wasn't in at 8 o'clock then you'd have to go and ask one of the other wards to open the door and let you in. You soon got told off in the morning if you did that. I never done that but it did use to happen. I stayed out of a lot of trouble, but some of the others did things what they shouldn't be doing, like staying out late. I don't think it's worth getting into trouble, you might just as well do what they want. And the day will come when you can go out and get about on your own.

You had to get up at half six, seven o'clock. In my time you didn't have choices. You just did as they said.

Meals

We all ate on the ward together, but not with the staff. The food was vile, I didn't like it. They used to bring the dinners up at 11 o'clock and they used to sit and talk till 12 or half past. The dinners were horrible. There was no choices. My friend Eva, she used to be one of the nurses, she used to heat it up for us.

Relationships

I made a friend and she used to work in one of the workshops in the hospital, and I used to go there. This was Eva. She was the staff, she was one of the nurses. Eva used to sit and talk to me sometimes but otherwise you don't get anybody because they'd say they hadn't got the time.

I made a few friends with some of the patients. There was Gloria, Gloria Ferris, I made friends with her. I still see her. I go out every Saturday with her.

A lot of them got married. I didn't have many men friends. I never had any visitors in the hospital, nobody at all, never.

I found my auntie because she wrote to me once or twice in the hospital. And I said I would like to visit this aunt and one of the nurses, Mary Mason, she said, 'Oh, I'll find out about it. I'll get a pass and I'll take you.' So she did. We phoned up, she phoned up auntie and I went to see her, and now I do go and see her regularly. She was living in Bedford then. She lived in London for a little while, and then she moved out of London and went to Bedford.

Trips out

You weren't allowed out of the hospital. You had to write up and ask could you leave the grounds. You had to ask the medical or write to the doctor and ask them. You couldn't just go across the road and look at the shops, it wasn't allowed not unless you wrote up and asked. I didn't go out because I got so used to not going out. You'd get lost if you're not used to it.

If you wanted to go out they would give you a card. And every time you went out, you could only go out from 2 o'clock till four. If you wasn't back by four then you would be in trouble. You could never go out on your own, you always had to go with somebody, like one of the staff. You could write up and get a pass for a Saturday afternoon, but you had to get permission every time. They would watch to see if you come in after four. If you didn't get back, they'd give you till six and if you weren't back then they would ring the police.

In the old days, you had to be very crafty, you had to be one ahead of them. You could get down the pipe. The pipes used to be very big and if you was on the third floor upstairs, and you went down on to the fire escape, there used to be a big pipe. You used to get down in that because it was wide, it was wide enough for you to fit. So they could get out of the bottom because the hole at the bottom was big enough for them to get out of. And it led you outside the gate which you couldn't get out of otherwise, because that was always locked.

You could go round the boundary. There used to be a big old church, it's not there any more they've built a school on there. You could go round the back of the church and by the fence there used to be an opening. We used to go out through that way and then get back in through that way. You could only get as far as the shop down the road, that was all. You could just go round and look, and come back again. At least it was something that you could do, till you got caught. I didn't do it much, I did it once or twice. Nobody else knew it was there.

In the hospital they used to have a church so you never went out of the hospital to go to church because they had one in there, on the corridor. I never went to church. I don't go now only because I can't read. And for me, it's ridiculous so I just don't go. In the hospital church the men sat on one side and the women sat on the other. They used to pass letters in through the church, underneath the seat the letters used to go. The women used to pass letters across. I never went to church so I never did that. You could go round the fields and, if there was no staff about, then you could do it that way but otherwise you couldn't.

If you went on holiday with the hospital you sat on the grass and didn't do anything. They just used to sit on the grass if it was a nice day. You didn't go on the beach or anything. We went to like a holiday thing and they had green huts and they used to go to them. They didn't used to take anybody else. They just used to take people from hospitals. We never saw anybody else because they didn't encourage it.

Punishment

They had a ward up in the hospital G3 and they used to put people in there. They used to get locked up. I never was in G3 because I never run away or anything like that. They used to make you wear your bed slippers and then you couldn't run away. The door was locked, but you could get out. If you got out though you couldn't get back in so you had to ring the bell. G3 was for women, D3 was for men.

Reflections

In them days if you had learning difficulties or anything that's where they used to put you. They didn't say, 'Oh, you could go into a house and somebody would look after you.' They would just say 'You, you've gotta go into a big hospital' and that's it. Years ago, if you wasn't married and you had a baby that was a disgrace and they would say, 'Oh the mother goes to a workhouse or a loony bin' as they had in them days, or the mother went into a workhouse or a loony bin and the child was put in care. I think that's why there was more women.

In the hospital if you wanted to do anything or to go anywhere it was so much of a bind because you had to keep asking someone to write for you, so a lot of the time I never did. I got used to the hospital. Not really because I wanted to be there, it was because that's what I knew. That's all you knew, you didn't know anything else not like I do now.

A lot of people, especially people like me, we always think if they didn't have enough money to keep us outside they would say, 'Right, you all have to go back in the hospital' and open them again. It's important they knock them down and then people like me and a lot more will know that won't happen. I think it worries a lot of people like me because they are still standing there because they could say 'OK, we're going to open all that again and all the people what were there go back up there.' Of course it saves them a lot of money. I know they have turned a lot of St Lawrence's off, they've built houses on there. Some of it's gone, but there's still a lot there.[1]

Leaving hospital

Whyteleafe House

Whyteleafe House was the same as St Lawrence's, the only difference is that it was a house. It was still a big place. It was no different because they still had nurses and what-have-you. You still had 50 people. It was all women. I shared a room with six others.

Whyteleafe House used to be for people what used to go out to work, they didn't take anybody else. And then they said, 'Oh well, we haven't got enough people now what go out to work, we'll have to change it and put other people there.' That's how I got to go to Whyteleafe House.

The hospital used to bring me in the car and they used to take me back to Whyteleafe in the car. I lived at Whyteleafe House, they used to pick me up at the house and take me to the hospital for the day. At night time they used to take me back. I never went on the bus that we go on now. If you didn't go out, like me and a few of them, you still had to wait for someone to go with you. Eventually I just said could I go and try myself and they said I could. I went by myself but they don't like it.

I was about 31 when I went to Whyteleafe House. I've been out of St Lawrence's 16 years now. I asked to leave. My friend, Eva, she wrote and asked. She said I might be able to cope a bit. She got in touch with the social worker what used to be in the hospital. If you wanted to go to work or anything then they would just get in contact with one of the social workers.

First impressions of the outside world

When I first came out of there I thought the children were midgets. People have laughed because they said to me, 'Was that the difficultest part of coming out of there and finding children are midgets?' I never saw children, only children in wheelchairs and what-have-you, not children running about and doing all the things they're doing. So really the children fascinated me, seeing them it really did fascinate me.

I'd never been on a bus or on a train. Because you never went. These are all the things you didn't do. It's not like ordinary people going out and doing what they want to do. In them places, you didn't. So going on a train or going on the underground all them are new to me. In fact going on the underground and on the moving stairs and all that is quite new to me. I'm used to the bus now because I go so much. I don't have to buy a ticket, I've got a pass.

Early days in the community

I lived with a family in Caterham Valley but she used to keep having nervous breakdowns. She used to be ever so funny. And then, because there was nobody in the house when I went home one day, I got frightened and ran off.

I went to Eva's house but I couldn't stay there so Eva phoned up and I went in where I worked, at the old people's home. I lived there, stayed there. I used to help look after the old people in Caterham. I used to help them do the cleaning. I lived there for a little while, and then they said, 'Oh, you can't live here any more.' They said, 'You know, it's not really for you.'

So I went to live with another lady, she had a Down's syndrome boy. A social worker, a man, decided this, but that was only supposed to have been for a short time. It was at Old Lodge Lane. I was there for a year and a half, then I went to Isabel's. I went because the other lady only wanted someone to play with her little boy and I didn't want to do that, not really. I don't want to keep somebody company.

When I first went to Isabel's she found me a morning job but they were again being a bit difficult because Isabel had to keep coming up and getting social workers to come and talk to them. I just gave it up. There was only me and Anne in the beginning at Isabel's. And then she said she was gonna have another one, and she had Gloria. Then they started to get more and more and more, till there was 13 living there.

I had my own front door key at Isabel's and she made sure always that you had money in your pocket. I had my own room and since I'd been at Isabel's I'd got my own telly and my own tape recorder. I stayed at Isabel's six years and a half and I thought, well, now it's time for me to adventure a bit more. Gloria got like me, she asked to move out of Isabel's because there was too many, like I did, and she went to live with two sisters.

I thought it was time I adventured. I got friendly with a lady called Anne Evans, one of the boarding-out ladies and a friend of Gloria's. I went to dinner one day with Gloria and Anne and I said to Anne 'Do you know I'm thinking of asking to move out of Isabel's? It's just too noisy.' There were 13 people then. I stayed as long as I thought I could stand it. And I said, right, this is enough, and I asked. I said to Anne, 'I am thinking of moving, definitely' and she said, 'Oh, leave it with me and I'll sort it out for you.' I went to a few places and I said no, and then I went to Mary's.

I've been at Mary's a year, gone a year now. I moved there in May 1992.

Life now

Mary is my carer now. She buys the clothes for me because I find that's difficult. Mary does it for me because my eyesight's not that brilliant and the writing's so small. I can't read the labels so Mary does it. Jean lives at Mary's, she's all right, she helped me write a letter last night. She can't walk very much but otherwise she's OK. So I've got Jean and I've got Mary, so there is people there.

Gloria lives in South Croydon with Nora. Nora is like Mary, a carer. So Gloria lives there and on Saturdays I go there to see her. We're good friends but I don't think I could live with Gloria. And I've got Flo, I've got quite a few friends what don't live, what hasn't been in hospital – but I've got some what have.

I go down the seaside, I go places. I just tell Mary I'm off and I go. Because when I first came out I had to learn to get on the bus and go to the places I want to do. I taught myself to go to Brighton. I had to. They showed me what train to get on. And then I didn't sit on the grass, I went to the fair because I like the fair. That was new to me as well. I even go to Margate. You have to go to Victoria and get a train from Victoria.

I joined People First two or three years ago, when Isabel asked me would I like to join. There were about ten people when it first started in Croydon, now there's loads. I didn't join in very much at the first time or for a couple of weeks, something like that. Then one of the men what was chairperson, he didn't turn up so they asked me would I take it on. So I said, 'Oh, all right, I'll take it on for one week.' And one week got more weeks than ever. This was last year sometime.

Because of being in the People First Group I went to Canada. That was the biggest conference yet, that was bigger than Mencap put together. That was good, Canada is one of the good ones. But I think I would have liked somebody else to come because it would have been more exciting with somebody else. Declan said it would have been nice for somebody else from Croydon to come as well. I do a few jobs for Declan, like going out talking to people, and help tidying their office, and doing all the little jobs they need to do on a Monday. Declan pays and keeps the money for me, so it pays for my trips and what–have–you.

The group I'm doing now is coming out in the community. Me and another fellow is going to do that, two days a week for three months. Two days every week, for three months. We've also been into one of the day centres in London but a lot of people, they don't understand. One of them we had to ask could they go out because she was making so much noise. But I said to them, 'You know, she must be allowed to come back again,' I said, 'because she's out this time she mustn't stay out, she must come back and join in.' They said, 'Could the carers come in?' and I said, 'No, not carers, just the people what's got the learning difficulty.' I said 'otherwise they're not going to talk.' So no carers. They talked about different things, they want more money to go to day centres.

Reflections on life now

Work

I had a job for a little while but I find outside work difficult. I don't think they understand really. I've had so much trouble with them I said I wouldn't work again. I just said I wouldn't do it again, I won't work, so I haven't worked since. I'm quite happy doing what I do.

Skills

At Isabel's there was too many to learn. I've learnt to do quite a lot with Isabel because of the cooking and that but I think because there's so many you don't get enough attention. It's just you might as well be back in the hospital. I think the smaller places are much better because I think the carer can help a bit more and she can teach you to do the things that you want, you should be able to do.

I can't fill in the forms yet. Mind you I'm going to the class and they're teaching me. I never learnt to read or write but I'm learning now. I think they should take people who've got learning difficulties in the proper school. I think they are starting to do that now.

Self-advocacy

I think being in a group teaches you you've got to learn to say what you want to say and not what everybody else wants you to say. The others feel the same. We've stopped the children, for starts. We've stopped them calling us names, the children don't do it so much. They used to call us horrible names, some of the names you would never dream of. They stopped it, even in Purley, and the teachers go with them now.

There's a little Down's syndrome boy, he comes off the bus to go home because he lives in Purley. And the children would not leave him alone, they used to tease him and everything, and he used to sit on the floor. They called him names, and they squirted water out of the window at me a few times and threw tins but they don't do it any more. That's because I told Keith and he said, 'Well, we'll write to the schools.'

It stops the children but then you don't stop the adults because they never learn. One Saturday I was with one of my friends and one of the women was so rude my friend was really shocked. This woman said, 'Bloody well get out of the way!' My friend was really shocked. It really did upset her because she said, 'You know, you have told me about it, that people are rude but I had to believe it to listen to it.' She had said, 'I'll come with you just to find out, to see what it's like.' And she said, 'It's damn disgusting that people ought to be allowed to do that.'

I'm more confident since I've been in the People First group. You do what you want to do and not get anybody else to do something for you.

I'm chairperson, but it's just the same as anybody else. You just help the people what can't do it for themselves.

Living in the community

It's hard for the ones what live out on their own mostly the ones what have the flats. They do miss out. I think they get a bit frightened. Living out in the community, a lot of it, even for me, was new when I first started, so how must they feel? For people what's lived in the hospital for so many years, and then expect them to live on their own, it's wrong. If they've lived with their parents and that, and they go into a flat and they have a little support, they're OK. But for somebody what's lived in a hospital all their life and then to come out and go into a flat, that's murder. To me that is murder because that's just like putting somebody out in the street. They put them out on their own in a house, or by themselves in a flat, and they can't cope with it. I wouldn't do it, and I don't see why anybody else what's been in a long-stay hospital has to do it.

If they lived with their mum, OK, because their mum could watch over them. But if they come out of a big institution like I have, or a few of the others, they are not going to be able to do it. Because they've always had it, they've always had somebody there. They need support and somebody to teach them to do the things they should be able to do. To put them in a flat is murder. And you could find them dead one day, and then say, 'Oh, why, how did it happen?' Because somebody put them in a flat by themself and they've never been used to it. To live on one's own it's cruel. They shouldn't put people what's been in a long-stay hospital on their own. I think that's the worst cruelty ever.

I've been taught to cook and everything because the places I've been in they've taught me how to do that. But if I had to go into a flat and pay all the bills and what-have-you it would worry me to death, and I think it would worry anybody else as well. I don't think they should do it. I think I would worry just a little bit for the bills and that because I wouldn't know what to do. I quite like where I am, I think I'll stay for a little while. I don't want a flat, I think it would frighten me. I think it would upset me, and the least little thing upsets me.

A lot of people might not like it, some of them not at all, but I'm quite happy as I am.

Note

1 The rest of the hospital has subsequently been demolished. Mabel was guest of honour at the party held to mark the end of its life.

Mabel Cooper's life story provides an important first hand account of a system that once segregated some children and adults from the rest of the community. It is inspiring for those concerned with inclusion as it shows that society's structures and practices can be changed, for the better, within one person's lifetime. As with other chapters in this book it highlights the importance of listening to, and learning from, those whose voices have often been silenced.

Chapter 3

'The stairs didn't go anywhere!'

A self-advocate's reflections on specialised services and their impact on people with disabilities[1]

Michael F. Giangreco

> The information included in this article is based on a semi-structured interview conducted with Norman Kunc by Michael F. Giangreco on July 4, 1995 in Montreal, Quebec, Canada. The interview was tape recorded with Mr. Kunc's permission and was transcribed. The contents include selected portions of that interview and have been reviewed by Mr. Kunc to ensure that his opinions and ideas have been accurately presented in his own words.
>
> Norman Kunc (pronounced Koontz) is a sought-after consultant and speaker on a wide range of educational, disability, and social justice issues. He was born with cerebral palsy and attended a segregated school for students with disabilities from the age of three until 13 when he was included in a general education school. Earning a Bachelor's Degree in Humanities and a Master's Degree in Family Therapy have augmented a lifetime of learning from his experiences of being labeled 'disabled' in North America. I have had the pleasure of being in the audience on a number of occasions when Norman has spoken, and each time I have come away with more to think about and act upon. His message is at times provocative and his insights are undeniable. Here is a bit of my afternoon with Norman Kunc.

Michael: Norman, thanks for taking time to sit down with me. Let's start by establishing what specialized services you received when you were in school.

Norman: Physiotherapy, occupational therapy, and speech therapy. Each specialist had her own room and they would pull me out of my classroom for a half an hour to an hour to get therapy, two to three times a week.

Michael: Could you tell me about some of your memories receiving those services?

Norman: First, I'd like to say that it's fitting that we are talking about rehabilitation issues on none other than Independence Day! To answer your question, I remember thinking that the physical therapy room was a very weird place.

Michael: Why do you say that?

Norman: They had all this strange equipment and weights and mirrors and bars. But the weirdest part of the physical therapy room was the staircase. There was this staircase with a handrail on either side but the stairs didn't go anywhere – they went right into the wall! The physical therapist would come up to me and say, 'Walk up the stairs.'
And I'd say, 'Why? They don't go anywhere.'
But she'd say, 'Never mind, walk up the stairs.' So, I'd walk up the stairs and nearly kill myself getting up there. When I got to the top the physical therapist would say, 'Good! Now walk back down the stairs.'
I'd say, 'Wait a minute! If you didn't want me up here in the first place, why did you ask me to walk up here?'

Michael: Did she give you a reason?

Norman: She would say, 'You want to walk better, don't you?' I didn't know any better, so I said, 'Yeah.' And what I learned at that moment in life was that it was not a good thing to be disabled and that the more I could reduce or minimize my disability the better off I would be. When I was in segregated school, I fundamentally saw myself as deficient and abnormal. I saw myself as inherently different from the rest of the human race. The implicit message that permeated all my therapy experiences was that if I wanted to live as a valued person, wanted a quality life, to have a good job, everything could be mine. All I had to do was overcome my disability No one comes up and says, 'Look, in order to live a good life you have to be normal,' but it's a powerful, implicit message. Receiving physical and occupational therapy were important contributors in terms of seeing myself as abnormal. Every part of my life, from the minute I was born, told me that I was abnormal, whether it was getting physical therapy, going to Easter Seal Camp, or wearing leg braces at night.

Michael: How did you react at the time?

Norman: Well I wanted all those things, to have a good life – so I ended up declaring war on my own body. It was me against my disability; and my disability was my enemy. I was bound and determined that I was going to conquer that disability.

Michael: How did you propose to do battle with yourself?

Norman: I turned into a kid that physiotherapists only see in their dreams. If they wanted me to do ten repetitions of a certain exercise, I did 20. If they wanted me to hold a precarious balance position to the count of ten, I held it to the count of 30. I was determined I was going to get to be a valued person. And if that meant conquering my disability, so be it.

Michael: These early experiences happened when you were in a segregated school. What happened when you went to a regular school?

Norman: I thought I could overcome my devalued status as a person with a disability by being in the regular school. At first the school administration wanted to send me to a special class for students with physical disabilities in a regular school about ten miles from my home. I said, 'The hell with that!' First of all, I wanted to go to the regular school in my neighborhood because, for me, I guess that represented being valued. Secondly, I was offended by the stigma of being in a special class. I didn't want all my non-disabled neighborhood friends to see me getting on that big blue bus for kids with disabilities. Why not just hang flowers around my neck with a sign that says 'crippled'. I wanted to avoid all of that.

Michael: From what you are saying it sounds like there were a lot of professionals who saw your disability but didn't see you as a person.

Norman: That's true. If I had to describe myself to you now I'd say that I have an undergraduate degree in humanities and Master's in family therapy. I got divorced, now I'm remarried and I live with Emma and two step kids. I like classical music and jazz. Having cerebral palsy is one small aspect of who I am: it's part of who I am, but it's not the defining characteristic that makes me who I am.

Michael: When people disproportionately focus on your disability, how have they treated you?

Norman: People make unwarranted assumptions about who I am as a person because of my disability. People in airports sometimes think I have a mental disability or treat me like a child. Sometimes they assume that I need their help. People sometimes assume that people with disabilities are asexual, have unresolved anger, are in denial, or that all of us must be lonely or sad, that our lives are filled with frustration. The fact is that a very small part of my life gets blown up into a very big part. Unfortunately, too many people see me as nine-tenths disability, one-tenth person.

Michael: What has been the impact of these assumptions on your life and the lives of other people with disabilities?

Norman: It makes you feel that you are not quite human. Almost like you have to earn your right to be human. In earning your right to be human, what do you get? Human rights! So when you are perceived as less than fully human, what typically are rights for non-disabled people become privileges for people with disabilities. It's like if you have a disability they are doing you a favor by letting you live in the community. As soon as I demonstrate I am mentally capable then I have earned my right into the community. I see this going on not only with people with disabilities but also around the whole issue of poverty. You have to demonstrate your merit. It's categorizing people as producers versus non-producers. When people see that I am intelligent and articulate, the message is, 'Even though this guy has a disability, he can make a contribution to society. Therefore we'll let him in!'

Michael: It sounds like what you have experienced is a classic example of what Marc Gold called the 'competency/deviancy hypothesis' where the more competent the person is perceived to be, the more others will tolerate deviance in him. Of course, even that language, the term 'deviance', is so loaded with negative connotations.

Norman: I prefer to think of my disability as type of diversity rather than deviance or deficiency; my disability is just one characteristic or attribute among many that make me who I am. People do not need to prove their worthiness. Obviously, what we are talking about here is a human rights issue. We need to establish the unconditional and inherent worthiness of people regardless of what combinations of diverse characteristics they present.

Michael: When did you start feeling as though your disability was a characteristic of your personal diversity rather than a deficiency?

Norman: Let me tell you a story from when I was a university student. One night I was at this pub with a bunch of my friends. At one point, one of the guys started imitating my voice. It surprised me and I didn't like that he was doing it. So, afterwards I went up to him and said, 'Why did you imitate my voice?'

He said, 'Because that's how you talk.'

I told him, 'Hey, I'm articulating my words. I'm using my voice clearly. I'm not drooling. You imitate my voice and my whole show goes out the window.' And he said, 'Norman, why are you trying to be non-handicapped?' And that caused a categorical shift in my thinking. We talked for a long time that night and went through a lot of beer. Finally it dawned on me that I had *the right to be disabled.* And rather than seeing my disability as a deficiency, I began to see it as part of the inherent differentness among people; it was simply a characteristic. I came to understand that it really was no different from any other characteristic like height or weight or race or gender. So to say it another way, prior to that incident in the bar, I saw myself as abnormal. You were the normal people, I was abnormal. You are all non-disabled, I'm disabled. I saw myself as categorically different from most of the human population. I was part of a group with all the other abnormal, deficient, broken, disabled people. Once that shift happened to me I said, 'Wait a minute, I'm part of the normal diversity of the human community. I'm normal in that I am diverse.' I began to think, 'Wait! Why has this small characteristic of who I am been used as a criterion to put me in a segregated school, to do this to me, to do that to me?' Everything that happened to me suddenly came up for evaluation.

Michael: Let me back up for a moment and ask you about your experiences receiving therapy services when you went to regular school. Did you continue to receive the same types of services to the same extent?

Norman: No, it pretty much stopped.

Michael: Who made that decision?

Norman: Well, I think the therapists actually made the decision because they thought I could do a lot of things, plus I wanted to stop anyway. Ironically, my speech improved the most the year I quit speech therapy.

Michael: It sounds like by high school you had strong ideas about what you wanted for yourself. Did those coincide with what your therapists thought was best for you?

Norman: I believe they *thought* they knew the best destination for me, but they were mistaken. The therapists usually saw the destination as one of two things. The more naive therapist often perceived the destination as being one of normalcy; to make me more valuable in society's eyes. So that was one destination. This may not even have been conscious to the therapists; I think it may have been unconscious.

Michael: Do you think people in special education and rehabilitation fields are professionally socialized and trained to think that way?

Norman: Yes, absolutely, but it goes beyond that. I think the field of rehabilitation is to people with disabilities what the diet industry is to women. We live in a society that idolizes a full and completely artificial conception of bodily perfection. This view of the 'normal' body tyrannizes most, if not all, women so that far too many women in our culture grow up believing that their bodies are inadequate in some way. The issue here is that I want professionals to think about the whole parallel between dieting and rehabilitation. That's why I always tell people with disabilities, 'Never do physical therapy with a therapist who is on a diet!' If she hates her own body, she'll inevitably hate yours!

Michael: You said there were two views. You talked about people who want to strive toward 'normalcy', whatever that is. What is the second view you alluded to earlier?

Norman: Now there may be some therapists who say, 'Wait a minute, I don't want to make people more normal. I want to help them function better so that they can do more things.' Although that seems to be a far more enlightened perspective, I still have serious concerns about it because professionals mistakenly equate functioning level with quality of life and that may not be what's going on for some folks. Professionals say, 'If I can help you function better, then your quality of life will improve.'

Michael: This is a very mainstream view. What are your concerns with that way of thinking?

Norman: If you think about it, non-disabled people often don't equate the quality of their own lives with their ability to function in a certain way, so why apply it differently to people with disabilities? Rather than functioning level, I think most people would agree that the quality of life has to do with important personal experiences, feelings, and events, like relationships, having fun, and making contributions to the lives of other people. If you think about the most meaningful moments in life, they probably don't have to do with your functioning level. I'd bet they have more to do with other things like getting married, the birth of your first child, your friendships, or maybe going on a spiritual retreat; they probably don't have to do with your functioning level. Ironically, developing relationships, the opportunity to make contributions to your community, even fun itself is taken away from people with disabilities in the name of trying to get them to function better to improve, presumably, the quality of their lives. So I didn't get to go to regular school and then I missed the opportunity to make friends. Why? Because professionals were trying to improve my quality of life by putting me in a special school where I am supposed to learn to function better. So they take away the opportunity for me to have friends and subsequently they actually interfere with the quality of my life.

Michael: Are you saying that people with disabilities don't need to learn to function better?

Norman: No. For me I guess the key is the difference between what I call 'ease of living' and quality of life; many people confuse the two. Ease of living would be something to minimize the physical struggle, time, or energy that has to be expended in daily tasks. But just because life gets easier doesn't necessarily mean that my quality of life has improved.

Michael: Could you elaborate on what you mean?

Norman: Sure. In our society I think that many people assume that if they make their life 'easy enough' that the quality of their life will naturally follow. So they focus on making their lives easier through earning more money, or getting a better house, whatever, assuming that this ease will bring about quality. Now, while I see ease of living as partially contributing to quality of life, I believe it's overly simplistic to assume that quality comes from ease. Instead, I think many things contribute to a quality life, like relationships, having a sense of belonging, fun, making a contribution, and to some degree, struggle itself.

Michael: In your presentations I have heard you talk about some very sensitive personal experiences you had receiving physical therapy and the impact it had on your life. Could you share some of those experiences?

Norman: When I was doing my Master's Degree program in family therapy, we did a section on sex therapy. We did exercises involving touch, comparing our reactions to those of people with sexual dysfunctions.

Jokingly I said to my sex therapy professor, 'I can teach it, just don't ask me to believe it.'

He said, 'What do you mean?'

I replied, 'I hate being touched.' At that time I was involved in a sexual relationship where I could touch the other person, but I did not like to be touched. About four months later we were studying the side effects of post traumatic stress disorder, specifically how it related to victims of rape and sexual assault. As we reviewed the symptoms, like resistance of touch, lack of trust, and all things they were talking about, I kept thinking, 'Yep, that's me.' Then I thought, 'Wait a minute? Why do I fit all these categories?' That's when I first made the association between sexual assault and my own life. My body carried the memory, and these discussions triggered me to think back to physical therapy.

Michael: Are you saying that you were sexually assaulted by a therapist as a child?

Norman: It depends on how you define sexuality. If you define sexuality as in a forced sexual act, then no. But if you define sexuality as it is being defined today, in terms of physical space, in terms of your own control over your own body, then yes, it was sexual assault because the ramifications for me were sexual around the whole issue of touch. What I am saying is that the very practice of physical therapy in some of its historically common forms can have abusive outcomes.

Michael: Could you elaborate on what you mean?

Norman: If you think about it, from the age of three until the age of twelve, three times a week, women who were older than I was, who were more powerful than I was, who had more authority than I had, brought me in to their room, their space, their turf. They took off some of my clothes. They invaded my personal space. They gripped me and touched me, manipulating my body in ways that were painful — it hurt. Some of the exercises that were done in physical therapy were very painful, others were threatening. For example, there was the one where you are sitting or kneeling on the floor and the therapist kneels behind you and pushes you in different directions forward, sideways. The stated purpose of that activity is to improve reactive balance responses, but when I do this with non-disabled people as a training activity they find it enormously threatening when a person behind them is shoving them, especially when they never know what direction they were going to get pushed. When I was in school, I didn't know I had any other choice than to go along with it. So when you think of it, what did I have from the age of three up? People, women, who had more power than I did, took me in to their space, they took some of my clothes off, touched me in ways that were painful, and I felt that I had no choice in it. To me it's a form of sexual assault even though it was completely asexual. It's the power and domination that is part of the abuse. It's important for professionals to understand and acknowledge the power differential that exists between themselves and the children with disabilities they are supposed to be serving.

Michael: Norman, I am sure you realize that there are many people reading this who would say that the therapy procedures you describe are done to people with disabilities for their own good, after all it has a medical basis and it's considered a 'helping profession'. How do you respond to people who say that there is nothing abusive about what therapists do, that they obviously have only the best of intentions for people with disabilities?

Norman: I am only speaking of my own experience, but my response has to do with the whole issue of intent. Sometimes people get hung up on my ideas because obviously the therapist does not have the same intent as a rapist. Obviously their intent is different, it's positive, but there still can be a similarity of action and a similarity of consequence. My problem is that we can minimize the significance of the similarity of the action and consequences simply because the intent was positive.

Michael: So is part of your purpose to have professionals rethink what their intent really is and whether it matches their actions and the consequences that follow?

Norman: There is a difference between caring and competence. Many human service professionals assume that because they care for people their actions are inevitably competent. As soon as you challenge the competence of their actions, you're seen as questioning their caring for the person. It seems that competence, in their mind, is inextricably interwoven with caring. And they say, 'But how could you say I'm sexually abusing this little boy? I like this little boy. I would never do a thing to harm him.' You say, 'Yes, I know you care for him and your actions may be cruel.'

Michael: So what do you say to well-intentioned professionals who want to be of service to people with disabilities?

Norman: We've got to slow down. First of all, very often the temptation of many professionals is to ask, 'Tell me how to do it differently,' rather than saying, 'Help me think about this.' I hope people come to understand the complexity of the issues. That's what I'm concerned about.

Michael: Is there other advice you would offer to people who want to reflect on their practice to improve it?

Norman: I tell teachers and therapists all the time, 'If you really want to work on professional development, keep a journal.' Spend a half hour every night and write about what your students are doing. You don't gain the ability to deal with the complexity of people just by acquiring an abundance of strategies. You gain the ability to deal with the complexity of people from the depth of thought. And many people avoid seeking depth of thought because they are too busy acquiring this endless library of disjointed strategies.

Michael: We certainly have a lot of strategies out there. Can you suggest any actions people can take to put them in some sort of perspective?

Norman: Read the stories of people with disabilities. Read the self-advocacy and disability rights literature.

Michael: If I am hearing you correctly, you are saying that there are no cookbooks, no easy answers about what is the 'right' thing to do.

Norman: That's right. It's the same as being a man in our male dominated society. At some point, as a man, I have to enter the world with fear and trembling knowing that I will, through my functions of power and privilege, do damage to women. I try not to, but I will. There is no recipe for me to say, 'If I do this, this, and this, I will be fine.' It would be nice, but it's not the way it is.

Michael: What do you hope professionals gain from hearing this perspective?

Norman: I hope professionals will recognize that the very nature of their role is an oppressor because of the massive power differential between themselves and the children they work with, or should I say 'work on'? The good news is there are things we can do.

Michael: Like what?

Norman: Everyone can start with themselves and draw on their own experiences. For example, as a man I need to listen to the stories of women. Not with my own arguments going on in my head, 'Yes, but, yes, but …' Instead, I need to listen to what it feels like to be a woman who fears for her own safety when getting out of a car alone in an underground parking garage. I need to really listen to that. I need to really hear that story rather than beating myself up with guilt or shame because men historically have dominated women in our society. I need to listen to that story in a way that overlaps with my own experience with fear as a person with disabilities. When a woman listens to my story about airline agents being overly condescending to me, rather than her feeling guilty and saying, 'Oh my God, I've done things like that to people with disabilities,' I would like her to listen to that story and remember a time when a car salesman or an auto mechanic was condescending to her: 'Yes dear, you wouldn't understand that.' Relating people's stories to your own experience is part of developing that depth of thought and reflection.

Michael: So how does one avoid being oppressive when providing specialized services?

Norman: First of all, I think all advocates have to be self-advocates. On Monday morning, the professional may not always do the best thing, but that is not the point. I think the question is not so much how can I guarantee not to do damage; the question is to recognize oppression, recognize the issues, and be willing to struggle with them.

Michael: What kinds of actions can you envision as an outgrowth of recognition of the issues, reflection, and struggle?

Norman: I can envision three different therapists reading this interview and in the most positive ways having different ways of coming at therapy. One may talk about it with her colleagues; another might change the nature of how she does certain exercises with a child; another might keep a journal to help her reflect on her work. All are relevant, but the important part is that they have listened to it and in some way tied it to their experience and then decided to take actions based on who they are as people, not as professionals, as people. I hope they will move forward conditionally, continuing to be cognizant that other stories may come up that will challenge them again; this is an ongoing struggle. Reflection, personal commitment, and the beauty of struggling with ambiguity is where real connections get made between people that raise them above the oppressor/oppressed scenario.

Michael: In that way will these professionals become better advocates for people with disabilities?

Norman: Let me back up a moment. My point was that all advocates need to be self-advocates. What I meant by that was I don't want professionals to advocate on my behalf believing that they now have this new found knowledge about what people with disabilities want. I don't want therapists to say, 'I've read ten issues of the *Disability Rag*' and then spout out all the politically correct jargon. No! I want therapists to tap into her experience as a woman, to tap into her experiences of being in a position of less power, to pull that whole experience of women's rights and their own oppression into that therapy room. So when a case conference comes up where there is some issue being raised around intervention, around touch, or whatever, I want her to tie it to her own experience and challenge things not just from the stories of other people, but from her own experiences.

Michael: Does that mean only people who have had some significant level of personal experience being oppressed can relate to the stories they hear from people who have been oppressed in other ways?

Norman: Do you mean, what do I recommend to you, Mike, as an able-bodied, straight, white, middle-class male? Listen well. I think people don't need to be members of an oppressed group in order to listen. I have met people of an oppressed group who can't listen. I think you are listening to my story more intently than many women have listened to my story. Sometimes I think I can get a short-cut with women or with African-Americans. I can use analogies about used car salesmen, diets, or racial discrimination.

Michael: Any final thoughts?

Norman: Just listen.

Note

1 Reprinted, with permission from Giangreco, M. (1996) '"The stairs didn't go anywhere!" A self-advocate's reflections on specialised services and their impact on people with

disabilities.' *Physical Disabilities: Education and Related Services*, **14**(2), 1–12. © Council for Exceptional Children.

We chose to include this interview for its powerful and challenging ideas, particularly about the personal impact of accepting diversity, rather than striving towards and enforcing standards of an artificial perfection. As with other chapters in the book, this chapter illustrates the damaging outcomes of seeing a person in terms of a single attribute or characteristic. Importantly, Norman Kunc calls for professionals to listen to the voices of others, and reflect on their own practice in order to transform it.

Chapter 4

'Race', gender and educational desire

Heidi Safia Mirza

In the government, media and public mind, the relationship between race and education is overwhelmingly negative. This chapter explores the ways racialized people, particularly women, have a positive and enduring relationship with education. This is in contrast to more pervasive talk in Britain where when we talk about people identified as being from Black and minority ethnic groups we think of underachievement, rising exclusions and low aspirations. Drawing on historical, archival, personal and research evidence, Heidi Mirza looks at the pervasive myths behind the link between 'race' and education and asks, 'Why is there a crisis in "multicultural education" in twenty-first-century Britain?

[...]This paper centres around three consuming issues which I address in my academic work. The intersection of 'race', gender and the relationship this has with educational aspirations, what I call 'educational desire'. Reflecting on my scholarship over the last 25 years I realize it has been underpinned by a need to ask a fundamental question, 'Why is it that those who are the most committed to education often struggle the most to succeed?' To answer this question, I bring together seven stories of educational desire. [...]

Telling stories is traditional in many cultures. The African Griot or storyteller uses the oral tradition to pass on tales from generation to generation. In India the Hindu *Ramayana*, with its miracle plays and parables, tells epic stories of the battle between the Gods for good and evil. In the academic world we use critical race theory which is based on situational and reflexive knowledge to illuminate hidden or marginal social realities. Stories are a powerful way to talk.

Story 1: the quilt

[...] In Tamil Nadu I met a woman who weaved and stitched. In the shameful face of vast capitalist profits of high street shops this woman made cloth for

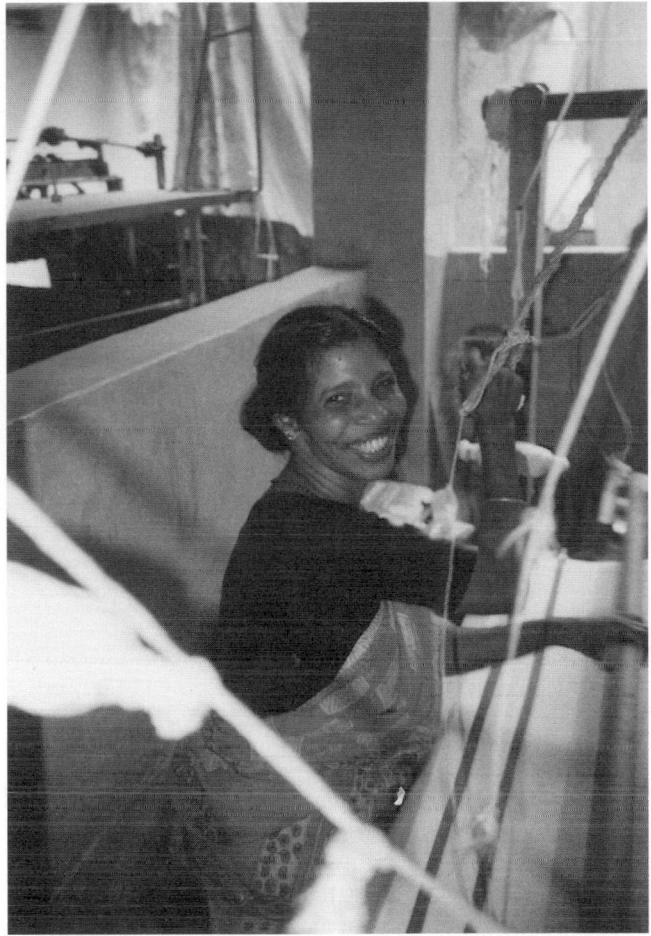

Figure 4.1 Woman weaver in Southern India at her loom, September 2004.

less than a dollar a day. She was so proud of her craft and showed me her loom where she sat for 12 hours a day. She asked for a pen for her children's schooling. She touched my soul. Why is education so important? A way up, a way out, a way to transform your life? What is the relationship between the marginal and dispossessed and the desire for education as transformation? I needed to know. I needed to find the answer.

On that trip I brought a beautiful quilt, a tapestry made of fragments of bridal dresses worn by the women who made it [...] Quilting is the art of stitching together pieces of cloth, fragments of memory, linking the past to the present and making it whole (Flannery, 2001). This has a powerful meaning for women across cultures and time. The women are marginal on the peripheries of their societies, yet in slow painstaking silent rhythm they take scraps of cloth making patterns for us to see. With care, warmth and love

Figure 4.2 Indian bridal tapestry quilt – Tamil Nadu.

they rework the quilt over and over again, remaking their story. The batting and back layers are unseen, but without them the patches have no foundation. When we stand back and look at their finished quilt the whole experience becomes coherent.

Black British feminism (Mirza, 1997), the framework that has inspired me, is like the quilt. It is about situated knowledges, building a framework for understanding whose stories we hear or choose to hear in the construction of our reality. The hidden voice of the women or the dominant paradigm of the powerful? We hear of policies, plans and acts of parliament but what can we see if we look at things differently? In so doing how can we build a new science of critical understanding that centres gender and 'race' as a critical space? *Black British feminism* asks critical questions about processes, relationships and power from the standpoint of women who are rarely seen and heard. We map hidden patterns in subjugated and suppressed knowledge, illuminate 'other ways of knowing'.

[...] In this paper I want to unpick the stitches and look beneath the patches, see the backing, and hear the voices which tell stories of educational desire among tails of educational despair in the women's struggle for themselves and their children.

Figure 4.3 My grandmother Theresa Hosein circa 1940.

Story 2: the Caribbean awakening

[...] In Trinidad last Christmas I visited a contemporary of my grandmother, Mrs Nobbee, now 92. She told me my grandmother had been the force behind the founding of one of the most prestigious girls' schools on the north of the Island, St Augustine Girls. I went to the sister school in the south of the Island, Naparima Girls. This picture here (see Figure 4.4) is how I remember it [...]

Yet it was my grandfather, one of the first local men to become a Christian minister on the island, who is remembered as a social reformer in our history. Not my grandmother, not his wife Theresa, one of the first 'bible women' who travelled the island to teach catechism to daughters of impoverished labourers, like herself. I was indignant and excited by this revelation! My grandmother must have been a feminist like me! A kindred spirit! But the things Mrs Nobbee told me did not fit my neat paradigm. She told a proud

Figure 4.4 Naparima Girls High School, Trinidad (circa 1960).

and different story of women's campaigning, not a story of radical women fighting for radical change. But a story about women working within the system. Conservative, traditional tropical 'genteel' women, schooled in Victorian colonial manners. They were trained to be good accomplished wives and mothers who cooked, sewed and sung hymns while doing algebra and Latin. They worked with the men to do the negotiating, and never asked, or got recognition. Women like my grandmother were transformative agents and educators. They worked not against the grain but within and alongside the mainstream, in order to challenge and change from within the structures and institutions in which they found themselves. As women they are too often forgotten souls in history of time.

[...] In the UK there are thousands of women and mothers who give up every weekend to teach their children in the Black community. Often becoming ill with overwork, they are the vanguards of change in their important work to 'raise the race'. [...] These schools are amazing places, set up by and for the Black community to 'supplement' the failing education system, they are hidden from the mainstream. They are autonomous, getting little or no state funding yet working alongside the mainstream. These schools have been core grassroots Black organizations since the 1970s. Here is a rare picture from this time.

[...]

Story 3: the Golden Fleece

[...] I heard a touching story about a Nigerian father who told his son to go to England and get educated. 'Leave,' he said, 'go in search of the Golden Fleece.' I think the idea of a Golden Fleece, a journey that transforms your life, is a useful way for us to think about the postcolonial educational experience.

My father and mother were part of the post-war migration to Britain. My mother came from Austria. My father from Trinidad. He was part of what John la Rose the Black activist and author calls the 'heroic generation' (La Rose, 1999). [...] He arrived in December 1950 and to keep warm he took hot showers in his bed-sit. His theory was the hot and cold made him lose his hair! He struggled to get into college, get a job and raise his family. It was a difficult time of overt racism. 'No Blacks, no dogs, no Irish' was the landlord's slogan of the day. He had a Muslim name and even in the 1950s, 50 years before the wave of Islamophobia after September 11, he had to change his surname to protect us, get a job and get a house. In 2005 my daughter too had to do the same, change her Muslim name just to get a job interview.

[...] When I came to England at 16 years old I was deemed a failure. They said I couldn't speak English and put me down a year. They even thought I cheated when I passed my entrance exams with flying colours. I had to remake my identity to succeed. I learnt to speak like them. But like bell hooks the Black feminist writer, I too kept alive in my heart and mind 'other ways of knowing' when I moved from the margin to the centre (hooks, 1990, p. 150).

[...] Young Black and Asian people are nearly three times more likely to be in university than their White counterparts. Though they are only 6 per cent of the working population they make up 15 per cent of students (NAO, 2002). Black and minority ethnic women are the highest participants of all – 60 per cent are in higher education, as are 48 per cent of ethnic minority men. I am privileged to teach many of these students here at Middlesex University. Young Black woman appear to transcend many obstacles and work their way through the cracks of educational opportunity in Britain. But what if these cracks are closing? A recent study by The Sutton Trust shows there has been little social mobility through educational routes since the 1970s (Blandon *et al.*, 2005). The expansion of higher education has benefited the middle classes, those who can afford to make choices. With the scrapping of grants, increasing tuition fees, and the realities of long-term debt, educational desire – the sheer motivation to succeed – is not enough if the structures and systems mitigate against you.

Many 'top down' schemes such as Widening Participation have been put in place to remedy the class bias in higher education. These schemes focus on motivating Black and working-class students to come in with the promises of access and support as the mechanism for change. But what about the cultural context of learning in ethnic communities? What about the complex interrelationship of educational desire linked to increasing debt? The issues are structural not cultural.

Inequalities are now inbuilt into the monolithic educational market system. You may want the Golden Fleece, but now it is more illusive than ever.

Story 4: the motherland

This is a hard story to tell, it is the story of racism and xenophobia in Britain. It is the backing on the quilt, the part we don't like to see but is always there giving shape to everything else. In this story we begin by asking 'How do mothers and fathers protect their children in a place where you are told you don't belong? [...] How do you protect your children and feel safe in a country where young people are still killed for simply being Black like Stephen Lawrence, among many others? How do you keep your dignity in a country where they spit at you in the street, where they whisper Paki under their breath (something I know about)?' In this story of the motherland, the Britain to which we came, Denise Lewis and Kelly Holmes, our Black female Olympians may wrap themselves in the British flag, and we may celebrate 'our multiculturalism' with chicken tikka masala, but as Gary Younge writes in *The Guardian* on the elections and immigration, there is still no sense of a truly inclusive Britishness [...] A haphazard and piecemeal resentful acceptance of the ethnic postcolonial presence. Now on the census you can tick the box to be 'Black British' and 'Asian British' (whatever that means), but after four generations here we are still not plain old English, Scottish or Welsh. This is the tightrope of multiculturalism, a balancing act. As the Black feminist Sara Ahmed (2004) has eloquently argued, multiculturalism is a 'love/hate' relationship.

If you show 'love' for the nation by not rejecting its 'hospitality', if you are not too different, not too outstanding, don't make too many claims – like insisting on wearing your hijab – you can be embraced and tolerated. All can belong in a state of 'mutual tolerance' as Roy Jenkins once famously said, if you accept the common norms, sign up for the citizenship test, and support the English cricket team. In the British Council lecture on Britishness, Gordon Brown, the then Chancellor of the Exchequer, talks of the golden

Figure 4.5 My parents, Ralph and Hilda Hosier; wedding picture, London 1956.

thread that runs through Britishness. The thread of liberty, tolerance, fair play, social justice and the rule of law. But, he argues, the shame of post-imperial national economic decline hangs like a shadow over any proud sense of celebrating these threads. This is what Paul Gilroy calls the British condition of melancholia (Gilroy, 2004). This is the backward looking nostalgia for Britain of old. [...]

Story 5: assimilating hope 1960–1970

Forty years ago there were many theories as to why Black children may not do well at school. In 1960s Britain Black children were bussed out to cool out and water down White fears whipped up by the conservative politician Enoch Powell during the racist Smethwick by-election, and the Notting Hill riots. It was believed the children of migrants needed to assimilate, lose their cultural markers and blend in. It was believed they were not only culturally and socially deficit coming from less civilized societies but also that they were inherently intellectually lacking. The now discredited pseudo-scientific IQ tests of Jensen and Eysenck claimed to show Black children were racially different and as such had lower intelligence (Mirza, 1998).

But 'natural ability' is still an issue. In what Gillborn and Youdell call the 'new IQism' (2000), the pressures of educational policy, such as league tables, causes the sifting and sorting of pupils into tiers and streams by perceived ability. The patterns are often racialized with Black children locked into the lower streams.

I was a little girl in the 1960s, but I remember being given a doll and asked which one I liked. Later refined into the Milner's scientific doll studies in the 1970s, the study suggested that if you chose a White doll rather than a dark one like yourself you were exhibiting negative self-esteem and low self-concept (Milner, 1975). This in turn affected your feelings of alienation and disaffection to be integrated and thus learn.

Does this seem improbable now? Work on raising achievement of young Black people through raising self-esteem is still with us today, though in its more sophisticated form of positive role models and mentoring. While it has been a lifeline to many young Black and Asian people who have been damaged by the effects of racism, we still need to acknowledge its roots in the cultural deficit model and understand its limitations.

Immigrants with English as a second language were also seen as a problem by the authorities. Not just, for example, Pakistani communities speaking Urdu, but also Patois speakers from the Caribbean. Thirty years ago Bernard Coard (1971) brought to light, in his seminal pamphlet, the scandal of disproportionate numbers of Caribbean children being labelled as educationally sub-normal (ESN). Many were deemed unable to speak good English and hence uneducable. They were put in special units, what were then called 'sin bins'. The Black Parents Movement was an important grassroots political response by the Black community to the criminalization and the wanton discarding of their children.

This seems long ago, surely it is not happening now? But now we have PRUs (pupil referral units). The issue that drives it now is the discourse on discipline and antisocial behaviour. As Tony Sewell (1997) has shown in his research there is no doubt that Black masculine peer pressure to be 'cool', urban youth culture and interracial gangs are issues for schools. This clearly relates to underachievement. However, there has been no attempt to decouple these issues of social control from the issues of 'race' and racism. David Gillborn's research shows we have effectively criminalized generations

Figure 4.6 Me, with my brother Gerard at our primary school, Balham, London 1962.

of Black children, particularly the boys, by not recognizing the subtle consequences of stereotyping, particularly what he calls the 'myth of the Black challenge to authority' (Gillborn, 1990, p. 30), which has seeped into the classroom and the consciousness of teachers. We find now Black boys are three times more likely to be excluded from school. It's an epidemic, a *real* crisis for the children and the parents.

Story 6: the multicultural dream? 1980–1990

Barry Troyna, one of our important educational theorists, called this period the three 'S's: somas, saris and steelbands (Troyna, 1992). It was an apt description of the day-to-day interpretation of Roy Jenkins's famous call for multiculturalism as, 'not a flattening out process but one of equal opportunity and cultural diversity in an atmosphere of mutual tolerance'. Aliya my daughter was at primary school then and we did a lot of sari wearing and bringing of food. Here she is with her class being an African bird (see Figure 4.7).

In the 1980s, about 30 years ago, there were the Brixton uprisings. Aliya was just born and we lived near Brixton. I remember being caught up in the riots. The hate was consuming, but this explosion of anger and frustration

Figure 4.7 My daughter Aliya (centre front) in her South London primary school 1985.

was also a watershed. The Scarman Report (1981) that followed uncovered the racism of the criminal justice system. The Rampton (1981) and Swann Reports (1985) on multiracial education showed educational underachievement had taken root, and for the first time linked it to socio-economic concerns of race and class. In this time dedicated scholars saw the visionary potential of multicultural education and engaged in radical, expansive and inclusive scholarship. [...] In a critique of existing theories and the limitations of the 1988 Educational Reform Act they called for a more coherent approach to multicultural education. [...] Schools make a difference, as does the curriculum, poverty and class inequality, and regressive colour-blind government policy.

The antiracist teachers movement also identified institutional and structural racism in the school system. Teacher expectations had always been at the core of theories on the self-fulfilling prophecy of how educational underachievement operates in a cycle of low expectations followed by low pupil outcomes. But 20 years on there is still no integral antiracist training for teachers; 70 per cent of newly qualified teachers say they do not feel equipped to teach pupils from different ethnicities (Multiverse, 2004). They may get an hour class on diversity in their whole training, and often I am the invited guest speaker! In the 1980s the right-wing backlash against multicultural education was all consuming. From the US to the UK they ridiculed any attempts at cultural inclusion as 'political correctness' and 'dumbing down'. Now, after the 2001 summer disturbances in the northern towns of Bradford and Oldham, Trevor Phillips, the Head of the Commission for Racial Equality, has also declared 'multiculturalism is dead'. It is argued it has led to segregation and caused ethnic enclaves, particularly in school, which have held young people back. But now in the government's sophisticated language of social cohesion and social inclusion – which embodies the notion of interfaith and intercultural understanding, citizenship and community engagement – we see again that communities must integrate and lose their cultural markers to become viable (Home Office, 2005). Is this a return to assimilationism? Has the wheel turned full circle? Are we back where we were 40 years ago? Is this just a new take on the same old problems? What is our vision for a *real* multicultural Britain?

Story 7: the difference of diversity: 2000–2005

We have entered a new era in 'race talk'. Now we talk of 'diversity and difference'. This has fundamentally changed the patterns on the quilt. [...] Now, in the wake of the identity politics of the 1980s, we celebrate our differences; being a woman, being Black, being Muslim, being gay. Discrimination based on gender, sexuality, race, disability, age and religion are now high on the legislative agenda.

This politics of recognition enabled those who had been marginalized to find a voice. It was a liberating time but not without its problems. It has been translated into a bureaucratic approach to diversity which monitors our progress and tracks our differences. We now have glossy brochures with our multi-coloured faces and wonderful policies and institutional statements that promise inclusion and change. But in reality, as a recent LDA report (2004) shows, there has been little progress toward equality. Good intentions remain locked in an institutional paper trail, unable to translate to our hearts and minds. Now we hear of diversity as 'good business sense'. We can expand the market more effectively by embracing difference. Diversity, we are told, opens up human potential and enables the best to excel. Ironically in the market place difference and diversity has led to the 'declining significance of race'. Now in a colour-blind approach we are told we are all the same. Fair treatment is based on merit. But what if we don't all have the same equal opportunities to get that merit?

In the story of education how does this notion of merit translate? Underpinning the Aiming High programme (DfES, 2003) to raise achievement

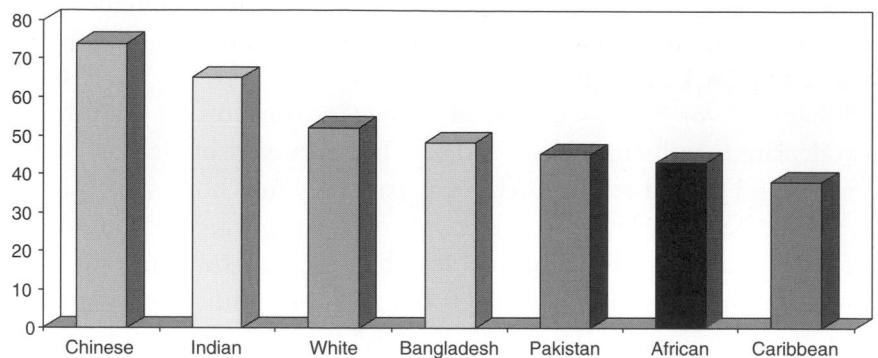

Figure 4.8 Percentage of ethnic minority pupils with 5 Grade A*–C GCSEs.
Source: DfES (2005) National Statistics First Release SFR 08/2005, 24 February.

for Black and minority ethnic young people, we see tables that chart hierarchies of difference between ethnicities (DfES, 2005).

Here we use the measure of getting five examination subjects at GCSE to rank ethnic groups in order of ability. It is seen as a good thing, with Indian and Chinese (the so-called 'model minorities') at the top and Africans and Caribbeans (the so-called 'failing' minorities) at the bottom. But what does this tell us? Some are gifted, others are not? Are Asians docile and hardworking (like coolies of the past)? Do Blacks have a chip on their shoulder and rebel (like uppity slaves of the past)? What do you think? What do we think? What do teachers think? We can ask, 'What about class, gender and regional difference in attainment?' We know these make a difference, but this complexity is rarely highlighted in the 'race' and achievement debate (Gillborn and Mirza, 2000).

Now, as in this graph, ethnicity and cultural difference have become signifiers for 'race'. This is the new racism. We have moved from biological notions of innate differences in the nineteenth century to religious, national and cultural notions of innate differences in the twenty-first century. It is as if cultural and religious differences are embodied in nature. In the new cultural construction of 'race', cultural and religious difference is played out when we say 'Blacks are good at sport, not so good at school. Chinese are good at maths, and make good food. Asians are good at business and love family life. Muslims cannot be trusted, they are aggressive, sexist and under all those clothes, usually a bit wild-eyed.' Racism in this cultural and religious guise seems less overt. We understand these differences. Recently a student said to me, 'What do you mean by "We"?' What I mean is the pervasive way *we* all talk about race, as if cultural and religious differences are fixed and immutable. It is a racialized way of being that infiltrates our daily language, personal interactions, professional practice, and what's more our social and education policies. [...]

Conclusion: where is the love? Towards a sociology of gendered aspirations

Where do these seven stories take us? There are always two sides to every story and the story of 'race', gender and education is no different. On one side is the harsh story of failure and being failed by the educational system. It is the story of racism and hate. But on the other hand educational desire remains hopeful and enduring. It is the story of love.

In my research women weave together stories of love, transcendence and hope. Hope, as Paulo Freire the Brazilian educational visionary says, is at the centre of the matrix between hope, indignation, anger and love – this matrix is the dialectic of change (Freire, 2004, p. ix). Like him I too argue for an understanding of the energy and commitment and love of education through teaching and learning as the mechanism for social change.

Plato argued education is fundamentally about love. Raimond Gaita the philosopher draws on this and tells us nothing goes deep in education unless it is under the inspiration and discipline of a certain kind of love. A teacher's privileged obligation is to initiate their students into a 'real and worthy love' for their subject, 'there is nothing finer that one human being can do for another' (Gaita, 2000, p. 231). The struggle for humanity, as the Black and Asian communities know, is fundamentally linked to the struggle for education. For a Black person to become educated is to become human. Franz Fanon the Black philosopher writes in his seminal text *Black Skin White Masks*, 'Nothing is more astonishing than to hear a Black (woman or) man express him (or herself) properly, for then they are putting on the White world' (1986, p. 36). Education in this sense is not about the process of learning or teaching; it is about refutation. [...]

If we look at the story of the racialization of education – where young Black men are three times more likely to be excluded and failed at school; where theories and approaches to Black and Asian educational underachievement have been based on low intelligence, cultural confusion, negative self esteem, alienation and bad behaviour – then the struggle for education becomes a battlefield. And if it is a battlefield, then the women are postmodern warriors. They are, as *The Guardian* said recently, a 'quiet riot' (Carter, 2001) strategically using their social and cultural knowledge drawn from their experience to educate themselves and their children. [...]

But is all this talk of love and new social movements naive, a Black feminist utopia? In the ideological and actual war against racism nothing stays the same, nothing is what it seems. You have to be contingent, strategic, strong and vigilant. When I was appointed to the Labour Government's Task Force on Standards in Education in 1997, David Blunkett, the then Secretary of State for Education and Employment, was interested in capturing the energy and commitment of the Black community to drive forward the schools standards agenda. Since then I have seen supplementary schools prevalent in the 1970s and 1980s decline as the government swallows them up and uses them to build its 'out of school' programmes. This is the new outsourcing. Just as the socialist Sunday schools set up by the working-class communities at the turn of the twentieth century were absorbed by the expansion following the 1944 Education Act, so too are these supplementary schools being absorbed by educational reforms to 'raise standards' since 1997. What goes around comes around. For the government, education is always a major election issue, but as Paulo Freire cautions, a dark cloud is enveloping education. When education is reduced to mere training, as is happening now with neo-liberal education markets, it annihilates dreams (Freire, 2004, p. 102).

References

Ahmed, S. (2004) *The cultural politics of emotions* (Edinburgh, Edinburgh University Press).

Blandon, J., Gregg, P. and Machin, S. (2005) *Intergenerational mobility in Europe and North America* (London, The Sutton Trust).

Carter, H. (2001) The quiet riot, *The Guardian*, 12 July, 8.

Coard, B. (1971) *How the West Indian child is made ESN in the British school system* (London, New Beacon Books).

Connor, H., Tyers, C., Modood, T. and Hillage, J. (2004) *Why the difference? A closer look at higher education minority ethnic students and graduates* (London, HMSO).

DfES (2003) *Aiming high: raising achievement of ethnic minority pupils* (London, HMSO).

DfES (2005) *National curriculum assessment GCSE and equivalent attainment and post-16 attainment by pupil characteristics, in England 2004*. Available online at: www.dfes.gov.uk/rsgateway/DB/ SFR (accessed 24 February 2005).

Fanon, F. (1986) *Black Skin White Masks* (London, Pluto Books).

Flannery, M. (2001) 'Quilting: a feminist metaphor for scientific inquiry', *Qualitative Enquiry,* l7(5), 628–645.

Freire, P. (2004) *Pedagogy of indignation* (Boulder, CO, Paradigm).

Gaita, R (2000) *A common humanity: thinking about love and truth and justice* (London, Routledge).

Gillborn, D. (1990) *Race, ethnicity and education: teaching and learning in multi-ethnic schools* (London, Unwin Hyman).

Gillborn, D. and Mirza, H. (2000) *Educational inequality: mapping race, class and gender: a synthesis of research evidence* (London, Ofsted). Available online at: www.ofsted.gov.uk (accessed 25 April 2005).

Gillborn, D. and Youdell, D. (2000) *Rationing education: policy, practice, reform and equity* (Buckingham, Open University Press).

Gilroy, P. (2004) *After empire: melancholia or convivial culture?* (Oxfordshire, Routledge).

Home Office (2005) *Improving opportunity, strengthening society: the government's strategy to increase race equality and community cohesion* (London, Home Office).

hooks, b. (1990) *Yearning: race, gender and cultural politics* (London, Turnaround).

La Rose, J. (1999) *Remembering the past forging forward to the future* (Crofton Park, Root and Branch Consultancy).

LDA (2004) *The educational experiences and achievements of Black boys in London schools 2000–2003* (London, London Development Agency).

Milner, D. (1975) *Children and race* (Harmondsworth, Penguin).

Mirza, H. S. (1997) *Black British feminism: a reader* (London, Routledge).

Mirza, H. S. (1998) 'Race, gender and IQ: the social consequence of pseudo-scientific discourse', *Race, ethnicity & education,* 1(1), 109–126.

Multiverse (2004) 'Exploring diversity and achievement', *Newsletter Issue 1,* February. Available online at: www.multiverse.ac.uk/ (accessed 21 March 2005).

NAO (2002) *Widening participation in higher education in England* (London, National Audit Office).

Rampton Report (1981) *West Indian children in our schools* (London, HMSO).

Reay, D., David, M. and Ball, S. (2005) *Degrees of choice: social class, race and gender in higher education* (Stoke-on-Trent, Trentham Books).

Sewell, T. (1997) *Black masculinities and schooling* (Stoke on Trent, Trentham).

Scarman Report (1981) *The Brixton disorders 10–12 April 1981: report of an inquiry* (London, HMSO).

Swann Report (1985) *Education for all: final report of the committee of inquiry into the education of children from ethnic minority groups* (London, HMSO).

Troyna, B. (1992) 'Can you see the join? An historical analysis of multicultural and antiracist education policies', in D. Gill, B. Mayor and M. Blair (eds) *Racism and education: structures and strategies* (London, Sage).

Heidi Mirza argues that by understanding the Black and Asian collective desire for education, we can begin to reclaim the meaning of education, reinstating it as a radical site of resistance and refutation, so evident in the postcolonial experience. She also shows us how we need to look for patterns in the quilt, patterns which go against the grain of formal social expectations. We have to 'see around the corners' and look at things differently, chart the hidden histories. Overwhelmingly, this chapter has been a story of the power of love to transcend the struggle for education. We need to hold on to our love, hopes and dreams, the fabric that makes the heart of the quilt.

Chapter 5

Brushed behind the bike shed

Working-class lesbians' experiences of school

Yvette Taylor

This chapter presents the experiences of women in schools grappling with class-based notions of femininity, the promotion of heterosexuality and the support of hetero-normative, middle-class families against, and in contrast with, their own working-class families, identities and experiences. Two interconnecting but relatively neglected issues in education, those of sexuality and class, are addressed in order to highlight the interconnections in living out these often analytically separated categories. This chapter draws upon research on working-class lesbians, based upon in-depth interviews with 53 women in the United Kingdom, and explores interviewees', mostly retrospective, class and sexual encounters, 'realisations' and resistances in schools.

[...] All of the women I interviewed reported being very conscious of class as children, manifest by accent, lifestyle and money, made apparent in school settings. Children, it would seem, quickly learn to reproduce wider social divisions and inequalities (Renold, 2000; Youdell, 2005). The sense of inequity, apparent throughout interview accounts, also featured in recalled childhood encounters between classed 'others': middle-class children who were treated better, expected more and often got it—from better meals and clothes to better attention and better grades. Many women spoke of the emotional impact of feeling and being reminded of their 'difference' through the class signifiers of appearance and housing, which often formed the basis of negative judgements. This highlights the common circulation and awareness of class signifiers and the use of these, which may in fact be in operation even without the explanatory language of class; women often reflected back on their 'pasts' and spoke about 'knowing', 'realising' and being 'conscious' of class while also being unsure and uncertain about what (classed) judgements 'were about'.

Correspondingly, in a similar vein of confusion, uncertainty and merging articulation, sexuality was variously enacted, denied and 'achieved' in school settings. For the women I interviewed, the 'best days of their lives' more often than not were not, and in recounting their experiences the dominant narrative was often one of hostility and struggle as opposed to football stickers and school trips. [...]

'Periods, poofs and pregnancy': sexuality in education

Instead of imparting knowledge and offering 'protection', many women experienced varied invalidations, confusions and uncertainties within schools, as a result of who they were. For many, recalling schooling experiences brought back memories of playground taunts, laughable or non-existent sex education lessons, and a sense of being let down and left out. [...] Experiences of poor or missing sex education lessons were recounted and, as a result, many interviewees had no language to express their feelings or to 'come out' as lesbians (Renold, 2000). At best sex education was taught in a brief and embarrassing one-off lesson, which emphasised heterosexual reproduction, with women across the age range reporting similar experiences, unfortunately suggesting a lack of improvement in this area. [...]

For all of the women in my study, learning about sex and sexuality was indeed experienced as paradoxical as they had to negotiate the in/visibility of heterosexuality as well as the formal silencing of lesbian and gay sexuality (Epstein, 1994). This silence contrasted with the very loud informal messages that many received in school playgrounds through homophobic taunts, indicating that children quickly learn and re-enact social norms, which have been both overtly and subtly conveyed to them, even if they do not fully understand them. Such 'policing' points to the powerful presence of an informal sexual 'subculture' within schools (Lees, 1986), suggesting that the women's realisations were mediated interpersonally as well as structurally. [...]

For many women an initial sense of difference was compounded by verbal and physical attacks, which went unnoticed and unpunished. In such circumstances, the 'correct', socially legitimised norm was quickly recognised. The 'right thing to do' is easy to recognise when there is little alternative. Lauren (age 18, Edinburgh) felt 'different' at school and this difference had to be managed: 'I just sort of said "Right I'm just going to have to, you know, grit my teeth and bear it."' This strongly illustrates the uncertain and unconfident awareness of sexuality and the (temporary) inability to resist expectations, which features throughout interviewees' accounts of schooling. Despite having the responsibility as knowledge providers, many women spoke of teachers who refused to tell them what a lesbian was—yet knowledge was somehow confusingly received, sometimes through the 'obligatory' (token) lesbian teacher. Speaking of her physical education teacher, Jo (age 30, Glasgow) says 'She was also a lesbian, by the way. Do you know the story?' The story always seems to be the same and yet must always be different.

Informal knowledge was subject to pressure, homophobic bullying and name-calling. Rumours also circulated, based on ignorance, about the illegality of homosexuality, producing fear, which served to generate conformity, as Rita remembers:

> I had a kiss with this girl in the school playground and they [school pupils] saw me and they told me it was wrong and that it was dirty and naughty and I would get locked up for it 'cause it was illegal. So I thought 'Shit!'
>
> (Rita, age 52, Manchester)

Apparently harmless questions about who had a boyfriend still caused many difficulties for interviewees in identifying their sexuality and claiming their difference. It is the playground catch 22—'Yes' makes you a liar in fear of being found out, 'No' makes you sad, stupid or highly suspect. Which is easier to live with? [...]

Many spoke of the negative consequences, such as isolation, of coming-out to themselves and to others while at school. Consequently, school was negatively experienced and many women excluded themselves or left at an early age. Many 'opted' not to spend time in a place where they were often hated, ridiculed or despised. Jo moved school when her sexuality became known (why stay when nobody really wants you?), whereas Jeannette was asked to leave. Jeannette feels resentment towards the school system, which should have offered her protection. Her situation reveals the classed process of exclusion—her working-class mother, unwilling and unable to confront the middle-class authority of the school, did not challenge her exclusion (see Ball, 2003; Devine, 2004). This is made more complicated by the fact that any protest would have required Jeannette to 'come out' to her mother; Jeannette's anger is recollected and, apparently, ongoing:

> I came out when I was still at school and I got kicked out of school, I didn't have much option. I was given an option to either leave or I had my parents come down, that was my mother, come down and discuss the situation. And things that were happening at home at the

time … It didn't really feel like I had an option to get her to come down and discuss my acting out because I was feeling isolated and scared I suppose … So I chose to leave, which then made me really quite angry 'cause up until then, the system had really worked fairly well for me in terms of schooling and, you know, achieving and stuff. It had worked ok. It was only when I started to come out and my sexuality became an issue that the system stopped working. So that made me really, really angry. I still get really angry about it … I think that's where class left me being working-class left me much more vulnerable to, you know, slipping out the system.

(Jeannette, age 39, Glasgow)

The events and situations recounted in this paragraph are a lot to pile on a teenager, especially one who is already confused and uncertain. No wonder getting out often seems a sensible option. Jeannette lacked support and affirmation from the school and her ability to challenge their views was constrained by her unwillingness to put more pressure on her mother, aware of the daily stresses that she already had to manage; she was then more vulnerable to authoritative judgements and devaluations, lacking the economic and social capital and time to contest this. The failure is not Jeannette's but she will have to bear the brunt of its impact. Leaving school at an early age has obvious implications for qualifications and subsequent employment opportunities (Taylor, 2005); it can begin a cycle of disadvantage that can be very difficult to break and that must be heartbreaking if the reason behind it is the unfortunate interface of class and sexuality. [...]

By resisting the official and middle-class ideology for girls in schools (neatness, diligence, appliance, passivity) and by replacing this with a more feminine, even sexual one, working-class girls have been seen to display both a class instinct and an awareness of the nature of gender oppression within school (Skeggs, 1997). In my study, working-class women were often 'marked' with (hetero-sexualised) meanings and expectations, as Kelly and Lisa suggest, and lacked the 'neutrality' available to their middle-class counterparts—although such neutrality is still gendered and disempowering.

Jude reports feeling different while at school not only in terms of sexuality but also in the ways that the story of 'the family', told at school, is a particularly heterosexual and middle-class version; alternative models are not validated because they are not spoken about or appear as pathological. For Jude, class is an *additional* problem, combining with her feelings about her sexual identity and causing greater uncertainty. To think you might be 'one of those' is difficult enough without the added burden of being from the wrong class in the first place. A hypothetical comparison is made with middle-class women and their struggles (or 'ease') in 'coming-out', although Jude notes the push towards heterosexuality across social class:

> What class does then in terms of sexual identity is that it, em, makes you feel even more insecure about thinking differently, because you don't have access to certain things that make you feel more normal … So if you were middle-class and didn't have the same degrees of deprivation if you like, then of course you're going to feel a lot more comfortable with the challenges of exploring your sexual identity. It's going to be a hell of a lot easier to do that, than to deal with two, em, two more things that impinge upon your self-identity.
>
> (Jude, age 31, Yorkshire)

The interface in this case is one of two issues coming together to produce a weighty burden. If you are stuck in the maze of being working-class in a society that normalises the middle-class experience, then it is going to be even harder to find the route to sexual acceptance within the heteronormative context. If certain voices are silenced and certain experiences delegitimised, then to be on the receiving end on both counts is quite something to deal with. It means that to come out, to tell the story of class and sexuality, you really are going to have to shout very loud to be heard and understood.

But many chose to avoid the issue of sexuality, which was easy to do in the context of formal silence. Identifications were mediated and constrained through these silences. Keeping your head down can become an art form, saying nothing to nobody about anything—ever. As Alice (age 25, Edinburgh) puts it 'As long as you kept it hidden you were alright. If you mentioned it out loud you'd get your head kicked in'. The silence on the issue does not mean it is not there. Instead, silence generates confusion and fascination, which, although reflected on with amusement, can be very distressing:

> I remember being actually so confused in school as to which one's 'hetero' and 'homo', that I'd gone to the library and tried to find a book. And I can remember in a maths class, they were going 'Are you hetero or homo?' and I didn't want to answer first 'cause I didn't know what one it was and they all said 'hetero', 'hetero', 'hetero', so the answer you've got to say is hetero but as I said it I felt like I was betraying myself, you know, not to put a homosexual label on it but just say what if I fancy you?
>
> (Mandy, age 22, Yorkshire)

Such processes are indicative of the enforced and acceptable identities apparent within schooling, creating confusion rather than clarity and generating feelings of shame and embarrassment. Positions, identities and confusions become structured through the educational curriculum, which operates with specific purposes and effects, apparent in the promotion of heterosexuality. Mandy spoke of the promotion of heterosexuality via sex education lessons: 'It was more like passing around condoms and how they fit and that'. The school sex education curriculum is thus not only about what is taught but how it is taught: this praxis in turn affords space for some possible identities and elides others (Thomson and Scott, 1991; Buston *et al.*, 2001).

Many respondents felt that their class position, and the consequent standards of schooling and expectations placed upon them, also limited opportunities. For example, Sharon speaks of (university) education as providing a safe environment to discuss sexuality and possibly providing alternative options through this. She notes the contrast between this taken for granted aspect of middle-class existence compared with her own progression from working-class background to heterosexual marriage:

> Well I think there's more opportunity for you to come out and meet your own full potential if you have ... have had the opportunity to explore yourself, emotionally, it's usually doing it through education ... I mean I was married at one point about a month before I was 18 but I knew I was gay but I thought 'Maybe every woman's attracted to women but you just get married anyway!' because it was never spoke about at school so if they said to me at school 'You can be attracted to women and that's ok' then I would have went 'Click'. Whereas I didn't want to ask. I think there is maybe a lot of women out there like me and then they get married and they don't particularly like it, don't like the sex of it but just put up with it for the sake of the kids. Then just get caught up with their everyday lives ... Whereas if you're maybe in a middle-class background and a woman and you're encouraged to go out and do education, when you go to college or university you're able to have the discussions and the talks with other women and realise 'Hey, there's nothing wrong with me'.
>
> (Sharon, age 47, Glasgow)

Sharon highlights the gendered and classed messages and assumptions behind socially sanctioned expectations, which impacted upon many women's ideas of what was possible and achievable. Her account also implies resistance and empowerment— Sharon is now speaking from hindsight. Societal expectations shaped future possibilities and opportunities and many respondents were adept at recognising their manifestations, conscious of the classed channelling of themselves as children. They were in effect saying 'if you are not offered the options, how can you make the choices, how can you realise what you could be?'

Have you thought about factory work?

[...] Schools are attached to particular areas—the 'catchment' area is also a classed area. Often schools in middle-class areas are able to celebrate the 'success' of their pupils, while schools in working-class areas, and their pupils, are deemed 'failures'—the old school tie can close as many doors as it opens. But although schools significantly contribute to generating inequalities, they are not the only or ultimate cause of them.

On reflection, many criticised the hidden curriculum operating in schools. Functioning subtly, often through unspoken mechanisms, schools make assumptions about the 'proper' place of their pupils based on class, race and gender, and school them accordingly (Mac an Ghaill, 1994; Skeggs, 1997). Many interviewees challenged classed expectations, making attempts to 'fight against the system'. But, lacking economic, social and cultural resources and capitals to entirely resist the authoritative devaluation of them, and facing a double depreciation via class and sexuality, they were often dismissed as angry, incompetent individuals; 'quiet at the back and less of your lip'. [...]

As well as being restricted by pre-conceived ideas regarding their abilities and social positions (their 'places'), several women spoke of being able to challenge these negative associations: there is no success like failing to fail. For example, Kelly (age 23, Yorkshire) insisted that she do 'A'-level mathematics, despite being warned that she was incapable and would fail. She effectively subverted their expectations and judgements, although not without a degree of emotional cost (and benefit): 'They made me sit on my own for two years but I got a C in Maths. I felt like I'd beaten the system.' Several women sought to challenge the low expectations of them by excelling academically, although they still had to manage the low provisions and resources. Dawn (age 22, Yorkshire), a 'high achiever' at school, speaks of her academic enjoyment of school, even though her school was 'rubbish'. Many women spoke of being 'let down' by the educational system, for example, Ali (age 42, Manchester) told how she was not allowed to do the re-sits offered to middle-class pupils because she got 'what she deserved', what was 'appropriate' for a working-class girl.

Some respondents were able to take advantage of patronising attitudes—but only if they were otherwise 'good girls'. Others suggested that, although they had made direct verbal challenges to teachers, this then served to reinforce existent low opinions of them, ultimately producing silence rather than debate: a situation where the 'gobby girl' in the corner is left to doodle in the margins. There was a careful path to negotiate, between the good/bad girl and the un/deserving poor, but 'advantage' was sometimes accrued through accepting 'patronising' help. For example, Sukhjit spoke of taking advantage of the patronising attitudes of teachers, but the 'advantages' were set against bitterness and anger, after all nobody likes to feel like an intellectual Oliver Twist:

> There was one woman she treated me like a *specimen* I think, like I was from a rough area and she was always very proud of me and I thought 'You twat' [laughs]. But at the time I just thought she was being nice but it was really patronising some of the stuff.
>
> (Sukhjit, age 29, Manchester)

There was also an awareness of a hidden curriculum operating within schools, in/validating certain experiences. The hidden curriculum may have more effect than the formal one in channelling children into social positions and in maintaining 'social cohesion', or social inequality. With the introduction of the National Curriculum in England and Wales, and with other provisions in Scotland, subjects are, in theory, open to both girls and boys, yet girls are in fact still channelled into certain subject areas, perhaps more so in working-class areas where there is an expectation that young girls will become (heterosexual) mothers with caring responsibilities (Mac an Ghaill, 1994; Skeggs, 1997). Teachers and careers advisors can make powerful and enduring judgements and can restrict pupils' careers; the 'hidden' curriculum can in fact be very explicit. Rita, however, challenges the lack of worth associated with working-class women's typical career options. Despite what she was taught at school, she has learnt the value of her own skills:

> When I was in school I was told 'Oh, you'll never amount to anything', 'cause I was always in the loos doing everybody's hair and I was being told off because in those days if you were clever with your hands that didn't mean anything, you had to be academic … They used to say to me in the high school 'You'll never amount to anything, there's no point you even bothering' … So I never learnt how to learn and I just wanted

to leave school and work. I grew up thinking I was stupid and only fit for hairdressing. Not realising how clever you have to be and how artistic, I'm a bloody good hairdresser.

(Rita, age 52, Manchester)

Much of the women's class awareness was formed through such painful judgments, exclusions and challenges, creating emotional and economic 'costs', which were daily experienced and moved through—and against. Such exclusion, pre-judgment and channelling made it difficult for many to positively claim their (classed and sexual) 'difference' (Dunne, 1997).

Attendance at middle-class schools, experienced by only three women, as 'placing requests', or as a result of being 'kicked out' of school because of sexuality, produced feelings of inferiority, due to the judgments of both teachers and pupils. In Cathy's case this resulted in silence, a fear of opening her mouth as well as being 'closeted' about her sexuality, vividly demonstrating another embodied intersection of class and sexuality. Cathy demonstrates failure to protect at an emotional level, portraying her previous working-class school as more physically 'rough', yet more comfortable. The exclusions within middle-class schools can often operate at hidden and underhand levels:

… 'Cause with working-class kids if you've a problem with someone you go out into the playground and beat the crap out of them and you sort it all out. Whereas those middle-class girls they've got a completely different way of dealing with stuff. It's all to do with ostracism and bitching and if they'd just get together and have a fight and sort it all out, you know. So it was just really hard for me to deal with that, going to the school where you had to act like a lady and I've just got this memory of being about 11 years old … so you've gone through this working-class school where everybody is pretty rough, into this middle-class environment where everybody's wearing little white gloves and they were handing out books in English class and I got my book and I went 'Sir there's a dirty great hole in my book!' and he just looked at me and went 'Catherine, the whole is neither dirty nor is it great' [laughs]. I didn't speak again for the next three years. I just thought 'Right, ok, I've got it now!' … All through my teens I was a closet case, 'cause I realised I was a lesbian when I was seven or eight or something, so that then affected it as well. I just thought, with all this other shit going on, I'm not going to announce it, I'm not going to draw attention to myself.

(Cathy, age 37, Manchester)

It is one thing to speak, it is quite another to speak and be accepted for that voice. Words mean different things depending on how they are pronounced and some women reported being told to speak 'properly', with the 'correct' accent. I speak therefore I am, but what happens when that speech—that being—is not quite right? The embodied aspects of class, such as accent and appearance, are clearly demonstrated, as are the enduring effects of these, which Cathy connects to (not) 'coming out'. It would seem that for Cathy the dominant recollection of her time at school is of not fitting in terms of class and so not even trying to broach the subject of sexuality. A double silence, a double discomfort.

Cathy's comments, like so many others, link the embodied and emotional aspects of class in school with the objective and material components, as charted throughout this article. A feature of all interviewees' comments was 'dealing with the consequences', managing and resisting the devaluations of them, their families, their areas—what they were, what they wore, where they came from, where they could go and who they could be, positionings to be negotiated, 'achieved' and resisted in terms of both sexuality and class. Such mediations affected realisations and identifications, moving between the 'obvious', the comparative 'other' and the socially il/legitimate.

I have highlighted the continued and enduring intersecting impact of class, gender and sexuality across family and school settings. A lot is learnt at school and not all of it is mathematics, English and chemistry. The experience of education stays with you, after all it takes up at least ten years of your life and that is a long time to feel undervalued, sidelined and written off. As the women I spoke to have clearly illustrated, the school system works on the common denominator, as long as it is not too common. (Working) class and (homo)sexuality are often perceived to be unwanted visitors at a middle-class hetero-normative educational tea party. This was clearly illustrated in the women's attitudes to and recollections of education and schooling. Their narratives of education are often narratives of 'failure' and missed opportunities; their stories represent the intersection of class and sexuality even if the official literatures often do not.

References

Ball, S. (2003) *Class strategies and the education market: the middle-class and social advantage* (London, Routledge/Flamer).

Buston, K., Wight, D. and Scott, S. (2001) Difficulty and diversity: the context and practice of sex education, *British Journal of Sociology of Education*, 22(3), 353–368.

Devine, F. (2004) *Class practices: how parents help their children get good jobs* (Cambridge, Cambridge University Press).

Dunne, G. A. (1997) *Lesbian lifestyles. Women's work and the politics of sexuality* (London, Macmillian Press Limited).

Epstein, D. (1994) *Challenging lesbian and gay inequalities in education* (Buckingham, Open University Press).

Lees, S. (1986) *Losing out* (London, Hutchinson).

Mac an Ghaill, M. (1994) *The making of men: masculinities, sexualities and schooling* (Buckingham, Open University Press).

Renold, E. (2000) 'Coming out': gender, (hetero)sexuality and the primary school, *Gender and Education*, 12(3), 309–326.

Skeggs, B. (1997) *Formations of class and gender* (London, Sage).

Taylor, Y. (2005) What now? Working–class lesbians' post-school transitions, *Youth and Policy*, 87, 29–43.

Thomson, R. and Scott, S. (1991) *Learning about sex: young women and the social construction of sexual identity* (London, Tufnell Press).

Youdell, D. (2005) Sex–gender–sexuality: how sex, gender and sexuality constellations are constituted in secondary schools, *Gender and Education*, 17(3), 249–270.

Yvette Taylor's chapter illustrates how expectations of young women in schools tend to be based on certain understandings of hetero-normativity, as well as their understanding of being classed. The tales told here also highlight the similarities and differences between working-class heterosexual women's and lesbian's experiences of schooling, and presents the multifarious ways working-class lesbians face an intersecting burden of class and sexuality, and a dual positioning as 'failures', even as they resisted and 'opted out' of (hetero) normalised positions.

Part 2

Looking forwards

The development of new thinking

Chapter 6

Has classroom teaching served its day?

Donald McIntyre

This is an abridged version of a chapter by Donald McIntyre. Given the importance of pedagogy in developing inclusive education we have selected McIntyre's discussion of how classroom teaching practices, developed over two centuries, are reaching the limits of their effectiveness. He highlights areas where change is essential and proposes a way forward.

Introduction: what is teaching?

Teaching is a relatively easy concept to define: teaching is acting so as deliberately and directly to facilitate learning. While *what* is done to achieve the purpose of teaching may be almost infinitely diverse, it is the purpose of these activities, not the activities themselves, which is definitive. Similarly, teaching of important kinds is undertaken in many different contexts and by many people in diverse roles. The concept of teaching has no implications for *where* or *by whom* teaching is done. It is only the purpose of the activity, that of facilitating learning, that is crucial to the definition.

This definition of teaching is of course a crude one, which might properly be the subject of various elaborations and qualifications. Yet the central truth that it offers is of much more than semantic importance, since it emphasises the point that, in a world where the importance of learning is beyond debate, nothing can be taken for granted about the importance of any kind of teaching, except its purpose of facilitating learning. Answers to the question of what kind of teaching is needed or is useful must always be contingent on answers to other questions, primarily about what will best facilitate the kinds of learning that we most want.

We have become accustomed to having various institutions designed for the facilitation of learning, and it is a matter of judgement as to whether it will be helpful to go back to first principles to question the value of any of these institutions. Two such institutions which each have a history of at least two or three millennia are those of *professional teaching* and *schools*. Arguments have certainly been offered, some decades ago, for questioning the usefulness of these institutions for the twenty-first century (Illich 1976; Reimer 1971). Yet the scale of the learning in which everyone needs to engage for twenty-first-century living makes the idea of doing without schools look increasingly like a romantic dream. For the purposes of this essay it will be assumed that schooling is necessary, and that professional teaching is necessary to make it work. But it will not be assumed that schooling needs to be organised as it was in the twentieth century. On the contrary, this essay argues that a more significant issue concerns the dominant way in which professional teaching in schools has been structured during the last century or two, and it asks how well suited that way of structuring professional teaching is for the contentious and problematic tasks which schoolteachers currently face. That dominant way of structuring professional teaching in schools is taken to be classroom teaching.

In raising this issue, the essay seeks quite explicitly to challenge current suggestions that the central issues facing schooling are to be construed primarily in terms of *teachers'* skills:

> Expectations of politicians, parents and employers of what schools should accomplish in terms of student achievement, broadly conceived, have been rising for over twenty years. And they will continue to accelerate as we take further steps into the information age or the knowledge society. [...] It is plain that if teachers do not acquire and display the capacity to redefine their skills for the task of teaching, and if they do not model in their own conduct the very qualities – flexibility, networking, creativity – that are now key outcomes for students, then the challenge of schooling in the next millennium will not be met.
>
> (Hargreaves 1999: 122–3)

While David Hargreaves' above diagnosis of the situation must be very largely correct, the argument here is that he, together with the British government, its Teacher Training Agency and many others, is wrong to suggest that the solution can be found simply through the further development of teachers' expertise. The general thesis of this essay is instead that, however hard teachers work, however sensitive they are to what is needed, however skilled they become, there are limits to what is possible through the classroom teaching system that we have inherited. Furthermore, we may be approaching these limits now, at a time when much more is being expected of schools; and so it is unlikely that expectations can be met except by going beyond the classroom teaching system.

The system of classroom teaching

During the last two centuries, and therefore during the entire history of public systems of schooling in most countries, classroom teaching has been the dominant form of schoolteaching. The most fundamental characteristics of classroom teaching are that a teacher is located in one enclosed room with a group – a class – of pupils for whose teaching he or she is directly responsible. Schools, on this model, are little more than organised collections of classrooms, with virtually all the organised teaching and learning being classroom based. Gradually, during the history of classroom teaching, there has been a trend towards classroom specialisation, with differentiation according to the subjects being taught in them: gymnasia, laboratories, art and music rooms, technical workshops of various kinds and latterly computer rooms. In general, however, these specialist spaces have been types of classroom, with the fundamental characteristics identified above, rather than alternative ways of organising teaching and learning. Libraries, and sometimes resource centres of a broader character, have tended to be the only places in schools other than classrooms designed for learning, but even these have rarely been designed for alternative ways of organising teaching.

Classroom teaching became the dominant pattern of schoolteaching in England after a long period of competition, in the first half of the nineteenth century, with the monitorial system, in which one teacher was responsible for the teaching of all pupils in the school, but only indirectly for most of them. Only the senior pupils were taught by the teacher, and they in turn were responsible for teaching their juniors. [...]

The dominance of classroom teaching has been such that, throughout the twentieth century, it was very widely taken for granted as the 'natural' way of organising teaching and schooling. It clearly has very considerable merits as a way of organising schooling, from both managerial and pedagogical perspectives. Managerially, it makes the individual teacher unambiguously responsible for the teaching and learning in his or her classroom; it allows pupils to be categorised tidily and allocated to teachers according to whatever variables are deemed appropriate: age, prior attainments, general or subject-specific ability, and/or course; and it allows teachers and/or classes to be matched with appropriate rooms.

Pedagogically, Hamilton (1986) informs us, it was attractive to early advocates of classroom teaching such as Adam Smith because it allowed direct two-way communication between the teacher and the pupils (currently known as whole-class interactive teaching) and because it allowed pupils to observe each other's performances easily and so encouraged emulation of the most successful. In some respects, it has also proved to offer a highly flexible framework for teaching, adaptable to group and individualised working, and to various kinds of practical as well as language-based activities.

Perhaps the key feature of classroom teaching as a system for schooling is that all responsibility for facilitating pupils' learning is concentrated on the individual teacher. Whatever has been decided or demanded by government, parents, headteacher, head of department or others has to be 'delivered' by the classroom teacher, who is unambiguously accountable for everything that happens in the classroom. This simple truth is, furthermore, not lost on the other inhabitants of the classroom: the pupils too learn quickly that it is the teacher who has total authority over their classroom activities and is responsible for facilitating their learning, which militates strongly against the development of learning activities not planned by the teacher (cf Holt 1969, 1971). As school effectiveness scholars are gradually coming to understand, the effectiveness of schooling under this system depends overwhelmingly on what the individual teacher, alone in the classroom with his or her pupils, is able to do.

Having been developed and adapted over two centuries, unquestioned as the appropriate way of delivering schooling on a mass scale, classroom teaching must be assumed to be the pattern for schooling in the future unless there are very persuasive arguments to the contrary. Here I shall aim first to understand something of what classroom teaching involves from the perspective of teachers themselves. Next, I shall consider some of the demands for development which schools are currently being asked to meet; and I shall explore the relationship of these demands to the nature of teachers' classroom expertise. We can then consider some of the possible implications for the future.

Life in classrooms

The above subheading is borrowed from the title of a book by Philip Jackson, published in 1968. It was one of the first and most influential of the many studies which, in the last 30 years, have sought very usefully to stand back from the question 'What ought teachers to be doing?' to ask the prior question 'How can we best understand what teachers do?'

One of the features of classrooms that Jackson noted was that they are busy and crowded places, which led to 'four unpublicised features of school life: delay, denial, interruption, and social distraction' (Jackson 1968: 17) and imposed severe constraints upon how teachers and pupils could work. Later investigators have picked up this theme of the complexity of classroom life. [...]

For example, the tension between 'covering' a set curriculum and preparing pupils for external assessments on one hand, and trying to teach for understanding or the development of autonomy on the other, can be a major complicating factor in teachers' work. Similarly, trying to ensure thorough learning while at the same time trying to 'sell' the subject can add to the complexity. And the ever-widening range of responsibilities given to teachers, for example for identifying pupils' special needs or possible symptoms of child abuse, or checking immediately on unexplained absences, makes classroom teaching an extraordinarily complex job.

How do teachers cope with this complexity?

It seems that, very rationally, teachers prioritise and develop sophisticated skills for dealing with priority aspects of their task. [...] Teachers must, to survive with any degree of satisfaction, be able to deal with the unpredictable, immediate, public, simultaneous, multidimensional demands of classroom life in ways that win and maintain some respect from their pupils, their colleagues, their managers and themselves. What precisely that means will vary according to the particular context, including for example the age of the pupils and whether they have come willingly to school. [...]

The sophisticated skills that teachers develop for dealing with classroom life are far from adequately understood. This is partly due to the inherent isolation of traditional classroom life: the teacher, alone in the classroom, has to make things happen and has to deal with what happens. Unlike the doctor, the lawyer, the engineer or the architect, the teacher cannot discuss with colleagues most of the priority decisions that need to be made before making them; and, to judge from teachers' practice, there seems little point in discussing them afterwards. Since there is no apparent point in talking about their classroom expertise, the inherently tacit nature of that expertise is compounded by the lack of need to articulate it. Many commentators have remarked on teachers' lack of any specialist language for discussing their work. Jackson, for example, noted that 'when teachers talk together, almost any reasonably intelligent adult can listen in and comprehend what is being said' (Jackson 1968:143). It is only in recent years, therefore, that researchers have begun to find out, through purposeful investigation, something of the nature of teachers' expertise. [...]

Expert teaching seems then to involve the use of complex schemata of diverse kinds, developed through experience, through which teachers intuitively recognise typical situations or pupils and relate these to what they themselves want to achieve and to the ways they have learned to achieve these goals. They are able, from the vast amount of information constantly available, both to filter out irrelevant information and to use the relevant information in highly efficient ways. It is not of course simply a matter of teaching various *types* of lessons to different *types* of pupils, using appropriate *types* of activities and making appropriate *types* of reaction to whatever *types* of situation arise: each lesson, each pupil, each activity, each situation and each reaction is unique. Part of the importance of thinking intuitively seems to be that instead of recognising examples of formally defined categories and then responding to 'the type', experienced teachers generally appear to recognise situations or pupils as being 'like' others that they have encountered in the past. They seem to be guided by their past experience both in being able to tune in to the general nature of the situation and also in knowing which distinctive features of the unique new situation need to be taken into account.

Studies of teachers' thinking while engaged in interactive teaching (e.g. Brown and McIntyre 1993; Cooper and McIntyre 1996) consistently suggest that teachers take account of a very large number of situational and pupil factors in making classroom choices about how to go about achieving their purposes, and also in judging what standards are appropriate in assessing how well things go. For each of the many 'decisions' that teachers appear to make almost instantaneously in the course of most lessons, there are likely to be several factors involved. Many of these factors are elements of teachers' knowledge about their pupils, both individually and as groups: for example, how able, attentive, confident, tenacious or mature they are. Other factors relate to the current state of pupils, as observed by the teacher: for example, whether they are excited, tired, bored, bewildered or enthusiastic. In addition, there are a wide variety of other conditions of which teachers take account, including their own stable or temporary characteristics (e.g. expertise, tiredness), the availability of accommodation, equipment, materials and time, characteristics of the content of the lesson, the weather, and other things going on. […]

Teachers are not, of course, engaged in interactive teaching all the time. They also spend a good deal of time planning for their teaching, making and recording assessments of students' work, and preparing materials. One might expect their thinking to be very different in these quite different circumstances, when they are away from their pupils. That does indeed seem to be the case, but experienced teachers' planning does not contrast with the intuitive nature of their classroom decision-making to the extent that it approximates to the widely prescribed 'rational planning model'. Far from focusing first on desired outcomes and then planning how to attain them, experienced (and novice) teachers' planning seems generally to focus first and most on teaching content and on pupil activities, to involve a cyclical process through which initial ideas are gradually developed, and to be heavily dependent on visualisation of the intended teaching activity in the specific context of their own classrooms (Clark and Peterson 1986): a feel for the situation is apparently very important in preactive teacher thinking also. Significant too is the consistent research finding that, among the many kinds of planning in which teachers regularly engage, 'lesson planning is rarely claimed as an important part of the repertoire of experienced teachers' (*Ibid.*, 262). Presumably, given that one has a general idea of how the lesson will fit into longer-term plans, the unpredictability of classroom life makes dependence on one's interactive skills a more fruitful and flexible way of dealing with detailed aspects of a lesson than planning in advance; this is another way of prioritising what is important. [...]

The argument in summary

Research on the nature of expert classroom teaching suggests that expert classroom teachers are highly impressive in the complexity of the information that they constructively take into account in order to achieve their purposes. Their expertise seems exceptionally well tuned to the realities of classroom teaching. It involves:

(1) very sophisticated, experience-based schemata;
(2) highly intuitive judgements and decision-making;
(3) largely tacit, individual and quite private expert knowledge;
(4) prioritisation and simplification geared to teaching purposes, for example, through

- short-term perspectives
- working within classroom walls
- simplification of differences among pupils
- practicality.

Some limitations of current classroom teaching

Having developed as a very distinctive type of expertise over the last two centuries, classroom teaching is at its best very good at doing certain kinds of things, less good at others. Of course, not all good classroom teaching is the same: most strikingly, classrooms for different age-groups tend to be very different. The early years classroom, in which the teacher is not only with the same class throughout the school day, but also aspires to the multifaceted development of each 'whole child', is very different from the narrowly focused A-level classroom in which the teacher's expertise may be directed solely towards examination success. But these are, it is claimed, variations on a central theme: classroom teaching, with one adult figure responsible for the learning of a substantial number of young people within one large room for substantial periods of time, has its distinctive strengths and limitations.

Its strengths, as already argued, are reflected in its total and virtually unchallenged dominance of schooling throughout the twentieth century. It has allowed mass schooling on an unprecedented scale not only to be possible but also to achieve enormous success: it has kept millions of young people of ever-increasing ages off the labour market and generally peaceful and law-abiding; and it has enabled most of them to be literate, numerate and to acquire diverse qualifications and knowledge which have allowed them more or less to thrive in societies that have been changing at an accelerating rate.

None the less, it is the limitations of this classroom teaching system which are most frequently commented upon. […] Many of the complaints made about the inadequacies of schoolteaching in recent years can best be understood as complaints about teachers' failure to take account in their teaching of various kinds of information or evidence. These complaints are therefore seen as fundamental challenges to the sophisticated kind of classroom expertise upon which teachers have learned to depend, with its emphasis on the intuitive and the tacit, on prioritisation and on simplification. It is not suggested that it is impossible for classroom teachers to respond to any such demands: there is plenty of evidence that classroom teaching is, within limits, quite flexible, and that classroom teachers can, when motivated by strong convictions or pressures, adapt their teaching to take account of new kinds of information. It is suggested, however, that classroom teaching is not at all well suited as a system to meeting the demand that all these multiple kinds of information should be used by teachers. It is further suggested, therefore, that it is this unsuitability of classroom teaching as a system that has led teachers to be generally unresponsive to these demands and complaints, even though the use of each of these kinds of information can plausibly be argued to contribute to increased teaching effectiveness.

Four ways have already been discussed in which classroom teachers characteristically make their task more manageable by prioritising, and simplifying, the information available to them. Each of these has brought with it complaints and demands for change from critics who believe that pupils' learning could be more effectively facilitated if such prioritisation and simplification were avoided. On the other hand, informed observers might reasonably argue that, unfortunate as it is that teachers do not make fuller use of the wider range of information potentially available to them, neglect of that information is a reasonable price to pay for the benefits of skilled classroom teaching. However, if it is the case that mounting complaints of diverse kinds are all to be understood as consequences of the complexity of classroom life and of teachers' best efforts to cope with it, then it might seem that the balance of the argument has swung against the classroom system, and that the costs to be paid for continuing to rely upon it are too great. The focus of the essay now turns to five major areas of concern:

(1) differentiation;
(2) formative assessment;
(3) home–school partnership;
(4) students' own perspectives;
(5) teaching as an evidence-based profession.

These will be examined in turn below.

Differentiation

Teachers widely depend on notions of 'general ability' in their classroom teaching. They do so in varying the materials they use, the tasks they set, the questions they ask, the explanations they offer and the standards they set, according to the perceived needs of pupils of differing abilities. Although strongly opposed by many commentators because of its oversimplifying dependence on 'general ability' (e.g. Hart 1996, 1998), such differentiation tends to be officially encouraged in the UK, both by politicians and by Her Majesty's Inspectorate, as a realistic way of taking account of differences among pupils. Alongside such encouragement, however, come repeated complaints that teachers do not differentiate adequately among their pupils.

Both inspectors and researchers have sought to judge the adequacy with which teachers vary tasks to take account of differences in ability (HMI 1978; Bennett *et al.* 1984; Simpson 1989), and have with some consistency concluded that, both for more able and for less able pupils, tasks are often poorly matched to student needs. Teachers, it appears from these studies, tend in practice to overestimate the capabilities of children whom they see as 'less able' and to underestimate the capabilities of pupils whom they see as 'more able'.

Why does this happen? The researcher who was conducting one of these studies (Simpson 1989) fed her findings back to the primary school teachers involved and asked them to comment. The teachers agreed that the tasks they set probably did over-and underestimate pupils' capabilities as the research report suggested, and commented as follows.

(1) There were limits to the number of different groups or distinctive individuals with which they could cope at any one time.
(2) Having a wide spread of ability in their classes was greatly preferable for both teachers and children to grouping children into classes according to ability.
(3) Whereas the study had been concerned only with children's 'academic' needs, it was also important to cater for their diverse social and emotional needs.
(4) They deliberately gave special attention and extra resources to the lower ability pupils, because their need for teaching help was greater.
(5) More able children in the classroom were a valuable resource in that they offered models of effective learning and problem-solving which could help the learning of the other children.
(6) It was more useful for children's education to be broadened than for them to 'shoot ahead' of their peers; however, the provision of breadth depended on the availability of appropriate resources and time.
(7) While the research had concentrated on number and language tasks, it was necessary to provide a wide curriculum.
(8) If able children appeared to be over-practising, it was almost certainly related to the teachers' concern to ensure that the basic skills had been thoroughly mastered; the teachers had to be mindful of the prerequisites for the children's learning with the next teacher, the next stage of the curriculum, or the next school to which they were going.

The problem, these teachers suggest, is not with teachers' knowledge of the different learning needs of different children, nor even with finding ways of catering for these needs. The problem is that the careful professional prioritisation which is necessary in dealing with the complexity of classroom teaching involves the simplification or neglect of much available information, with the inevitable consequence that interested parties whose priorities are different from those of the teachers will, to some extent, be disappointed. We must recognise, they are telling us, the limits of what is possible through classroom teaching.

Formative assessment

In the last few years, the concept of differentiation seems to some extent to have been replaced as a solution to the problems of classroom teaching, as offered for example in inspection reports, by that of formative assessment. Here the focus is less on stable differences among children and more on the use of information about their current individual achievements and problems, as discovered through their teachers' assessments, to guide their future learning. Unlike assessment for other purposes, for this purpose 'the aspiration is that assessment should become fully integrated with teaching and learning, and therefore part of the educational process rather than a "bolt-on" activity' (James 1998: 172).

Formative assessment is a much less contentious idea than differentiation by ability, and indeed it is difficult to find any cases of people arguing against it. It is such an obviously sensible idea that academic commentators have been queuing up for around 30 years to commend it to teachers (e.g. McIntyre 1970; Scriven 1967). It has recently been given new impetus and importance by an authoritative review of research in the field by Black and Wiliam (1998), whose main conclusion is 'The research reported here shows conclusively that formative assessment does improve learning. The gains in achievement appear to be quite considerable … among the largest ever reported for educational interventions.' They also report, however, that there is 'extensive evidence to show that present levels of practice in this aspect of teaching are low' (*Ibid.*).

Why is it that, despite 30 years of propaganda, teachers appear to make little use of formative assessment in their classroom practice? Is it, as Black and Wiliam suggest, because there has not been sufficient external encouragement and support for such good practice? A more plausible hypothesis might be that regular effective formative assessment so adds to the complexity of classroom teaching as to make it an impracticable option for teachers. […] Torrance and Pryor (1998:151) conclude that the impact of formative assessment is 'complex, multifaceted, and is not necessarily always as positive as might be intended by teachers and as some advocates of formative assessment would have us believe'. They describe two ideal types of classroom assessment. *Convergent assessment*, which is 'routinely accomplished', is characterised by 'analysis of the interaction of the child and the curriculum from the point of view of the curriculum' and is close to what is done in much current classroom assessment practice. *Divergent assessment*, which 'emphasises the learner's understanding rather than the agenda of the assessor', is 'aimed at prompting pupils to reflect on their own thinking (or) focusing on … aspects of learners' work which yield insights into their current understanding' and 'accepts the complexity of formative assessment'. Developed instances of divergent assessment were found to be rare, to derive from 'ideological commitments to a "child-centred approach" and [to be] not necessarily as well structured as they could and (we would argue) should be'. While Torrance and Pryor consider that both types of classroom assessment have their place, they suggest that 'divergent assessment is the more interesting approach, and the one that seems to offer more scope for positively affecting children's learning' (*Ibid.*, 154); and they go on to make more detailed suggestions about how the quality of formative assessment may be improved.

Increasingly, then, researchers seem to be able to provide teachers with detailed guidance – about how they can use formative assessment in ways that will contribute significantly to their students' effective learning. There is, however, a problem: all the advice offered by Black and Wiliam and by Torrance and Pryor to teachers seems to involve sustained, high-quality, non-routine interaction – either orally or in writing – between the teacher and either individual students or small groups. How far does this advice take account of the complexity of classroom life, and of the sophisticated ways in which expert teachers have learned to work effectively in classrooms through rigorous prioritisation, simplification and intuitive decision-making? We can have a good deal of confidence in the validity of these researchers' conclusions that it is feedback from, and interaction with, teachers of the kinds they suggest which can best facilitate pupils' learning. What may well be doubted is that the current lack of frequency of such practices in classrooms is a consequence of teachers' ignorance or lack of understanding of what would be valuable, or the lack of external encouragement. On the contrary, it would seem much more likely that, sensing that effective formative assessment depends on such unrealistic, high-quality engagement with individual pupils, teachers do not attempt widely to build such assessment into their classroom teaching. Current efforts to encourage and support teachers in the fuller and more effective use of formative assessment may prove this wrong, and show instead that the researchers' insights into good classroom practice are far ahead of the insights of most teachers. However, a more plausible expectation would be that the researchers' guidance will founder on their failure to take account of the real constraints imposed by classroom teaching as a system.

The point of the argument is not, of course, that we must resign ourselves to the present levels of effectiveness achieved by classroom teaching. It is instead that, if our schooling system is to become substantially more effective, through for example taking account of new insights into the effective use of formative assessment, this improvement may depend on a questioning of the system of classroom teaching which we have learned to take for granted. It would be wrong to leave this section without noting that James, Black and Wiliam, and Torrance and Pryor offer some seeds of ideas about what such questioning might lead to, ideas to which I shall return.

Home–school partnership

British traditions of schooling have involved very limited levels of collaboration between the school and the home. Throughout the twentieth century, however, there has been a sustained critique of these traditions from progressive educational thinkers, including increasing numbers of teachers, especially in primary schools. They argue that 'meaningful' education of 'the whole child' depends, among other things, on children's experience of continuity across the home–school divide. The most important assault on the separation of schooling from home life came in the 1960s when successive studies, culminating in the Plowden Report (1967), demonstrated very clearly that children's progress and success throughout schooling were closely related to the nature of their home background. Although initially these research findings were often interpreted rather naively as showing a simple causal relationship between home characteristics and educational success, even this led to calls for closer home school relationships aimed at encouraging parents to take greater interest in their children's school learning and to become more involved in the work of the school. Subsequent thinking, much influenced by the powerful theoretical contributions of Bourdieu (especially Bourdieu and Passeron 1977) and of Bernstein (1970, 1975) and by research such as that of Tizard and Hughes (1984), has increasingly construed the problem not in terms of the deficiencies of working-class homes but as resulting from the gap between the home lives of many children and their school experiences. Accordingly it has emphasised the need for schools to work in partnership with parents, the primary educators of their children, in order to bridge that gap.

What is most needed, it has been argued, most forcibly by Atkins and Bastiani (1988), is for teachers to listen to parents. Teachers' classroom practice, it is suggested, can be made much more effective if they have the benefit of parents' authoritative insights into their children's lives away from school: their interests, their talents, their achievements, their aspirations and their learning needs. The argument is surely persuasive, since parents have much more opportunity, and generally more motivation, to understand their own children than teachers can have, especially secondary school teachers who are weekly teaching over a hundred students. Yet there is very little evidence of teachers being motivated to listen to such valuable information. The opportunities created for such sharing of information tend, again especially in secondary schools, to be rare and brief, and most of the talking seems generally to be done by the teachers. On the whole, parents do not complain. They have for the most part accepted the ideology of professionalism and are ready to accept that teachers know best; and so they learn not to offer their insights about their children to a system that clearly does not want to hear them.

It is very tempting to be critical of teachers because of their apparent unwillingness to work in genuine partnership with parents, and especially because of their lack of readiness to take advantage of the information that parents could provide. But classroom teachers have to select and to use the information that they find most conducive to the management of many pupils' learning activities in a classroom. The information that parents can provide, based as it is on a completely different perspective, may not be easily usable by teachers. Randell (1998), in a study of different perspectives on students' progress in their first year at secondary school, found that teachers talked about the individual students in a largely judgemental way – the two dimensions of ability and hard work/good behaviour suggested earlier – whereas parents talked predominantly about their needs. Teachers, it seemed, found it difficult, and also perhaps of questionable value, to adapt their classroom practice to take account of the distinctive needs that parents perceived their children to have.

It may thus be the case that the information which parents think they call usefully offer teachers to facilitate their children's learning cannot generally be effectively used to inform classroom teaching. The problem remains that the progress made by school systems in recent decades in serving the more socially and economically disadvantaged half of the population has been very slow; and it seems highly improbable that better progress can be made in future unless schools develop more genuine and effective ways of working in partnership with disadvantaged communities and families. It is probably unreasonable and unproductive to continue to place the major responsibility for engaging effectively in such partnerships on individual teachers working within the constraining framework of classroom teaching.

Students' own perspectives

While teachers are for the most part supportive, stimulating and selfless in the hours they put in to help young people, the *conditions of learning* that are common across secondary schools do not adequately take account of the social maturity of young people, nor of the tensions and pressures they feel as they struggle to reconcile the demands of their social and personal lives with the development of their identity as learners.

(Rudduck *et al.* 1996: 1)

That is how Rudduck and her colleagues summarise what they learned from secondary school pupils in their extensive study of pupils' own perspectives on their schooling. In introducing their book, they also quote Silberman and agree with his dictum that 'we should affirm the right of students to negotiate our purposes and demands so that the activities we undertake with them have greatest possible meaning to all' (Silberman 1971: 364). Teachers are under increasing pressure not only to take responsibility for students' attainment of learning targets but also to listen to students' voices and to take fuller account of their perspectives on their schooling. This seems to be partly in response to a view that students' rights need to be more widely respected in schools, but perhaps even more because of a recognition that improved school effectiveness will depend in large measure on the creation of conditions of learning which take fuller account of what students feel and think.

One of the major themes in the research reports from Rudduck and her colleagues concerns the significance of pupils' sense of having some control over their own learning:

It was noticeable that when pupils spoke about work that they had designed themselves and that they felt was very much their own – whether project work in technology or work in art – they had a strong sense of purpose, strategy and goal. [...] Clearly, the meaningfulness of particular tasks is greater when pupils have a degree of control over the planning and execution of the work: they have a greater sense of ownership.

(Rudduck *et al.* 1996: 48)

However, pupils did not *expect* to have control over their learning. [...] The researchers describe too 'pupils who *wanted* to learn but felt that they had little control over their own learning' (*Ibid.*, 46). Sometimes blame was attached to teachers, sometimes to their own past behaviour or absences, sometimes to other (disruptive) pupils, but rarely did the pupils feel that they themselves were in a position to overcome any learning problems they had.

In classroom teaching, it is the teacher who has responsibility for determining the activities to be engaged in and the learning tasks to be undertaken. The teacher can, of course, share this responsibility with pupils or take account of pupils' interests and felt needs in deciding what to do. Cooper and McIntyre (1996) found that the teachers whom they studied always took some account of their pupils' perspectives. They characterised the teaching they observed as varying from *interactive* teaching, in which pupils' contributions would be taken into account within the framework of teachers' predetermined plans, to *reactive* teaching, in which teachers were willing to take more fundamental account of pupils' concerns in deciding what to do. They found reactive teaching less common, and apparently more complex, since the teacher's plans depended on finding out and using information about the different perspectives of the pupils in a class as well as about the set curriculum.

Arguments that secondary school students are not sufficiently treated as partners in their own learning are highly persuasive, both in terms of their rights to have their perspectives taken into account and also instrumentally in terms of their commitment to learning. The lack of control which students generally have over their own lives in institutions that would claim to be serving their interests can indeed be seen as quite remarkable. Within the context of classroom teaching, however, the task for the teacher of treating students as partners while continuing to take responsibility for classroom activities and outcomes cannot but be seen as adding to the complexity of the teacher's task.

Teaching as an evidence-based profession

There has been vigorous debate over recent years about the usefulness of educational research. Although the obvious target of most of the criticism has been educational researchers, a much more fundamental challenge implicit in this debate has been in relation to classroom teachers. The aspiration of the powerful groups who have been promoting this debate – that teaching should be directly informed by research evidence about the relative effectiveness of different practices – gives research an importance hitherto undreamed of, but asks teachers to transform their ways of working. It asks that teachers should somehow integrate into their subtle, complex, tacit and intuitive decision-making the very different propositional kind of knowledge offered by research results. Teaching would therefore become a less idiosyncratic craft, and instead one informed by a standard but constantly developing set of validated generalisations about the consequences of using clearly specified practices in specified types of context. The Teacher Training Agency outlines this conception of teaching and research:

> Good teachers relish the opportunity to draw upon the most up to date knowledge. They continually challenge their own practice in order to do the best for their pupils. They want to be able to examine what they do in the light of important new knowledge, scientific investigation and evaluation, disciplined enquiry and rigorous comparison of practice in this country and in others – provided such resources are relevant to their field and accessible. Many of the resources they need to do this are, or ought to be, precisely those provided by good research.
>
> (Teacher Training Agency 1996: 2)

As yet there is a relatively modest corpus of such knowledge, especially in relation to the British context. However – and this is the complaint against educational researchers – this can in very large measure be explained by the neglect over the last 20 years by British researchers of the kinds of research which could have generated such knowledge. […] There is no reason to believe that a useful body of such knowledge could not be generated. […] Much more problematic, however, is the idea that such knowledge, if available, would be used by classroom teachers. The authors of the review of educational research commissioned in England by the Department for Education and Employment had some sense, on the basis of their assessment of current practice, that this could not be taken for granted:

> Whatever the relevance and the quality of the research and the user-friendliness of the output, its eventual impact will depend on the willingness and the capacity of policy-makers and practitioners to take research into account in their decision-making and their actions. This relies on a commitment to the principle, an understanding of what research can offer, and the practical capacity to interpret research.
>
> (Hillage et al. 1998: 53)

It depends on all that, but in relation to classroom teaching it depends much more on how such research-based knowledge can be integrated into the kind of classroom expertise on which teachers currently rely: the two kinds of knowledge are so different that this seems highly problematic. […]

Summary of the argument

Having first sought to outline the nature of the expertise which teachers have successfully developed for the distinctive task of classroom teaching, with its considerable strengths but also with some limitations, my aim in this section has been to exemplify the mounting pressure on the classroom teaching system. I have outlined five major kinds of information to which teachers are increasingly being urged to become more responsive, but there is as yet little sign of this happening. In each case, I have argued that it is not realistic to ask teachers to take account of the additional information while maintaining the kind of expertise which has made classroom teaching a viable and indeed very successful system. I have emphasised that classroom teaching has been quite flexible as a system, and that classroom teachers have shown themselves to be highly adaptable; so it may be quite possible for highly motivated teachers to incorporate any one of these five demands into their classroom expertise, or to go a little way towards absorbing all of them. None the less, I am persuaded that the classroom teaching system is near to its limits, and that it will not be able to respond adequately to the accelerating 'expectations … of what schools should accomplish' (Hargreaves 1999:122).

The argument here has been focused on the classroom teacher's position as solely responsible for what happens in his or her classroom, on the complexity of classroom life, on the teacher's need to find special ways of handling very large amounts and diverse kinds of information, and finally on the lack of realism in asking teachers to attend carefully to an accumulation of new kinds of information traditionally neglected. That is one kind of argument for believing that classroom teaching may have served its day. But we should note briefly that there are other very good arguments which could lead us to the same conclusion. One of these is that classroom teaching seems peculiarly ill-suited to most of the more exciting possibilities for using information technology to enhance the quality of learning in schools, as seems to be reflected in the very limited impact it has had on schooling in the last quarter century. Another might be that the very strong boundary which we have noted between classroom learning and learning in other contexts has been accepted for long enough, and that schools must, to enhance their effectiveness and usefulness, find ways of organising learning activities so that these *normally*, not just exceptionally, relate to pupils' learning in other contexts. More pragmatic arguments might emphasise the escalating costs of provision for 'lifelong learning' and consequent pressures for greater efficiency in schooling, or the likelihood that the shortage of well-qualified subject teachers in secondary schools will be endemic. The pressures on the viability of the classroom teaching system are of many kinds.

The way ahead

To offer a clear vision of how schooling might be more effectively organised than on the classroom teaching system would be as foolhardy as it is unnecessary. There seems little doubt that change via a new system will come, but – we must hope and seek to ensure – only gradually over the next 20 years. New approaches will need to be developed, tested, modified and perfected, preferably with the help of careful research. A major constraint will be the architecture of schools, very obviously designed for classroom teaching and very badly designed for anything else. So, as new approaches are tried and found useful, they will be built into the architecture of new schools and then, one hopes, found even more useful. The change should properly be piecemeal, but it may come about in relatively efficient, rational and well-researched ways under the control of professional educators, or chaotically and through a series of reluctant and unhappy compromises to cope with external economic and political pressures. If we are clear about why change is necessary and about the principles by which the changes should be guided, the benefits can be maximised and the pain of change minimised.

What should we be seeking in a new system? Some elements of what is needed are obvious and are already apparent on a small scale in changing patterns of teachers' work. The problems of the classroom teaching system may properly be viewed as resulting from an over-dependence on certain elements which in themselves have considerable merits. The aim must be not to abandon these valuable elements, but to achieve a new balance in which dependence on their strengths does not automatically lead to problems because of their limitations. There are at least four ways in which a proper balance will require radical change:

- *Especially in secondary schools, a very different balance must be achieved between students and teachers in terms of responsibilities for generating and using information about students' achievements and needs in making decisions about their learning objectives and activities.* The research on formative assessment strongly suggests that the improved learning which can come from formative assessment is most likely through students themselves gaining a thorough understanding of the criteria for effective learning, through them assessing themselves, individually and as peers, and through them having opportunities, encouragement and responsibilities for using the information from such assessment in order to improve their understanding and skills. Students, of course, have to learn how to do these things and how to take these responsibilities, and facilitating that learning must be an important task for schools; but while this move towards greater student responsibility is no doubt possible to some degree in classrooms, it seems much more likely to happen where the social settings more obviously reflect this shift in responsibilities.

- *A very different balance must be achieved between reliance on intuitive, tacit and private decision-making and on collaborative, explicit and evidence-based decision-making.* In all complex professional activities, as Dreyfus and Dreyfus (1986) and Schon (1983), for example, have argued, there is necessarily a heavy dependence on tacit and intuitive understanding and decision-making, just as in teaching. Classroom teaching is distinctive, however, in the scale of its dependence on such decision-making, with very little use being made traditionally of attempts to evaluate and synthesise available evidence, explicitly or rationally or collaboratively, as a basis for decision-making. The astonishingly wide acceptance of Schon's idea of reflective practice as an ideal for classroom teaching might reasonably be interpreted as a recognition of the rarity and difficulty of such explicit consideration of the evidence and of the choices to be made for important classroom decisions. The need for a change springs both from the inherent merits of rational thinking and use of evidence for the most important decisions, and also from the current state of affairs where – as has been demonstrated – even expert, intuitive, classroom decision-making cannot take account of much of the evidence which could be highly relevant for facilitating learning. Already in recent years, a greater proportion of the time and professional energy of teachers has been spent on gathering information, explicitly analysing it, sharing it and discussing its implications with colleagues, and planning collaboratively for pupils' learning. The work of schoolteachers should move increasingly in this direction, with more and more decision-making being explicit, rationally justified and corporate, and with such decision-making being a larger part of teachers' work, while face-to-face teaching, though still important, will occupy less of teachers' time. As in other professions, teachers' capacities for expert intuitive decision-making must continue to be of great importance, but it should cease to be all-important. How it can best be used to complement more explicit decision-making is a matter that will require extensive research and learning from experience.

- *A very different balance must be achieved between exclusive decision-making by professional schoolteachers and shared decision-making with adults who are not professional teachers.* Schoolteachers have, and will continue to have, a crucial and distinctive kind of expertise for facilitating learning. However, partly because they have been fully occupied with classroom teaching, and partly in order to simplify their classroom teaching work, teachers have denied themselves a great deal of valuable information and insights, and have failed to develop vital shared understandings with others. A slightly greater proportion of teachers' time and professional energies seems currently to be being spent on collaborative planning with other adults who are not fellow-teachers. The work of schoolteachers should move much more in this direction, with increased consultation and joint decision-making with learning support staff, with parents, with community members, with employers and with other specialist professional workers: again, this will be possible only in so far as less time is spent in face-to-face teaching.

- *A very different balance must be achieved between the amount of pupils' learning done in classroom teaching groups and the amount done in other kinds of social groups and settings.* Individual work in resource centres, on work experience and other contexts has increased and should increase further, as should small-group work on joint projects and investigations in different contexts. Much of this work in contexts other than classrooms is likely to be related to diverse uses of computers and other modern technology. Teachers should spend much more of their time in planning and evaluating and in negotiating, with other teachers, with students and with others. However, they should continue to spend much of their time in face-to-face contact with students, individually and with groups of different sizes. Teaching – deliberately and directly facilitating learning – must continue to be their overriding responsibility.

The problem inevitably seems a good deal clearer than the solution. This essay has aspired only to offer a tentative formulation of the problem and some very preliminary ideas towards a solution. It seems likely that the changes needed will be of different kinds and different degrees in different contexts and for different groups of pupils, for example perhaps being much more fundamental at secondary school level than at primary. Much of the school-based research and development work of the next 20 years should be directed towards formulating and investigating possible solutions.

References

Atkins, J. and Bastiani, J. (1988) *Listening to Parents: An approach to the improvement of home–school relations*. London: Croom Helm.

Bennett, N., Desforges, C., Cockburn, A. and Wilkinson, B. (1984) *The Quality of Pupil Learning Experiences*. London: Lawrence Erlbaum Associates.

Bernstein, B. (1970) Education cannot compensate for society. In D. Rubinstein and C. Stoneman (eds) *Education for Democracy*. Harmondsworth: Penguin, 104–16.

Bernstein, B. (1975) *Class, Codes and Control, vol. 3*. London: Routledge & Kegan Paul.

Black, P. and Wiliam, D. (1998) Assessment and classroom learning, *Assessment in Education*, **5** (1).

Bourdieu, P. and Passeron, J. C. (1977) *Reproduction in Education, Society and Culture*. London and Beverly Hills: Sage.

Brown, S. and McIntyre, D. (1993) *Making Sense of Teaching*. Buckingham: Open University Press.

Clark, C. M. and Peterson, P. L. (1986) Teachers' thought processes. In M. C. Wittrock (ed.) *Handbook of Research on Teaching, 3rd edn*. New York: Macmillan, 255–96.

Cooper, P. and McIntyre, D. (1996) *Effective Teaching and Learning: Teachers' and pupils' perspectives*. Buckingham: Open University Press.

Dreyfus, H. L. and Dreyfus, S. E. (1986) *Mind over Machine: The power of human intuition and expertise in the era of the computer*. New York: Macmillan.

Hamilton, D. (1986) Adam Smith and the moral economy of the classroom system. In P. H. Taylor (ed.) *Recent Developments in Curriculum Studies*. Windsor: NFER–Nelson, 84–111.

Hargreaves, D. H. (1999) The knowlege-creating school, *British Journal of Educational Studies*, **47** (2), 122–44.

Hart, S. (ed.) (1996) *Differentiation and the Secondary Curriculum: Debates and dilemmas*. London: Routledge.

Hart, S. (1998) A sorry tale: ability, pedagogy and educational reform, *British Journal of Educational Studies*, **46** (2), 153–68.

Hillage, J., Pearson, R., Anderson, A. and Tamkin, P. (1998) *Excellence in Research on Schools*. Research Report RR74. London: Department for Education and Employment.

HMI (Her Majesty's Inspectorate) (1978) *Mixed Ability Work in Comprehensive Schools*. London: HMSO.

Holt, J. (1969) *How Children Fail*. Harmondsworth: Penguin.

Holt, J. (1971) *The Underachieving School*. Harmondsworth: Penguin.

Illich, I. (1976) *Deschooling Society*. Harmondsworth: Penguin.

Jackson, P. W. (1968) *Life in Classrooms*. New York: Holt, Rinehart & Winston.

James, M. (1998) *Using Assessment for School Improvement*. Oxford: Heinemann.

Lortie, D. C. (1975) *Schoolteacher*. Chicago: University of Chicago Press.

McIntyre, D. (1970) Assessment for teaching. In D. Rubinstein and C. Stoneman (eds) *Education for Democracy*. Harmondsworth: Penguin, 164–71.

Plowden Report (1967) *Children and Their Primary Schools*. London: HMSO.

Randell, S. (1998) Parents, teachers, pupils: Different contributions to understanding pupils' needs? Unpublished D. Phil diss., University of Oxford.

Reimer, E. (1971) *School Is Dead*. Harmondsworth: Penguin.

Rudduck, J., Chaplain, R. and Wallace, G. (eds) (1996) *School Improvement: What can pupils tell us?* London: David Fulton.

Schon, D. A. (1983) *The Reflective Practitioner.* London: Temple Smith.

Scriven, M. (1967) *The Methodology of Evaluation.* American Educational Research Association.

Silberman, M. L. (1971) Discussion. In M. L. Silberman *The Experience of Schooling.* New York: Holt, Rinehart & Winston.

Simpson, M. (1989) *A Study of Differentiation and Learning in Schools.* Aberdeen: Northern College.

Teacher Training Agency (1996) *Teaching as a Research-based Profession.* London: Teacher Training Agency.

Tizard, B. and Hughes, M. (1984) *Young Children Learning: Talking and thinking at home and at school.* London: Fontana.

Torrance, H. and Pryor, J. (1998) *Investigating Formative Assessment.* Buckingham: Open University Press.

McIntyre hopes that change will be a gradual and thoughtful process but the outcomes he envisages are still radical ones. Students will need to become more reflective and knowledgeable about their own learning and educational performance. Teachers working with such students will do so across a wide range of situations and activities. This requires a new social context, in which there is much greater collaboration with other members of the school community. The resulting organisation, should it evolve, would be much more inclusive and one in which the voices of students are more influential. Does his vision for twenty years hence seem just as far off as it did when this article was written in 2000? what has changed?

Chapter 7

The politics of education for all

Len Barton

This chapter is taken from a published conference paper that Len Barton presented at the International Special Education Congress in Birmingham in 1995 on the theme of Education for All. At this time he looked forward, from a political perspective, to significant challenges integral to the process of change and these retain their relevance in the early part of the twenty-first century. We must have a vision, he argues, and we must struggle to achieve it, and this includes tackling assumptions about education as a market place.

'Education for All' is one of the most important and urgent issues facing all societies concerned with the education of their future citizens. The pursuit of 'Education for All' will entail engaging with questions of social justice, equity and participatory democracy. It is thus part of a human–rights approach to education and living, one in which the barriers to the empowerment of *all* pupils must be removed.

It is essential, therefore, that we do not underestimate the serious, complex and contentious nature of the issues involved in the pursuit of inclusive policies and practice. The process will be challenging and disturbing, necessitating fundamental changes to the social and economic conditions and relations of a given society. This will include changes to the values informing the prioritisation and distribution of resources, how society views difference, how schools are organised, how teachers view their work, the styles of their teaching and the nature of the curriculum.

This paper will maintain that a fundamental barrier to the realisation of education for all is the growing emergence and implementation of policies and practices informed by a market ideology. The concept of the 'market' and its applicability to education will be explored and the paper will highlight the political nature of these developments.

The politics of education for all

All governments are concerned with controlling human service provision. This includes the issue of funding and the extent to which investment in particular institutions results in the sorts of economic and cultural reforms that are viewed as worthwhile.

Government priorities and decisions, and the values informing them, are all part of the public manifestation of the intentions and vision they hold with regard to the form of society they wish to see develop and continue. Thus, the allocation of human and material resources are fundamentally political decisions. Their significance is much more crucial in a social context in which there are both limited resources and extensive inequalities arising from the existing economic and structural relations. Questions of politics, power and control are central in this situation. The nature of discrimination and its impact on the lives of different groups must be carefully explored and exposed. This will be particularly important where a 'blaming the victim' mentality represents the official discourse used to explain these conditions and experiences (Ryan 1976).

Educational issues are complex and contentious and often involve passionately held beliefs and values. These entail making connections between schools and the wider society of which they are a part. This involves the capacity to range from the microcontexts of biographical and school life to the wider social and economic conditions and relations in which the former are embedded. One of the leading analysts of school change and improvement, Fullan (1993), has advocated that if schools and teachers are to make a difference then:

> Making a difference must be explicitly recast in broader social and moral terms. It must be seen that one cannot make a difference at the interpersonal level unless the problem and solution are enlarged to encompass the conditions that surround teaching ... and the skills and actions that would be needed to make a difference. Without this attitude and broader dimension the best of teachers will end up as moral martyrs. In brief, care must be linked to a broader, social, public purpose ... (p. 11)

Any serious consideration of education for all must therefore engage with questions of politics and power and encapsulate socio–economic conditions and relations.

Within the context of 'special education', this engagement is very underdeveloped. There are several reasons as to why this is so. First, special education has been dominated by a form of reductionism which gives a privileged status to individualistic explanations. Within-the-child factors are emphasised, encouraging 'special needs' to be viewed as a personal trouble and not a public issue (Mills 1970). In particular, medical and psychological ideas have powerfully informed policy and practice. This has had the effect of depoliticising the issues involved. Secondly, given the restrictive nature of this approach, attempts to introduce complex questions – for example, of power, politics, class, gender and race – into the analysis can be seen as unnecessary and unhelpful. This will be particularly so where the 'special' quality of such provision is justified on the grounds that all children are treated equally. Lastly, the strong traditional belief that professionals involved in special education provision are caring, patient and loving, and that politics should be kept separate from education, make it difficult to raise such questions.

The politics of disability

Disability is a significant means of social differentiation in modern societies. The level of esteem and social standing of disabled people is derived from their position in relation to the wider social conditions and relations of a given society. Particular institutions have a very crucial influence on social status. This includes the level and nature of employment, education and economic well-being (Equality Studies Centre 1994).

Status is influenced by the cultural images which, for example, the media portray about particular groups, the legal rights and protection afforded them and the quality and duration of educational experiences. How a society excludes particular groups or individuals involves the process of categorisation, in which the inabilities and unacceptable and inferior aspects of a person's make-up are legitimated. Through the act of the 'individualised gaze', problems are located within the individual resulting in a view of them as 'other' or negatively different.

A crucial feature of the oppression of disabled people has been the extent to which their voice has been excluded. Overcoming disabling barriers will include listening to the voice of disabled people and their organisations, especially as they struggle for choice, rights and participation. Jenny Morris (1992) has captured the concerns of disabled people in a booklet concerned with the issue of rights. The voice is unmistakably clear: 'Our vision is of a society which recognises our rights and our value as equal citizens rather than merely treating us as the recipient of other people's good will' (p. 10).

This must be the context within which the question of inclusive education needs to be explored. It is crucial, given the general unwillingness of national governments 'to think in terms of a national comprehensive plan to meet the needs of disabled people' (Daunt 1991: 174), as well as the difficulties a market approach to educational policy, planning and practice are beginning to generate with regard to issues of social justice, equity and entitlement.

Inclusive education

Inclusive education is part of a human rights approach to social relations and conditions. The intentions and values involved relate to a vision of the whole society of which education is a part. Issues of social justice, equity and choice are central to the demands for inclusive education. Disablist assumptions and practices need to be identified and challenged in order to promote positive views of others.

Inclusive education is concerned with the well-being of *all* pupils, and schools should be welcoming institutions. Special education entails a discourse of exclusion and this is seen as a particularly offensive aspect of such provision. This is clearly demonstrated in the concerns of a group of non-disabled parents over the education of their disabled children. In the introduction to a forthcoming book of the stories of their children, the editors (parents) maintain:

> For us the concept of segregation is completely unjustifiable – it is morally offensive – it contradicts any notion of civil liberties and human rights. Whoever it is done to, wherever it appears, the discrimination is damaging for our children, for our families and for our communities. We do not want our children to be sent to segregated schools or any other form of segregated provision. We do not want our children and our families to be damaged in this way. Our communities should not be impoverished by the loss of our children.
>
> (Murray and Penman 1995)

From this perspective, the goal is not to leave anyone out of school. Inclusive experience is about learning to live with one another. This raises the question of what schools are for. They must not be about assimilation in which a process of accommodation leaves the school remaining essentially unchanged (Wolfe 1994).

It is essential that the demand for inclusive education does not result in a critique of special schooling which becomes an end in itself. We are not advocating that these developments are merely in terms of the existing conditions and relations in mainstream schools. They too will need to change and there are certain features that are unacceptable, including the plant, organisation, ethos, pedagogy and curriculum. It will demand the transfer of resources, careful planning and continual monitoring. We are not advocating a dumping practice into existing provision.

Inclusive education needs to be part of a whole-school equal opportunities policy. If we are to resist complacency and recognise the degree of struggle still to be engaged with, and if official rhetoric is to be translated into reality in substantive terms in the lives of *all* pupils, then the question of inclusive education needs to be an integral part of a well-thought-through, adequately resourced and carefully monitored equal opportunities policy. By being an integral part of an equal opportunities approach, it will provide a basis for the identification of those features of the existing society, including policy and practices within specific institutions and contexts, that are offensive, unacceptable and thus must be challenged and changed.

The transition from segregated special schools to inclusive provision and practice will demand careful planning and sensitive implementation. In the current context, some parents prefer their children to attend a special day or residential school. From the perspective adopted in this paper, such choices should not be viewed as a defence for the continuation of special schools, but rather, as Dessent (1987) has forcefully argued:

> Special schools do not have a right to exist. *They exist because of the limitations of ordinary schools in providing for the full range of abilities and disabilities amongst children.* It is not primarily a question of the quality or adequacy of what is offered in a special school. Even a superbly well organised special school offering the highest quality curriculum and educational input to its children has no right to exist if that same education can be provided in a mainstream school.
>
> (p. 97; my emphasis)

The marketisation of education

The demand for education for all needs to be set within the wider context of the attempts by successive Conservative governments to restructure the welfare state. [...]

A powerful programme of change has been directed at the governance, content and outcomes of schooling, post-school and higher educational provision.

The ideological force behind such developments has become known as the 'New Right'. [...] The fundamental features of the new economic policy became those of efficiency and modernisation and, as Gamble (1994) also notes, the market was depicted as the 'best way of allocating resources, providing incentives and stimulating growth' (p. 42). [...] In this process, notions of 'citizenship', 'freedom' and 'equality' are invested with new meaning and informed by market assumptions. [...]

Under the guise of reducing state control, the role and powers of local educational authorities (LEAs) have been radically reduced, local management of schools (LMS) has been introduced and the working conditions and definition of teachers' work has been changed. A new form of language has been introduced by which we both think about and evaluate education – it is the language of business. Thus, 'quality', 'accountability', 'cost-efficiency', 'effectiveness', 'performance indicators', 'development plans', 'mission statements', 'targets', and 'appraisal' are key concepts in this discourse. Pupils are now viewed as 'units of resource'.

Within a market-driven system of provision, there will be winners and losers. The market is not a neutral mechanism: it involves socialising individuals into a new value system. Gewirtz, Ball and Bowe (1993) maintain that 'the market rewards shrewdness rather than principles and encourages commercial rather than educational decision-making'(p. 252). [...]

One of the fundamental features of the marketisation of education has been the intensification of competitiveness. The emphasis on competitiveness supports the celebration of individualism and the development of an increasingly hierarchically organised system of provision. In this context the question of access to particular schools raises the issue of selection and the existing 'cultural capital' of pupils entering particular schools (Walford 1992). One analyst has called this 'the rise of parentocracy' (Brown 1990). We already have indications that these policies and their implementation are leading to a more socially and divisive system of education (Ball 1993). [...]

Vincent et al. (1994) maintain that LEAs are finding it less possible to resist the influx of a more market-created culture. This is viewed as fragmenting and atomising educational provision. Legislative restrictions, the fragile financial climate and reduction in the amounts of reserves LEAs are permitted to hold have combined to decrease their ability to meet their general tasks, and special needs functions in particular. They conclude that a market-oriented discourse 'encourages an emphasis on individualism which is antithetical to the concept of a planned and pervasive approach to provision for "vulnerable children"' (p. 275).

In terms of the pursuit of education for all, the impact of market-led decision making on educational provision and practice raises serious concerns about the establishment of national policies supported by the political will of governments. Indeed, Bines (1995) contends that the marketisation of education is now resulting in the influx of a strong form of managerialism. […] Managers within schools increasingly face the dilemma that 'giving too high a profile to SEN work may not match with concerns to promote a market image based on a high level of pupil achievement'.

Some key questions can be identified as emerging from the analysis provided in this paper. They include:

- What view of 'difference' is enshrined within a market discourse?
- To what extent is the marketisation of education leading to an increase in special educational provision?
- To what extent does the populace discourse of 'parental choice' mask existing stubborn inequalities?
- How far will the marketisation of education reduce collaboration between schools?

Conclusion

In presenting this notion of the 'market', I am aware of reservations being expressed over its applicability to education. Clearly, education is not a 'free market' and has contradictory features resulting from explicit political interventions by government. These include the introduction of the National Curriculum and the use of various undemocratically elected 'quangos'. What we have, as Bottery (1992) so shrewdly notes, is 'a paradoxical mixture of a free market liberalism and centralist autocracy' (p. 4). Thus, it may be more appropriate to work with the notion of a quasi-market (Ranson 1994). This in no way detracts from the necessity of situating any discussion of education for all within a wider sociopolitical framework.

In the World Conference on Special Needs in Education (1994) held in Salamanca, Spain, a framework for action was adopted which will hopefully inform policy and practice on an international scale. Confirming a human rights approach and attempting to develop new thinking on this issue, the document states:

> The trend in social policy during the past two decades has been to promote integration and participation and to combat exclusion. Inclusion and participation are essential to human dignity and to the enjoyment and exercise of human rights. Within the field of education, this is reflected in the development of strategies that seek to bring about a genuine equalisation of opportunity. Experience in many countries demonstrates that the integration of children and youth with special

educational needs is best achieved within inclusive schools that serve all children within a community. It is within this context that those with special education needs can achieve the fullest educational progress and social integration. While inclusive schools provide a favourable setting for achieving equal opportunity and full participation, their success requires a concerted effort, not only by teachers and school staff, but also by peers, parents, families and volunteers. The reform of social institutions is not only a technical task; it depends, above all, upon the conviction, commitment and goodwill of the individuals who constitute society.

If we are to see the fundamental changes required in order for us to realise a truly inclusive society, then it will necessarily involve us addressing questions of politics and power.

What we are ultimately concerned with when we allude to the issue of education for all is determining what constitutes the 'good society': how is it to be achieved and what is the role of education in this task? We have no room for complacency but every reason to intensify our commitment to struggle for the removal of all disabling barriers – in this instance, an uncritical acceptance that a marketisation of education will lead to a better society for *all* citizens.

We need to dream, to have a vision, but one which arises from an informed understanding of the discriminatory factors of the material world we now live in.

References

Ball, S. J. (1993) Education markets, choice and social class. The market as a class strategy in the UK and US. *British Journal of Sociology of Education*, **14**(1), 3–19.

Bines, H. (1995) Special educational needs in the market place. *Journal of Educational Policy*, **10**(2), 157–72.

Bottery, M. (1992) *The Ethics of Educational Management*. London: Cassell.

Brown, P. (1990) The 'third wave': Education and the ideology of parentocracy. *British Journal of Sociology of Education*, **11**(1), 65–86.

Daunt, P. (1991) *Meeting Disability: A European response*. London: Cassell.

Dessent, T. (1987) *Making the Ordinary School Special*. Lewes: Falmer Press.

Equality Studies Centre (1994) *Equality, Status and Disability*. University College Dublin.

Fullan, M. (1993) *Change Forces: Probing the depths of educational reform*. Lewes: Falmer Press.

Gamble, A. (1994) *The Free Economy and the Strong State*. Basingstoke: Macmillan.

Gewirtz, S., Ball, S. J. and Bowe, R. (1993) Values and ethics in the education market place: The case of Northwark Park. *International Studies in Sociology of Education*, **3**(2), 233–54.

Mills, C. W. (1970) *The Sociological Imagination*. Harmondsworth: Penguin.

Morris, J. (1992) *Disabled Lives: Many voices, one message*. London: BBC.

Murray, P. and Penman, J. (1995) Draft Introduction, Sheffield.

Ranson, S. (1994) Public institutions for co-operative action: A reply to James Tooley. *British Journal of Educational Studies*, **43**(1), 35–42.

Ryan, W. (1976) *Blaming the Victim*. New York: Vintage Books.

Vincent, C., Evans, J., Lunt, I. and Young, P. (1994) The market forces? The effect of local management of schools on special educational needs provision. *British Educational Research Journal*, **20**(3), 261–77.

Walford, G. (1992) *Selection for Secondary Schooling*. Briefing Paper No. 7, London: National Commission on Education.

Wolfe, J. (1994) Beyond difference: Toward inclusion and equity. In F. Pignatelli and S. Pflaum (eds) *Experiencing Diversity: Toward educational equity*. California: Corwin Press.

World Conference on Special Needs Education (1994) Framework for action on special needs education. *International Review of Education*, **40** (6), 495–507.

This chapter has provided a broad context for the discussions in the following chapters of what we might envisage and want from inclusive services in the coming years. It has illustrated the policy tensions under which we currently operate and shown that seeing our way through the maze of mixed messages must be an important first step in thinking through our wish-list for inclusion and making it happen.

Chapter 8

Why it remains important to take children's rights seriously

Michael Freeman

> In this chapter, the author points out that, nearly 30 years ago, Ronald Dworkin (1977) urged us to 'take rights seriously', but that his argument did not specifically extend to children. This chapter makes the case to take children's rights seriously. Rights are invisible and inter-dependent. Human rights—for that is what children's rights are—include the whole range of civil, political, social, economic and cultural rights. This chapter reminds us of the need to maintain the struggle for the rights of children who many regard as not yet ready to exercise such rights.

It was Ronald Dworkin who, nearly 30 years ago, urged us to 'take rights seriously' (1977). It is a pity that his argument did not specifically extend to children. Indeed, that in a little noticed passage a decade later he stumbled on the dilemma of what 'Hercules' (the ideal superhuman judge) should do when he thought 'the best interpretation of the equal protection clause outlaws distinctions between the rights of adults and those of children that have never been questioned in the community, and yet he ... thinks that it would be politically unfair. ... for the law to impose that view on a community where family and social practices accept such distinctions as proper and fundamental' (Dworkin, 1986, 402). Nor has he ever returned to this dilemma; a pity because it beautifully encapsulates the problem of what to do when the supposedly 'right answer' is morally the 'wrong answer'.

When Taking Rights Seriously was published we were in the heyday of the children's liberation movement. This was the era of Farson (1978) and Holt (1975). Their thesis is ripe for reassessment, but it is clear that at the time its impact was limited. Dworkin was clearly unaware of it, as indeed he was of other children's rights literature of the 1970s and earlier.

My own first foray into writing on children's rights was in 1980, the text of a lecture given to celebrate the International Year of The Child in 1979 (1980).

The Rights and Wrongs of Children (1983) emerged four years later. Then followed the Brian Jackson Memorial Lecture in Huddersfield in 1987 (1988) which advocated that we take children's rights seriously, and a paper at a workshop on 'children, rights and the law' at the ANU in 1991 which emphasised the need to take children's rights' more seriously' (1992). By then, of course, there was the United Nations Convention on the Rights of the Child, which was swiftly ratified by virtually the whole world, and there were developments in legal systems which suggested that children's rights were indeed being taken seriously or at least a lot more seriously than previously.

There has since been a backlash: in part this is because rights themselves have come under attack. But this cannot be the sole reason. Many of today's critics of children's rights are passionate defenders of the rights of others, notably of the rights of parents. An example is the … deeply- flawed–book by the American lawyer, Martin Guggenheim (2005, and see Freeman, 2006).

The language of rights can make visible what has for too long been suppressed. It can lead to different and new stories being heard in public. Carrie Menkel-Meadow explains that 'Each time we let in an excluded group, each time we listen to a new way of knowing, we learn more about the limits of our current way of seeing' (1987, 52). An illustration from a recent English case may assist.

The Williamson case revolved about whether parents (as well as teachers) could exercise their right, as they saw it, to continue the practice of corporal punishment in their Christian schools. Legislation had outlawed it, but they claimed this was incompatible with their human rights to freedom of religion and to ensure that education was in conformity with their religious convictions. The case was fought right up to the highest court in the land, the House of Lords. And throughout it was conceived as a dispute between the State–its right to ban corporal punishment from schools–and parents and teachers. Children were the objects of concern, not subjects in their own right. They were not represented: their views were not sought or known. Yes, there is a clear suspicion that they would have agreed with their parents– echoes of the famous U.S. Supreme Court case of Wisconsin v. Yoder. And this raises a problem, which I discuss later. But that is not the issue. More significant than what these children want is the potential impact of the decision on children as a class. The courts found against the parents and teachers. But suppose they hadn't. Children would once again have been exposed to the rod to uphold the human rights of adults. It is significant that the state did not argue that corporal punishment necessarily involved an infringement of any of the rights of children. The practice is a clear breach of the UN Convention. But Arden L.J. was astute enough to observe that the common law 'effectively treats the child as the property of the parent'– corporal punishment by parents is still permitted in English law–and she adds 'the courts may one day have to consider whether this is the right approach'.

The clearest appreciation of these issues is in Baroness Hale's judgment in the House of Lords. Her judgment begins: 'This is, and always has been, a case about children, their rights and the rights of their parents and teachers. Yet there has been no one here or in the courts below to speak on behalf of the children. The battle has been fought on ground selected by the adults'. What she then has to say is 'for the sake of the children'. From this perspective the case is about 'whether the legislation achieves a fair balance between the rights and freedoms of the parents and teachers and the rights, freedoms and interests, not only of their children, but also of any other children who might be affected by the persistence of corporal punishment in some schools'. However, instead the argument focused on 'whether the beliefs of the parents and teachers qualified for protection'. How could it be otherwise? There was no litigation friend to represent children's rights. Nor any NGO. Had it been possible to argue this case from a children's rights perspective, it would have looked very different, even though, of course, the conclusion would have been the same.

The Williamson case draws attention to the importance of children's rights. But I see these as no more or less important than rights generally. It is impossible to underestimate the centrality of rights. Rights are important because they are inclusive: they are universal, available to all members of the human race. In the past, they have depended on gender and on race. Women were non-persons– the US Supreme Court even said this on one notorious occasion. Black people were kept in subservience by policies which justified institutions like slavery and apartheid and other discriminatory policies. And it is surely not insignificant that the word 'boy' was not infrequently applied to black men.

But, just as concepts of gender inequality have been key to understanding womanhood and woman's social status, so the 'concept of generation is key to understanding childhood' (Mayall, 2002, 120). It has always been to the advantage of the powerful to keep others out. It is not, therefore, surprising that adults should want to do this to children, and that they should wish to keep them in an often imposed and prolonged dependence, which history and culture shows to be neither inevitable nor essential. Think of the other side of inclusion–of exclusion, and what this generates both on the part of the excluded and their victims, the socially excluded. And observe how the powerful regulate space–social, political (Archard, 2004), geographical

(Valentine, 2004)–define participation, marginalise significance, and frustrate development.

Rights are invisible and inter-dependent. Human rights–for that is what children's rights are–include the whole range of civil, political, social, economic and cultural rights. Denying certain rights undermines other rights. So, for example, if we deny children the right to be free from corporal chastisement, we so undermine their status and integrity that other rights fall as well. And this point applies across classes of potential rights-holders. Thus, if we do not put in place structures to tackle domestic violence, we will not protect children from child abuse. And if we do not eradicate child abuse, we can never hope to conquer domestic violence.

Rights are important because they recognise the respect their bearers are entitled to. To accord rights is to respect dignity: to deny rights is to cast doubt on humanity and on integrity. Rights are an affirmation of the Kantian basic principle that we are ends in ourselves, and not means to the ends of others (Kant, 1997).

What the excluded often most lack is a right one rarely finds articulated.

It is Hannah Arendt who has explained this 'right' better than anyone. Her context is very different from ours. Commenting on the Holocaust, she observed that 'a condition of complete rightlessness was created before the right to live was challenged' (1986, 296). Thus, before the Nazis robbed Jews–and gypsies, homosexuals and others–of their lives, they robbed them of their humanity, just as generations had done with slaves. The most fundamental of rights is the right to possess rights. This is a right we deny animals: some are concerned about this.

We deny it also to trees, rain forests, mountains: this is less controversial, but they have their supporters too. And we do of course deny it to humans until they are born, which constitutes a major moral dilemma. For the powerful, and as far as children are concerned adults are always powerful, rights are an inconvenience. The powerful would find it easier if those below them lacked rights. It would be easier to rule, decision-making would be swifter, cheaper, more efficient, more certain. It is hardly surprising that none of the rights we have were freely bestowed: they all had to be fought for. It is, therefore, important that we see rights, as Dworkin so appositely put it, as 'trumps' (1977, ix). This is to emphasise that they cannot be knocked off their pedestal, chipped away at, because it would be better for others (in the case of children, perhaps their parents or teachers) or even for society as a whole were these rights not to exist.

Rights are important because those who have them can exercise agency. Agents are decision-makers. They are people who can negotiate with others, who are capable of altering relationships or decisions, who can shift social assumptions and constraints. And there is now clear evidence that even the youngest can do this (Alderson, Hawthorne and Killen, 2005 and Alderson, Sutcliffe and Curtis, 2006). As agents, rights-bearers can participate. They can make their own lives, rather than having their lives made for them. And participation is a fundamental human right. It enables us to demand rights. We are, of course, better able to do so where there is freedom of speech, so that orthodoxies (for example, about children and their abilities and incapacities) can be challenged; freedom of association, so that understandings can be nourished; and freedom of information. It is common to deny children all three of these freedoms.

Rights are also an important advocacy tool, a weapon which can be employed in the battle to secure recognition. Giving people rights without access to those who can present those rights, and expertly, without the right to representation, is thus of little value. But this is to acknowledge that we must get beyond rhetoric. Rights without remedies are of symbolic importance, no more. And remedies themselves require the injection of resources, a commitment on behalf of all of us that we view rights with respect, that we want them to have an impact on the lives of all people, and not just the lives of the powerful and privileged, who are often the first to exploit rights for their own purposes.

Rights offer legitimacy to pressure groups, lobbies, campaigns, to both direct and indirect action, in particular to those who are disadvantaged or excluded. They offer a way in; they open doors. It is thus hardly surprising that some of the best statements of the case for rights have come from minority scholars like Mari Matsuda (1987) Kimberlé Crenshaw (1988) and Patricia Williams (1997), or from those arguing the case for the excluded like Martha Minow (1990). For Crenshaw, adopting a rights-based discourse is a vehicle in which social movements can enter a debate into the validity of the dominant ideology as part of a counter-hegemonic strategy. And for Alan Hunt (1990): 'rights . . . have the capacity to be elements of emancipation'. He cautions, however, that they are neither 'a perfect nor exclusive vehicle' for such a loosening of bonds. They 'can only be operative as constituents of a strategy for social transformation as they become part of an emergent common sense and are articulated within social practices'. The message is, as Federle so eloquently puts it (1994, 343), 'that rights flow downhill'.

The task of the children's rights advocate is thus manifest, though no one can pretend it is easy. We must show that the case we are making is morally right, so right in fact that people will come to wonder how they can ever have thought—or more likely felt—otherwise. And we can help to negotiate this common sense through our social practices: certainly, the social practices of those who work with children can help to construct a new culture of childhood.

Rights then are also a resource: they offer reasoned argument. They support a strong moral case. Too often those who oppose rights can offer little if anything in response. For example, the opponent of anti-smacking laws who tells us that it never did him any harm (or perhaps none that he recognises!) Or, for that matter the one who, rather like the claimants in the Williamson case, reels off epigrams from the Book of Proverbs as if the 'wisdom' of an earlier millennium offered closure to a contemporary debate (and see Greven, 1992).

Rights then offer fora for action. Without rights the excluded can make requests, they can beg or implore, they can be troublesome; they can rely on, what has been called, noblesse oblige, or on others being charitable, generous, kind, co-operative or even intelligently foresighted. But they cannot demand, for there is no entitlement (Bandman, 1973).

References

Alderson, P., Hawthorne, J. and Killen, M. (2005) 'The Participation Rights of Premature Babies' *International Journal of Children's Rights*, 13, 31–50.

Alderson, P., Sutcliffe, K. and Curtis, K. (2006) Children as Partners with Adults in their Medical Care *Archives of Disease in Childhood*, 91, 300–303.

Archard, D. (2004) *Children, Rights and Childhood*, London: Routledge, 2004 (2nd ed).

Arendt, H. (1986) *The Origins of Totalitarianism*, London: André Deutsch.

Bandman, B. (1973) 'Do Children Have Any Natural Rights?' *Proceedings of the 29th Annual Meeting Of Philosophy of Education Society*, 234–246.

Crenshaw, K. (1988) 'Race, Reform and Retrenchment: Transformation and Legitimization in Anti-Discrimination Law', *Harvard Law Review*, 101, 1331.

Dworkin, R. (1977) *Taking Rights Seriously*, London: Duckworth.

Dworkin, R. (1986) *Law's Empire*, London: Fontana.

Farson, R. (1978) Birthrights, Harmondsworth: Penguin Books.

Federle, K.H. (1994) 'Rights Flow Downhill', *International Journal of Children's Rights*, 2, 343–368.

Freeman, M. (1980) 'The Rights of Children in The International Year of the Child', *Current Legal Problems*, 33, 1–31.

Freeman, M. (1983) *The Rights and Wrongs of Children*, London: Frances Pinter.

Freeman, M. (1988) 'Taking Children's Rights Seriously', *Children and Society*, 1, 299–319.

Freeman, M. (1992) 'Taking Children's Rights More Seriously', *International Journal of Law and the Family*, 6, 52–71.

Freeman, M. (2006) 'What's Right with Children's Rights', *International Journal of Law In Context*, 2, 89–98.

Greven, P. (1992) *Spare The Child*, New York: Vintage Books.

Guggenheim, M. (2005) *What's Wrong With Children's Rights*, Cambridge, Mass: Harvard University Press.

Holt, J. (1975) Escape From Childhood, Harmondsworth: Penguin Books.

Hunt, A. (1990) 'Rights and Social Movements: Counter-Hegemonic Strategies', *Journal of Law and Society*, 17, 309–337.

Kant, I. (1997) *Groundwork of The Metaphysics of Morals*, Cambridge: Cambridge University Press Originally published in 1783.

Matsuda, M. (1987) 'Looking To The Bottom: Critical Legal Studies and Reparations', *Harvard Civil Rights–Civil Liberties Law Review*, 22, 338.

Mayall, B. (2002) *Towards A Sociology of Childhood*, London: Routledge, Falmer.

Menkel-Meadow, C. (1987) 'Excluded Voices: New Voices in the Legal Profession Making New Voices In The Law' *University of Miami Law Review*, 42, 29–53.

Minow, M. (1990) *Making all The Difference*, Ithaca, N.Y: Cornell University Press.

Valentine, G. (2004) *Public Space and The Culture of Childhood*, Aldershot: Ashgate.

Williams, P. (1997) *The Alchemy of Race and Rights*, Cambridge, Mass: Harvard University Press.

Michael Freeman reminds us of the importance of engaging with children and young people on their own terms. We need to genuinely engage with their lifeworlds. His central persuasive argument is simple and straightforward: if children have rights and they are taken seriously and protected, then a better world will not only exist for all children, but for all people everywhere.

Chapter 9

Youth participation in the UK

Bureaucratic disaster or triumph of child rights?

Emily Middleton

The chapter begins with an outline of the history of the development of youth participation in the UK over the last 15 years. Emily Middleton, who wrote this article as a young person involved in youth participation explores its use by the government, as well as the methods various charities and other organizations use to involve children and young people in their work, on both local and national levels. The impact of youth participation on decision-making is assessed and the problems facing youth participation are also considered, with a particular emphasis on the issue of tokenism.

> You can't ignore children any longer and get away with it.
> Stephen Lewis, Deputy Executive Director of UNICEF, 1999

Youth participation is about giving children and young people (usually up to the age of 18) the opportunity to express their views on aspects of life that affect them, and to use these opinions to inform and influence decision-making. Youth participation has many forms, from school councils to youth forums, from young board members to surveys. I have chosen to discuss youth participation in the UK as I have been involved in several youth participation projects, and wanted to find out more about the history, methods and potential of involving young people. I want to go further than this, however, and ask: how effective is youth participation in the UK? There are many reports dedicated to why and how to develop youth participation, but very few evaluating the extent of its impact. I have looked at a wide variety of websites, articles, reports and research regarding youth participation. [...]

History of youth participation in the UK

The widespread participation of children and young people in decision-making is a relatively new phenomenon. Arguably, youth participation in public decision-making was triggered by the United Nations Convention on the Rights of the Child (1989) in which Article 12 clearly states that children and young people should have their opinions taken into account in all major decisions affecting their lives. Stephen Lewis, then the Deputy Executive Director of UNICEF, argued at the Commission on Human Rights in 1999 that in fact the UN Convention's most impressive effect was the wider inclusion of children and young people in decision-making:

> The most powerful change wrought by the Convention is the way in which children have become visible. Politicians, media, NGOs (non-governmental organizations) and broader civil society feel a clear obligation to include children in their respective public domains, interventions, dialogues, debates, mandates.
>
> (Lewis 1999)

Indeed, the period between 1989 and 1991 (when the UK government ratified the Convention) saw the beginnings of youth participation within several organizations. Katherine Harding of Save the Children told me: "Save the Children's project work in the area of participation has only had real emphasis since the late [19]80s." Since then, in the words of Katherine Harding, youth participation in Britain has been a "slow, evolutionary process." However, it now appears to be fairly well established in the UK that anyone with anything to do with children and young people should consult them:

> There has been a shift in thinking where participation of young people from being of marginal concern has now become a central issue for organizations working with young people.
>
> ("Child and Youth Participation," www.article13.com, accessed on 1 June 2010)

In the last seven years, the participation of children and young people has been included in seven separate pieces of legislation in the United Kingdom, ranging from the Crime and Disorder Act 1998 to the Children Act 2004. The involvement of young people in the government's work has been particularly important since 2001, however, when the European Youth White Paper stated a "Common Objective of more Youth Participation." The Department for Education and Skills (DfES) completed a report on the UK's progress on this objective in 2005. Another example of the UK government's commitment to youth participation was the guidance on pupil participation that was published for schools and local education authorities in 2004 entitled, "Working Together: Giving Children and Young People a Say."

Youth participation in practice

When I asked the Rt Hon Beverley Hughes MP (the then newly appointed Minister of State for Children, Young People and Families) why it was important to involve children and young people in the work of the Department for Education and Skills, she replied that it is

> vitally important—essential, in fact—that we involve children and young people directly in the work of DfES, consult them about our proposals … the decisions we take should be informed by the views of children and young people themselves.

These are fine, honorable sentiments, but does it actually happen in practice? Is the government's use of youth participation effective?

So far my limited experience has been fairly constructive. For example, the department seems to be working hard to obtain the responses of as many young people as possible to the youth Green Paper, Youth Matters, which was published in the summer of 2005. However, one young person I spoke to who had been on the Board last year said:

> The actual policy work we were told we were impacting on was actually decided way in advance to the Board's August start. I think we were just there to be DfES skivvies.

Such a response is far from positive, and suggests a complete waste of the time of the young people involved as well as the DfES.

It is not just the UK government that has become increasingly active in the area of youth participation. According to a report published by the National Youth Agency in 2004, around 80 per cent of both statutory and voluntary sector organizations currently involve young people in decision-making. Youth-controlled wings of children's charities are becoming increasingly common, many of which contain a "young advisory group" made up of young people. One of the first was started by the National Children's

Bureau (NCB). It took the lead by establishing Young NCB in 1999, which encourages young people to voice their opinions, and works hard to make sure the right people hear those opinions and take note of them.

But why use up valuable resources in establishing youth-led offshoots in the first place? Lucy Morris, who is currently in charge of Young NCB, told me it was

> with the aim of making sure that NCB practices what it preaches in our second mission which is to "work with children and young people to ensure that they are involved in all matters that affect their lives."

NCB's motive to set up Young NCB may also lie in its mission statement, which states that "NCB promotes the voices ... of all children and young people across every aspect of their lives."

This may well be the incentive behind similar projects that have been set up by other children's charities such as UNICEF, Save the Children and the Children's Rights Alliance for England; in the words of a report published by Save the Children:

> an organization that seeks to promote and speak on behalf of the rights of children needs to be directly accountable to children themselves.
>
> (Lansdown 2003, 5)

Some independent organizations have been set up specifically to encourage young people to participate in local and national decision-making. One such organization is the UK Youth Parliament, which was formed in 2001. Its aim is that

> by 2006 young people in the UK will be aware that they have their own Youth Parliament, and that ... they have the right to vote for an MYP, and the right to stand as an MYP if they so wish.
>
> (UK Youth Parliament website)

More unusual, however, is the practice of appointing young people on adult Boards of Management and including them within other meetings designed for adults rather than for children. This form of youth participation has been relatively recent. The research paper *Participation in Our Village* found that

> children and young people responded well when meetings were organized specifically for them ... but less well when they were asked to attend meetings designed for adults.
>
> (Forum for Rural Young People and Children 2005, 10)

There are, in my opinion, only two possible solutions to this problem: not inviting children to "adult" meetings, or altering the meetings to make them more child-friendly. In the early days of young people being included in NCB's Board of Management, the young members asked for lunch to be longer and earlier in the meeting, and for there to be a break later on. The necessary amendments were made, with the result that more than a few adult Board members thanked the young Board members and said that they had wanted a break but did not know how to ask for one. So it seems that in making meetings more child-friendly, they can be made more adult-friendly, too.

Yet apart from increasing the number of breaks, do young people actually have an impact on the decisions an adult Board or meeting makes? I have sat as a young member on NCB's Board of Management for almost a year and can report that in this particular organization, young people do have an impact—probably because our suggestions are taken seriously and we have sufficient support. As part of a discussion on NCB's policy on healthy school meals, for example, we reminded the Board of the importance of having unhealthy as well as healthy options in schools: we argued that healthy eating education is useless when adults do not trust pupils to put this knowledge into practice. As a result, NCB's policy position (which is referred to by many different professionals and organizations within the children's services sector) was altered accordingly.

The Children's Rights Alliance for England is looking to go a step further, however, and make some young people full trustees on its Board of Management. This would carry a legal and financial burden on the young people involved. Is this one step too far on the road to comprehensive youth participation? It is rarely acknowledged by youth participation reports that knowing where to draw the line is essential. In my opinion, youth participation is all about involving young people in the decision–making process, whether in schools, government or organizations, and using their opinions to help improve services and enhance the decisions that are made. Allowing children to assume responsibility for their own advisory groups and projects is an important part of this, but any financial responsibilities, I would argue, are beyond the remit of youth participation.

Effective change?

In recent years, local youth participation has grown considerably in the UK, with more opportunities for young people to have a voice in their local communities than ever before. Indeed, many local authorities and city councils have made commitments to encourage youth participation, such as the following statement made by Gloucester City Council:

> The City Council: upholds the right of young people to participate in decisions about public services that affect them...[and] encourages and supports the involvement of young people in the planning, delivery and evaluation of city council services.

(2002)

The achievements of local youth participation initiatives vary greatly, but some of the more successful results include a new bus service for young people in Chideok, Dorset and setting up a local youth club in Halgate ward, Cumbria (Forum for Rural Young People and Children 2005).

Youth councils, also known as youth forums, are one of the most popular forms of local youth participation. Many such groups provide focused, directed discussion as to how to improve their local area. The Wiltshire Agenda for Youth, for example, comprised of 22 elected young people from across the county, recently published an "Agenda for Action."

Under their policy promises, many local authorities should be supporting and nurturing such groups—yet the British Youth Council (BYC) reports that among their network (which comprises over 500 youth councils from across the UK) "only 16 percent of youth councils have some form of staff support." In my opinion this is clearly not good enough. After all, the UK government's green paper *Every Child Matters*, published in 2003, asserted:

> Real service improvement is only attainable through involving children and young people and listening to their views.

(10)

Local government in the UK is, with a few honorable exceptions, failing to recognize and support the young people who are trying to make a difference and setting up their own forums for debate. (BYC claims that the majority of youth councils are established by young people.) BYC cites "limited resources including staff, funding and appropriate expertise" as a major problem that limits the effectiveness of youth councils today.

Encouragingly, youth participation is undoubtedly on the increase—one report states that around eight out of ten respondents whose organizations involved young people said "that the amount of work they did to involve young people in decision-making had increased over the past four years"

(Oldfield with Fowler 2004, 3). The research report *Building a Culture of Participation* agrees:

> Increasingly, acceptance of the principle of children's involvement is being turned into practice through a variety of participation activities across a range of organizations.
>
> (Kirby with Lanyon, Cronin and Sinclair 2003, 3)

But is this increase of youth participation doing anyone any good? Are young people actually influencing decisions more than they used to or, as an article on the Carnegie Young People Initiative's (CYPI) website asks: "Will participation be another case of organizations ticking boxes but not fundamentally reforming?" The latter suggestion is an unhappy possibility. Governmental organizations certainly feel pressured to meet the targets set by the government in the area of youth participation. One young person I spoke to complained about the "restrictions and targets ridiculously imposed by the government." The CYPI report *Measuring the Magic?* talked about bureaucracy as one of the "barriers to involving young people in area-wide strategic planning" (Kirby with Bryson 2002, 6). Although targets might fuel local authorities into setting up more youth participation projects, they are not sufficient to encourage good practice.

Dangerously, the practice of ticking bureaucratic boxes can manifest itself in "tokenism": asking young people for their opinions but failing to ask enough young people to make a significant impact, or failing to act upon their opinions or take them very seriously. I heard one young person speak about a conference he attended a few years ago, organized by Margaret Hodge (who was at the time Minister of State for Children, Young People and Families). He said that one young person had angrily asked the Minister, "Why have you invited us here? ... To tick boxes on bits of government paper?" This incident highlights the dangers of tokenism at any level: the young people involved can feel mistreated and under-valued as a result.

> There is substantial evidence that good participatory work benefits the participating young people, but that token involvement may not.
>
> (Kirby with Bryson 2002, 6)

Another young person with whom I spoke told me, "tokenism is a very big problem today and I think it will be for months, if not years to come." At a conference at which I spoke on the youth green paper *Youth Matters*, one young person asked at the end of our presentation, "Don't you think that only inviting four young people to speak at this conference is a bit tokenistic?" He had a point. Out of numerous speakers on panels and in presentations throughout the day, just four were young people, and only three of them were in the 13–19 age range on which the green paper was focused. On the other hand, inviting young people to speak would have been unlikely to happen at all ten years ago.

It seems that an optimum level needs to be found for youth participation within events designed primarily for adults. Involving too many young people could prove impractical, but when young people are the subject matter, they should undoubtedly be involved. One youth worker told me proudly that a conference she was organizing would be attended by 25 young people—25 per cent of the total number of attendees. She had good reason to be pleased with this figure: it certainly surpassed the percentage of young people at the conference on the youth green paper that I attended.

Nevertheless, despite increased levels of involvement, the question of effectiveness should not be ignored. Are young people influencing decisions more than they used to? Unfortunately, some recent reports suggest that in general they are not. One report stated:

> the evidence from existing evaluations is that they [young people] are still having little impact on public decision making.
>
> (Kirby with Bryson 2002, 5)

Significantly, the report continues, "although this varies across contexts and between different types of organizations." It is in the latter extract that hope for successful youth participation can be found. A report by Save the Children stated:

> Children's participation within the organization has challenged some of the assumptions which underlie the organization's policies and thinking.
>
> (Lansdown 2003, 14)

One can only imagine what far-reaching consequences such an effect may have. It seems that the effectiveness of youth participation varies widely across different projects, but the fact that it can sometimes produce impressive results gives children and professionals alike a target at which to aim.

However, as asserted by an article on the Carnegie Young People's Initiative website, "there remains the danger that young people's participation will become yet another glossy policy which will be quickly forgotten." Admittedly, there is a long way to go before the ideals of the "glossy policy" produce impressive results across the board.

Future directions for youth participation in the UK

Having considered the evidence of numerous projects, reports and accounts, the following are the issues that I believe need to be addressed in order to develop youth participation over the coming years.

First, organizations outside the children's services sector need to embrace youth participation and use it to inform decisions that affect young people. The National Health Service (NHS), for example, is increasing their use of youth participation. In the Stockport NHS Foundation Trust, for instance, there is now a young person on the Board of Governors. More institutions as well as non-governmental organizations need to make youth participation a matter of course.

Second, the quality of youth participation needs to be improved. One young person said that, in his experience, "local Youth Community Services are over-stretched and under-resourced." Youth participation can only improve in local areas if more money and qualified staff become available. More resources and support for young people would also help to tackle the unintentional practice of tokenism. Youth participation would be more successful more often if the following were established:

> definite aims and outcomes, clarity about the basis on which children and young people are involved, and ensuring that children and young people have the support they need.
>
> (Oldfield with Fowler 2004, 5)

The development of a major new website will help foster these aims: www. participationworks.org.uk will become the centre for sharing good practice in the UK.

Third, youth participation needs to become more popular among young people themselves. The report *Measuring the Magic?* admitted "only a minority of young people get involved in public decision making" (Kirby with Bryson 2002, 5). The opportunities available and the possible benefits for young people need to be more widely advertised (a hopeful outcome of more resources being put into local projects). Youth participation also needs to become more accessible by bringing opportunities to young people rather than expecting them to find out about them, and also through using alternative methods such as "music, drama and dance to engage with young people" (Lucy Morris, NCB). If the opinions gained from young people become more representative of young people as a whole, perhaps they will be better listened to.

Conclusion

It is imperative that society does not give up on youth participation, however hopeless or ineffective it can seem at times. On the whole, the benefits of involving young people in decision-making outweigh the problems. It is important to remember that the involvement of young people in decision-making at a strategic level has only really got underway in the last five years in the UK: think what can be achieved in another five. [...]

References

British Youth Council (2005) *The Youth Green Paper Strong Local Voices: BYC's Vision for Building a Vibrant Network of Local Youth Councils*, London: British Youth Council.

'Child and Youth Participation.' Available from http://www.article13.com/A13_ContentList. asp?strAction=GetPublication&PNID=713 (accessed on 1 June 2010).

Department for Education and Skills (2004) *Listening to Learn 2004: How the Department for Education and Skills involves children and young people in its work*, London: Department for Education and Skills.

Forum for Rural *Children and Young People* (2005) *Participation in Our Village: Involving Children and Young People in the Development of Parish and Town Plans*, London: National Children's Bureau.

Gloucester City Council (2002) *Youth Participation Policy*, Gloucester: Gloucester City Council.

Harnett, Robert (2003) *Peer Advocacy for Children and Young People*, Highlight no. 202, London: National Children's Bureau.

HM Government (2003) *Every Child Matters*, London: The Stationery Office on behalf of HM Government.

HM Government (2004) *Every Child Matters: Change for Children*, London: The Stationery Office on behalf of HM Government.

HM Government (2005) *Youth Matters*. London: The Stationery Office on behalf of HM Government. Youth Participation in the UK: Bureaucratic Disaster or Triumph of Child Rights? 189.

Kirby, Perpetua with Sara Bryson (2002) *Measuring the Magic? Evaluating and Researching Young People's Participation in Public Decision Making*, London: Carnegie Young People Initiative.

Kirby, Perpetua with Claire Lanyon, Kathleen Cronin and Ruth Sinclair (2003) *Building a Culture of Participation*, London: Department for Education and Skills.

Lansdown, Gerison (2003) *Involvement of Children and Young People in Shaping the Work of Save the Children*, London: Save the Children UK.

Lewis, Stephen (1999) Commission on Human Rights press release HR/CN 912, 14 April.

Oldfield, Carolyn with Clare Fowler (2004) *Mapping Children and Young People's Participation in England*, London: Department for Education and Skills.

Save the Children (2005). *Practice Standards in Children's Participation*, London: Save the Children UK.

Examining the future of youth participation in the UK, the chapter concludes that organizations outside the children's services sector need to embrace youth participation and the quality of youth participation should be improved. The chapter asserts that youth participation needs to become more popular among young people and would benefit from a wider range of young people being involved.

Part 3

Looking from within
Barriers and opportunities

Chapter 10

Social model or unsociable muddle?

Richard Light

This chapter was taken from the Disability Awareness in Action website and provides a useful overview of the origins and evolutions of the social model of disability. It also highlights some of the tensions and controversies.

It is becoming increasingly clear that one of the key issues in disability activisim – the social model of disability – is subject to repeated attacks, particularly within the academic community. What is equally clear is that much of the 'bad press' has been prompted by interpretations of the social model that many of us would find particularly strange. As you might expect, academic discussion is often marked by both completely incomprehensible language and a startling lack of humility – each writer seems to assume that their contribution offers an invaluable new insight and that anyone who does not accept it must be hopelessly stupid or badly informed.

This article seeks to describe, in straightforward terms, what the social model means to a great many disabled activists, including those of us at DAA [Disability Awareness in Action]. We believe that it is time for disabled activists to remind academics that the social model originated with *us*, and that *we* still have use for it! Despite our concerns about harmful criticism of the social model, we wholeheartedly endorse attempts to offer a more comprehensive or inclusive social *theory* of disability. This article is not intended to condemn efforts to theorise disability and what it means, but it is a heartfelt plea for theorists to understand the damage that is done by sweeping claims as to the social model's shortcomings, without proposing alternatives that are acceptable to the disability community. We are in no doubt that repeated attacks on the social model, particularly where no acceptable alternative is proposed, cause harm. We hope that this article makes it clear why so much is at stake.

The origins of the social model

The origins of what would later be called the 'social model' can be traced to an essay by a disabled Briton: *A Critical Condition*, written by Paul Hunt and published in 1966. In this paper, Hunt argued that because people with impairments are viewed as 'unfortunate, useless, different, oppressed and sick' they pose a direct challenge to commonly held Western values. According to Hunt, people with impairments were viewed as:

- 'unfortunate' because they are unable to 'enjoy' material and social benefits of modern society
- 'useless' because they are considered unable to contribute to 'economic good of the community', and
- marked as 'minority group' members because, like black people and homosexuals, they are perceived as 'abnormal' and 'different'.

This analysis led Hunt to the view that disabled people encounter 'prejudice which expresses itself in discrimination and oppression'. The relationship between economics and cultural attitudes toward disabled people is a vital part of Hunt's understanding of the experience of impairment and disability in Western society.

The UPIAS definition

Ten years later, the Union of the Physically Impaired Against Segregation (UPIAS) developed Paul Hunt's work further, leading to the UPIAS assertion, in 1976, that disability was

> the disadvantage or restriction of activity caused by a contemporary social organisation which takes little or no account of people who have physical impairments and thus excludes them from participation in the mainstream of social activities.

It must be acknowledged that the UPIAS definition of 'disability' only refers to *people who have physical impairments*, and the failure to include any other types of impairment has led some people to claim that the social model only applies to wheelchair users.

We would make two responses to such criticism: firstly, that the group 'people who have physical impairments' includes many people who are not wheelchair users. Secondly, and far more importantly, the statement was made by an organisation whose membership was made up of people with physical impairments – *how could UPIAS speak for any other group of disabled people?* The vital feature of the UPIAS statement and, indeed, Paul Hunt's 1966 essay, is that for the first time disability was described in terms of restrictions *imposed* on disabled people by *social* organisation.

The social model is born

It was not until 1983 that the disabled academic, Mike Oliver, described the ideas that lay behind the UPIAS definition as the 'social model of disability'. The 'social model' was extended and developed by academics like Vic Finkelstein, Mike Oliver and Colin Barries in the UK and Gerben DeJong in the USA (amongst others), and extended by Disabled Peoples' International to include *all* disabled people. So, while the original formulation of the social model may have been developed by people with physical impairments, the insight that it offered was quickly seen as having value to all disabled people. To suggest that the social model amounts to a conspiracy by one group of disabled people against the remainder is, therefore, either incorrect or mischievous.

The social model – an evolving idea

It is an inevitable aspect of human development that new ways of interpreting the world around us are introduced by an individual or, more often, a small group of people. It is simply the support and agreement of a wider group that transforms these interpretations into a social movement – precisely what happened with the African-American civil rights movement and feminism. As more and more people are introduced to these new interpretations, so the original ideas are questioned, argued over, developed and refined – precisely what happened to the social model of disability.

For those of us at DAA, the evolving nature of the social model, made possible by the interest it has generated throughout the disabled community, is a positive and necessary thing. Knowledge is always partial – the best that we can achieve at a particular time and place – but subsequent debate has ensured that the social model remains relevant to our lives, primarily because it still has the power to change dramatically the way disabled people think about themselves and their place in the world. What can be more liberating than the discovery that being disabled does not have to be viewed negatively – as some failure or weakness in us – and that there are people all over the world who feel a sense of community because of disability?

The social model and different impairments

DAA's work is driven by an *inclusive* view of the disabled community – defined quite simply as those people who choose to identify themselves as 'disabled'. We are aware that not all groups of disabled people adopt such an inclusive approach, sometimes using both formal rules and informal sanctions to discourage people who are not seen as belonging to 'their' group, but such difficulties are caused by the individuals involved, not the social model! The construction of the social model which DAA adopts defines 'disability' quite simply as 'the *social* consequences of having an impairment'. It is unquestionably the case that using 'disability' to describe such a huge and very different group of people is difficult, not least because the label is artificial and because too much is usually taken for granted when the wider community talk about 'the disabled'.

It is also the case that all members of the disabled community have not had the same opportunity to have their opinions heard. Self-advocacy ultimately depends on individuals being prepared to advocate for themselves. Demanding the right to advocate for ourselves is a dynamic process, it is not something that others can give to, or provide for, us (although the space and opportunity to be heard may). No matter how much disability advocates might want to be joined by under-represented groups within the disability community, this requires those groups to want to be part of the wider community. Blaming the social model for the undoubted shortcomings of the disability movement is, quite simply, unreasonable!

While the academic community may view it differently, for the disability movement the social model provides a way of thinking about disability that accords with our experience of being disabled people – that disability is caused by the attitudinal, physical and communication barriers imposed on us, rather than the effects of our impairments. Despite the artificial nature of the label 'disabled', this shared experience of external barriers allows disabled people, irrespective of their different impairments, to feel a sense of shared identity. Having a shared identity as 'disabled people' need not and, in our opinion, should not, interfere with our identities as people with specific impairments, nor should they cause some impairment-specific needs to be promoted at the expense of others. The disability movement can only remain strong and effective when we each respect the enormous diversity within the movement.

After years of campaigning and persuasion, the social model has offered a valuable and effective tool for helping people, disabled and non-disabled alike, to view disability in a way that does not put the 'blame' for disability on the disabled person. Disability equality trainers, activists and academics have used the insight provided by the social model to make a real difference in all areas of social, political and economic life. It is also true that the changes won by disabled campaigners are unpopular with those who see their authority, power and, in some cases, wealth, being eroded by social model ideals.

Theorising disability is important, but it's time that some of those who do theorise adopt a little more humility and understanding before making public attacks on the social model.

While Richard Light is not attempting to contribute directly to the debates on equality, participation and inclusion, his honest appraisal here is relevant to inclusion. When we theorise about equality, participation and inclusion we should not shy away from forming and articulating our own ideas, but we will do this more effectively if we also listen to, and learn from, each other, recognising achievements and debates in other domains. This author writes from the multiple perspective of being a disabled person and someone with a long history in policy formation at (inter)national and regional levels. He reminds us that academic theorising can and does have an impact on real world struggles.

Chapter 11

Including all of our lives
Renewing the social model of disability

Liz Crow

In this chapter Liz Crow, a disabled feminist active in the disabled people's movement, gives one of the clearest explanations of the social model of disability we have found. Her narrative is rich with discussion of the complexities involved as disabled people take charge of the debates about their experiences. The chapter had its origins in an article written for *Coalition*, one of the journals of the British disabled people's movement, before appearing as an extended chapter in Jenny Morris' edited collection *Encounters with Strangers: Feminism and Disability*.

My life has two phases: before the social model of disability, and after it. Discovering this way of thinking about my experiences was the proverbial raft in stormy seas. It gave me an understanding of my life, shared with thousands, even millions, of other people around the world, and I clung to it.

This was the explanation I had sought for years. Suddenly what I had always known, deep down, was confirmed. It wasn't my body that was responsible for all my difficulties, it was external factors, the barriers constructed by the society in which I live. I was being dis-abled – my capabilities and opportunities were being restricted – by prejudice, discrimination, inaccessible environments and inadequate support. Even more important, if all the problems had been created by society, then surely society could un-create them. Revolutionary!

For years now this social model of disability has enabled me to confront, survive and even surmount countless situations of exclusion and discrimination. It has been my mainstay, as it has been for the wider disabled people's movement. It has enabled a vision of ourselves free from the constraints of disability (oppression) and provided a direction for our commitment to social change. It has played a central role in promoting disabled people's individual self-worth, collective identity and political organisation. I don't think it is an exaggeration to say that the social model has saved lives. Gradually, very gradually, its sphere is extending beyond our movement to influence policy and practice in the mainstream. The contribution of the social model of disability, now and in the future, to achieving equal rights for disabled people is incalculable.

So how is it that, suddenly to me, for all its strengths and relevance, the social model doesn't seem so water-tight anymore? It is with trepidation that I criticise it. However, when personal experience no longer matches current explanations, then it is time to question afresh.

Disability is 'all'?

The social model of disability has been our key to dismantling the traditional conception of impairment[1] as 'personal tragedy' and the oppression that this creates.

Mainstream explanations have centred on impairment as 'all' – impairment as the cause of our experiences and disadvantage, and impairment as the focus of intervention. The World Health Organisation defines impairment and related concepts as follows:

> *Impairment*: Any loss or abnormality of psychological, physiological, or anatomical structure or function. *Disability*: Any restriction or lack (resulting from impairment) of ability to perform an activity in the manner or within the range considered normal for a human being. *Handicap*: A disadvantage for a given individual, resulting from an impairment or disability, that limits or prevents fulfilment of a role that is normal, depending on age, sex, social or cultural factors for that individual.
>
> (United Nations Division for Economic and
> Social Information 1983: 3)

Within this framework, which is often called the medical model of disability, a person's functional limitations (impairments) are the root cause of any disadvantages experienced and these disadvantages can therefore only be rectified by treatment or cure.

The social model, in contrast, shifts the focus from impairment onto disability, using this term to refer to disabling social, environmental and attitudinal barriers rather than lack of ability. Thus, while impairment is the functional limitation(s) which affects a person's body, disability is the loss or limitation of opportunities resulting from direct and indirect discrimination. Social change – the removal of disabling barriers – is the solution to the disadvantages we experience.

This way of seeing things opens up opportunities for the eradication of prejudice and discrimination. In contrast, the medical model makes the removal of disadvantage contingent upon the removal or 'overcoming' of impairment – full participation in society is only to be found through cure or fortitude. Small wonder, therefore, that we have focused so strongly on the importance of disabling barriers and struggled to dismantle them.

In doing so, however, we have tended to centre on disability as 'all'. Sometimes it feels as if this focus is so absolute that we are in danger of assuming that impairment has no part at all in determining our experiences. Instead of tackling the contradictions and complexities of our experiences head on, we have chosen in our campaigns to present impairment as irrelevant, neutral and, sometimes, positive, but never, ever as the quandary it really is.

Why has impairment been so excluded from our analysis? Do we believe that admitting there could be a difficult side to impairment will undermine the strong, positive (SuperCrip?) images of our campaigns? Or that showing every single problem cannot be solved by social change will inhibit or excuse non-disabled people from tackling anything at all? Or that we may make the issues so complex that people feel constructive change is outside their grasp? Or even that admitting it can sometimes be awful to have impairments may fuel the belief that our lives are not worth living?

Bring back impairment!

The experience of impairment is not always irrelevant, neutral or positive. How can it be when it is the very reason used to justify the oppression we are battling against? How can it be when pain, fatigue, depression and chronic illness are constant facts of life for many of us?

We align ourselves with other civil rights movements and we have learnt much from those campaigns. But we have one fundamental difference from other movements, which we cannot afford to ignore. There is nothing inherently unpleasant or difficult about other groups' embodiment: sexuality, sex and skin colour are neutral facts. In contrast, impairment means our experience of our bodies *can* be unpleasant or difficult. This does not mean our campaigns against disability are any less vital than those against heterosexism, sexism or racism; it does mean that for many disabled people personal struggle related to impairment will remain even when disabling barriers no longer exist.

Yet our insistence that disadvantage and exclusion are the result of discrimination and prejudice, and our criticisms of the medical model of disability, have made us wary of acknowledging our experiences of impairment. Impairment is safer not mentioned at all.

This silence prevents us from dealing effectively with the difficult aspects of impairment. Many of us remain frustrated and disheartened by pain, fatigue, depression and chronic illness, including the way they prevent us from realising our potential or railing fully against disability (our experience of exclusion and discrimination); many of us fear for our futures with progressive or additional impairments; we mourn past activities that are no longer possible for us; we are afraid we may die early or that suicide may seem our only option; we desperately seek some effective medical intervention; we feel ambivalent about the possibilities of our children having impairments; and we are motivated to work for the prevention of impairments. Yet our silence about impairment has made many of these things taboo and created a whole new series of constraints on our self-expression.

Of course, the suppression of concerns related to impairment does not mean they cease to exist or suddenly become more bearable. Instead this silencing undermines individuals' ability to 'cope' and, ultimately, the whole disabled people's movement. As individuals, most of us simply cannot pretend with any conviction that our impairments are irrelevant because they influence so much of our lives. External disabling barriers may create social and economic disadvantage but our subjective experience of our bodies is also an integral part of our everyday reality. What we need is to find a way to integrate impairment into our whole experience and sense of our selves for the sake of our own physical and emotional well-being, and, subsequently, for our individual and collective capacity to work against disability.

As a movement, we need to be informed about disability *and* impairment in all their diversity if our campaigns are to be open to all disabled people. Many people find that it is their experience of their bodies – and not only disabling barriers such as inaccessible public transport – which make political involvement difficult. For example, an individual's capacity to attend meetings and events might be restricted because of limited energy. If these circumstances remain unacknowledged, then alternative ways of contributing are unlikely to be sought. If our structures and strategies (i.e. *how* we organise and offer support in our debates, consultation and demonstrations) cannot involve all disabled people, then our campaigns lose the contributions of many people. If our movement excludes many disabled people or refuses to discuss certain issues then our understanding is partial: our collective ability to conceive of, and achieve, a world which does not disable is diminished.

What we risk is a world which includes an 'elite' of people with impairments, but which for many more of us contains no real promise of civil rights, equality or belonging. How can we expect anyone to take seriously a 'radical' movement which replicates some of the worst exclusionary aspects of the society it purports to change?

Our current approach to the social model is the ultimate irony: in tackling only one side of our situation we disable ourselves.

Redefining impairment

Our fears about acknowledging the implications of impairment are quite justified. Dominant perceptions of impairment as personal tragedy are regularly used to undermine the work of the disabled people's movement and they rarely coincide with disabled people's understandings of their circumstances. They are individualistic interpretations: our experiences are entirely explained by each individual's psychological or biological characteristics. Any problems we encounter are explained by personal inadequacy or functional limitation, to the exclusion of social influences.

These interpretations impose narrow assumptions about the varying experiences of impairment and isolate experience from its disabling context. They also segregate us from each other and from people without impairments. Interpreting impairment as personal tragedy creates fear of impairment and an emphasis on medical intervention. Such an interpretation is a key part of the attitudes and actions that disable us.

However, the perception of impairment as personal tragedy is merely a social construction; it is not an inevitable way of thinking about impairment. Recognising the importance of impairment for us does not mean that we have to take on the non-disabled world's ways of interpreting our experience of our bodies. In fact, impairment, at its most basic level, is a purely objective concept which carries no intrinsic meaning. Impairment simply means that aspects of a person's body do not function or they function with difficulty. Frequently this is taken a stage further to imply that the person's body, and ultimately the person, is inferior. However, the first is fact; the second is interpretation. If these interpretations are socially created then they are not fixed or inevitable and it is possible to replace them with alternative interpretations based on our own experience of impairment rather than what our impairments mean to non-disabled people.

We need a new approach which acknowledges that people apply their own meanings to their own experiences of impairment. This self-interpretation adds a whole new layer of personal, subjective meanings to the objective concept of impairment. The personal interpretation incorporates any meaning that impairment holds for an individual (i.e. any effects it has on their activities), the feelings it produces (e.g. pain) and any concerns the individual might have (e.g. how their impairment might progress). Individuals might regard their impairment as positive, neutral or negative, and this might differ according to time and changing circumstances.

With this approach the experiences and history of our impairments become a part of our autobiography. They join our experience of disability and other aspects of our lives to form a complete sense of ourselves.

Acknowledging the relevance of impairment is essential to ensuring that people are knowledgeable about their own circumstances. An individual's familiarity with how their body works allows them to identify their specific needs. This is a precursor to meeting those needs by accessing existing information and resources. Self-knowledge is the first stage of empowerment and gives a strong base for individuals to work collectively to confront disability and its impact upon people with impairments.

We need to think about impairment in three related ways:

- First, there is the objective concept of *impairment*. This was agreed in 1976 by the Union of the Physically Impaired Against Segregation (UPIAS 1976) and has since been developed by Disabled People's International (DPI) to include people with a range of non-physical impairments:
  Impairment: lacking all or part of a limb, or having a defective limb, organism or mechanism of the body.
- Second, there is the individual interpretation of the *subjective experience of impairment* in which an individual binds their own meanings to the concept of impairment to convey their personal circumstances.
- Finally, there is the impact of the wider *social context* upon impairment, in which misrepresentation, social exclusion and discrimination combine to disable people with impairments.

It is this third aspect to impairment which is not inevitable and its removal is the primary focus of the disabled people's movement. However, all three layers are currently essential to an understanding of our personal and social experiences.

Responses to impairment

We need to reclaim and acknowledge our personal experiences of impairment in order to develop our key debates, to incorporate this experience into the wider social context and target any action more precisely. One critical area of concern is the different responses to impairment, for ultimately these determine our exclusion or inclusion.

Currently, the main responses to impairment divide into four broad categories:

- *avoidance/'escape'*, through abortion, sterilisation, withholding treatment from disabled babies, infanticide and euthanasia (medically assisted suicide) or suicide
- *management*, in which any difficult effects of impairment are minimised and incorporated into our individual lives, without any significant change in the impairment
- *cure* through medical intervention
- *prevention* including vaccination, health education and improved social conditions.

The specific treatments that emerge from these responses differ markedly according to whether they are based on the medical or social model. Currently, the treatment available is dominated by the medical model's individualistic interpretation of impairment as tragic and problematic and the sole cause of disadvantage and difficulty. This leads policy-makers and professionals to seek a 'solution' through the removal of impairment. Each of the above responses is considered, at different times and in different contexts, to be valuable in bringing about the perceived desired outcome of reducing the number of people with impairments. The result is often a fundamental undermining of our civil and human rights.

For example, although not currently legal in Britain, euthanasia and infanticide are widely advocated where the 'quality of life' of someone with an impairment is deemed unacceptably low. An increasing number of infanticide and euthanasia cases have reached the courts in recent years, with judgments and public responses implying increasing approval. Infanticide is justified on grounds that 'killing a defective infant is not morally equivalent to killing a person. Very often it is not wrong at all.'[2] Suicide amongst people with impairments is frequently considered far more rational than in people without, as though impairment renders it the obvious, even the only, route to take. Ruth Bailey's chapter in *Encounters with Strangers* has illustrated how assumptions of the inevitable poor quality of life with an impairment dominate the development of prenatal screening and abortion. These approaches have created a huge research industry, and foetal screening and abortion are now major users of impairment-related resources.

Prevention of impairment through public health measures receives only minimal consideration and resourcing. The isolation of impairment from its social context means the social and economic causes of impairment often go unrecognised. The definitions of prevention are also questionable, in that foetal screening and subsequent abortion are categorised by mainstream approaches as preventative, whereas in reality such action is about the elimination of impairment.

Where removal of impairment is not possible, mainstream approaches extend to the management of impairment, although this remains one of the most under-resourced areas of the health service. However, much of the work in this area, rather than increasing an individual's access to and control over the help that they might need, is more about disguising or concealing impairment. Huge amounts of energy and resources are spent by medical and rehabilitation services to achieve this. For example, many individuals are prescribed cosmetic surgery and prostheses which have no practical function and may actually inhibit an individual's use of their body. Others are taught to struggle for hours to dress themselves when the provision of personal assistance would be more effective.

There are a number of critical flaws in mainstream interpretations of impairment and associated responses. First, little distinction is made between different people's experience of impairment or different aspects of a single impairment – or indeed, whether there may be positive aspects to some impairments. Instead, resources are applied in a generalised way to end impairment, regardless of the actual experience and interpretations of the individuals concerned. With the development of genetic screening, intervention aims to eliminate people with specific types of impairment altogether. Rarely is consideration given to the positive attributes of impairment, for example, the cystic fibrosis gene confers resistance to cholera which is an important benefit in some parts of the world. Associations are being identified between some impairments and creative or intellectual talent, while impairment in itself requires the development of more cooperative and communitarian ways of working and living – an advantage in a society with so much conflict to resolve.

Second, impairment is presented as the full explanation, with no recognition of disability. Massive resources are directed into impairment-related research and interventions. In contrast, scant resources are channelled into social change for the inclusion of people with impairments. For example, research will strive to 'cure' an individual of their walking difficulty, whilst ignoring the social factors which make not walking into a problem. There is little public questioning of the distribution of funds between these two approaches.

Additionally, such assumptions inhibit many disabled people from recognising the true causes of their circumstances and initiating appropriate responses.

A third criticism is that, while these responses to impairment are seen as representing the interests of disabled people, they are made largely by people with no direct experience of impairment, yet are presented as authoritative. Disabled people's knowledge, in contrast, is frequently derided as emotional and therefore lacking validity.[3] Although mainstream interventions are presented as being for the benefit of disabled people, in fact they are made for a non-disabled society. Ingrained assumptions and official directives make it clear that there is an implicit, and sometimes explicit, intention of population control. Abortion, euthanasia and cure are presented as 'quality of life' issues, but are also justified in terms of economic savings or 'improvement' to populations.[4]

It is counteracting these and related concerns which motivates the disabled people's movement. The social model of disability rejects the notion of impairment as problematic, focusing instead on discrimination as the key obstacle to a disabled person's quality of life. The logical extension of this approach is to seek a solution through the removal of disability and this is what the disabled people's movement works towards.

As a result, the overriding emphasis of the movement is on social change to end discrimination against people with impairments. There is a strong resistance to considering impairment as relevant to our political analysis. When impairment is discussed at all within the disabled people's movement it tends to be in the context of criticising mainstream responses. We have, for example, clearly stated that foetal screening for abortion and the implicit acceptance of infanticide for babies with significant impairments are based on assumptions that our lives are not worth living. Our intervention in public debates in recent years about medically assisted suicide (euthansia) has exposed the same assumption. In contrast, we have asserted the value of our lives and the importance of external disabling barriers, rather than impairment in itself, in determining quality of life. The same perspective informs our criticisms of the resources spent on attempting to 'cure' people of their impairments.

It is this rejection of impairment as problematic, however, that is the social model's flaw. Although social factors *do* generally dominate in determining experience and quality of life – for example requests for euthanasia are more likely to be motivated by lack of appropriate assistance than pain (Seale and Addington-Hall 1994) – impairment *is* relevant. For fear of appearing to endorse mainstream responses, we are in danger of failing to acknowledge that for some individuals impairment – as well as disability – causes disadvantage.

Not acknowledging impairment also lays the disabled people's movement open to misappropriation and misinterpretation. For example, disabled people's concerns about genetic screening and euthansia have been used by 'pro-life' groups to strengthen their arguments. Equally, the movement's rejection of medical and rehabilitation professionals' approaches to treatment and cure has not been accompanied by an exploration of what forms of intervention *would* be useful. Our message tends to come across as rejecting all forms of intervention when it is clear that some interventions, such as the alleviation of pain, in fact require more attention and resources. In both cases, the reluctance of the disabled people's movement to address the full implications of impairment leaves its stance ambiguous and open to misuse.

It is also clear that, by refusing to discuss impairment, we are failing to acknowledge the subjective reality of many disabled people's daily lives. Impairment *is* problematic for people who experience pain, illness, shortened lifespan or other factors. As a result, they may seek treatment to minimise these consequences and, in extreme circumstances, may no longer wish to live. It is vital not to assume that they are experiencing a kind of 'false consciousness' – that if all the external disabling barriers were removed they would no longer feel like this. We need to ensure the availability of all the support and resources that an individual might need, whilst acknowledging that impairment *can* still be intolerable.

This does not imply that *all* impairment is intolerable, or that impairment causes *all* related disadvantage; nor does it negate the urgency with which disability must be confronted and removed. It simply allows us, alongside wider social and political change, to recognise people's experiences of their bodies. Without incorporating a renewed approach to impairment we cannot achieve this.

A renewed social model of disability

We need to take a fresh look at the social model of disability and learn to integrate all its complexities. It is critical that we recognise the ways in which disability and impairment work together. The social model has never suggested that disability represents the total explanation or that impairment doesn't count – that has simply been the impression we have given by keeping our experiences of impairment private and failing to incorporate them into our public political analysis.

We need to focus on disability *and* impairment: on the external and internal constituents they bring to our experiences. Impairment is about our bodies' ways of working and any implications these hold for our lives. Disability is about the reaction and impact of the outside world on our particular bodies. One cannot be fully understood without attention to the other, because whilst they can exist independently of each other, there are also circumstances where they interact. And whilst there are common strands to the way they operate, the balance between disability and impairment, their impact and the explanations of their cause and effect will vary according to each individual's situation and from time to time.

We need a renewed social model of disability. This model would operate on two levels: a more complete understanding of disability and impairment as social concepts; and a recognition of an individual's experiences of their body over time and in variable circumstances. This social model of disability is thus a means to encapsulating the total experience of both disability and impairment.

Our current approach is based primarily on the idea that once the struggle against disability is complete, only the impairment will remain for the individual and there will be no disadvantage associated with this. In other words, when disability comes to an end there will be no socially-created barriers to transport, housing, education and so on for people with impairments. Impairment will not then be used as a pretext for excluding people from society. People with impairments will be able to participate in and contribute to society on a par with people who do not have impairments.

In this non-disabling society, however, impairment may well be unaltered and some individuals will find that disadvantages remain. Removal of disability does not necessarily mean the removal of restricted opportunities. For example, limitations to an individual's health and energy levels or their experience of pain may constrain their participation in activities. Impairment *in itself* can be a negative, painful experience.

Moreover, whilst an end to disability means people with impairments will no longer be discriminated against, they may remain disadvantaged in their social and economic opportunities by the long-term effects of earlier discrimination. Although affirmative action is an important factor in alleviating this, it is unlikely to be able to undo the full scale of discrimination for everyone.

Our current interpretation of the social model also tends to assume that if *impairment* ceases, then the individual will no longer experience disability. In practice, however, they may continue to be disabled, albeit to a lesser degree than previously. Future employment opportunities, for example, are likely to be affected by past discrimination in education even when impairment no longer exists.

In addition, an end to impairment may trigger a massive upheaval to those aspects of an individual's self-identity and image formed in response to disability and impairment. It can also signal the loss of what may be an individual's primary community. These personal and collective identities are formed in response to disability. That further changes may be required in changing circumstances is a sign of the continuing legacy of disability.

Our current approach also misses the fact that people can be disabled even when they have no impairment. Genetic and viral testing is now widely used to predict the probability of an individual subsequently acquiring a particular impairment. Fear has been expressed that predisposition to impairment will be used as a basis for discrimination, particularly in financial and medical services.[5]

There are also circumstances in which disability and impairment exist independently, and change in one is not necessarily linked to change in the other. For example, disability can dramatically ease or worsen with changes to an individual's environment or activities even when their particular impairment is static. Leaving a purpose-built home to go on holiday, for example, may give rise to a range of access restrictions not usually encountered, even though an individual's impairment remains the same. Equally, an employee with an impairment may find their capacity to succeed at work is confounded within one organisation but fully possible in another simply because of differences in the organisations' equality practices.

Where level of impairment increases, disability does not necessarily follow suit if adequate and appropriate resources are readily available to meet changes in need. A new impairment, a condition which fluctuates or a progressive impairment may mean that an individual needs additional or changing levels of personal assistance, but disability will remain constant if that resource is easily accessed, appropriate and flexible.

Perhaps most importantly, however, disability and impairment *interact*. Impairment must be present in the first instance for disability to be triggered: disability is the form of discrimination that acts specifically against people with (or who have had) impairments. This does not mean that impairment causes disability, but that it is a precondition for that particular oppression.

However, the difficulties associated with a particular impairment can influence the degree to which disability causes disadvantage. For example, an individual with a chronic illness may have periods in which their contact with the social world is curtailed to such an extent that external restrictions become irrelevant. At times of improved health the balance between impairment and disability may shift, with opportunities lost through discrimination being paramount.

Impairment can also be caused or compounded by disability. An excessively steep ramp, for example, might cause new impairment or exacerbate pain. An inaccessible health centre can restrict the availability of health screening that would otherwise prevent certain impairments, whilst inadequate resourcing can mean that pain reduction or management techniques are not available to many of the people who need them. Medical treatments – including those used primarily for cosmetic purposes – can cause impairment; for example, it has now emerged that a 'side effect' of growth hormone treatment is the fatal Creutzfeldt-Jakob disease.

Discrimination in general can also cause major emotional stress and place mental health at risk. Our reluctance to discuss impairment obscures this aspect of disability. If we present impairment as irrelevant then, even where impairment is caused by disability, it is, by implication, not a problem. This limits our ability to tackle social causes of impairment and so diminishes our campaigns.

Like disability, other experiences of inequality can also create or increase impairment. For example, abuse associated with racism or heterosexism, sexist pressure to modify physical appearance and lack of basic provision because of poverty can all lead to impairment. A significant proportion of people become active in the disabled people's movement as a result of such experiences, or through a recognition of these (and other) links that exist between oppressions.

Different social groups can also experience diverse patterns of impairment for a variety of social and biological reasons. Impairment for women, for example, is more likely to be associated with chronic pain, illness and old age (Morris 1994: 210–12). Excluding the implications of impairment risks reducing the relevance of the social model of disability to certain social groups. For example, the most common cause of impairment amongst women is a chronic condition, arthritis, where the major manifestation of impairment is pain. Unless the social model of disability incorporates a recognition of the patterns of impairment experienced by different social groups, there will be a failure to develop appropriate services.

Impairment can also be influenced by other external factors, not necessarily discriminatory, which may be physical, psychological or behavioural. Differences in cultural and individual approaches to pain and illness, for example, can significantly affect the way a person feels, perceives and reacts to pain. The study of pain control has revealed that pain can be significantly reduced by a range of measures, including by assisting individuals to control their own treatment programmes and through altered mental states associated with meditation or concentration on activity. Yet the limited availability of such measures to many people who could benefit extends this to the sphere of disability.

Social factors can, at the most fundamental level, define what is perceived as impairment. Perceptions of norms and differences vary culturally and historically. As mainstream perceptions change, people are defined in and out of impairment. Many people labelled 'mentally ill', for example, simply do not conform to contemporary social norms of behaviour. Other inequalities may contribute to the identification of impairment. For example, racist classifications in the school psychological service have led to a disproportionately high number of black compared to white children in segregated units for 'the emotionally and behaviourally disturbed', whilst it is relatively recently that the sexuality of lesbians and gay men has ceased to be officially defined as 'mental illness'.

Mainstream perceptions tend to increase the boundaries of impairment. The logical outcome of a successful disabled people's movement is a reduction in who is perceived as having an impairment. An absence of disability includes the widespread acceptance of individuality, through the development of a new norm which carries an expectation that there will be a wide range of attributes within a population. With an end to disability, many people currently defined as having an impairment will be within that norm. Impairment will only need definition as such if *in itself* it results in disadvantages such as pain, illness or reduced options.

Conclusion

I share the concerns expressed by some disabled people that some of the arguments I have put forward here could be used out of context to support the medical model of disability, to support the view that the experience of impairment is nothing but personal tragedy. However, suppression of our subjective experiences of impairment is not the answer to dealing with these risks; engaging with the debates and probing deeper for greater clarity might well be.

I am arguing for a recognition of the implications of impairment. I am not supporting traditional perspectives on disability and impairment, nor am I advocating any lessening of the energies we devote to eliminating disability. Acknowledging our personal experiences of impairment does not in any way disregard the tremendous weight of oppression, nor does it undermine our alignment with other civil rights movements. Certainly, it should not weaken our resolve for change. Disability remains our primary concern, *and* impairment exists alongside.

Integrating those key factors into our use of the social model is vital if we are to understand fully the ways that disability and impairment operate. What this renewed social model of disability does is broaden and strengthen the current social model, taking it beyond grand theory and into real life, because it allows us to incorporate a holistic understanding of our experiences and potential for change. This understanding needs to influence the structure of our movement – how we organise and campaign, how we include and support each other. A renewed approach to the social model is vital, both individually and collectively, if we are to develop truly effective strategies to manage our impairments and to confront disability. It is our learning and support within our own self-advocacy and political groups, peer counselling, training and arts that enable us to confront the difficulties we face, from both disability and impairment. It is this that allows us to continue working in the most effective way towards the basic principle of equality that underpins the disabled people's movement.

It is this confronting of disability and aspects of impairment that underpins the notion of disability pride which has become so central to our movement. Our pride comes not from 'being disabled' or 'having an impairment' but out of our response to that. We are proud of the way we have developed an understanding of the oppression we experience, of our work against discrimination and prejudice, of the way we live with our impairments.

A renewed approach to the social model is also relevant in our work with non-disabled people, particularly in disability equality training. Most of us who run such courses have avoided acknowledging impairment in our work, concerned that it confirms stereotypes of the 'tragedy' of impairment or makes the issues too complicated to convey. Denying the relevance of impairment, however, simply does not ring true to many non-disabled people: if pain, by definition, hurts then how can it be disregarded? We need to be honest about the experiences of impairment, without underplaying the overwhelming scale of disability. This does not mean portraying impairment as a total explanation, presenting participants with medical information or asking them to fantasise impairment through 'experiential' exercises. Instead, it allows a clear distinction to be made between disability and impairment, with an emphasis on tackling disabling barriers.

The assertion of the disabled people's movement that our civil and human rights must be protected and promoted by the removal of the disabling barriers of discrimination and prejudice has gained significant public support in recent years. It is this social model of disability which underpins the civil rights legislation for which we have campaigned, and civil rights will remain the centre of our political attention.

At a time when so many people – disabled and non-disabled – are meeting these ideas afresh, we need to be absolutely clear about the distinction between disability and impairment. The onus will remain upon disabled people to prove discrimination and there will still be attempts to refute our claims by using traditional perceptions of impairment. To strengthen our arguments we must peel away the layers and understand the complexities of the way disability and impairment work so that our allegations of discrimination are watertight. This is necessary now in our campaigning for full civil rights and will remain necessary when we claim justice under the legislation which will inevitably follow that campaign.

At this crossroads in disabled people's history, it is time for this renewed approach to the social model and the way we apply it. Disability is still socially created, still unacceptable, and still there to be changed; but by bringing impairment into our total understanding, by fully recognising our subjective experiences, we will achieve the best route to that change, the only route to a future which includes us all.

Notes

1 Along with many disabled people I feel some discomfort at the word impairment because it has become so imbued with offensive interpretation. Perhaps we need to replace impairment with an alternative term.

2 Professor Peter Singer, Director of the Centre for Human Bioethics, Monash University, Australia: quoted in Erika Feyerabend, 'Euthanasia in the Age of Genetic Engineering', *Reproductive and Genetic Engineering*, Vol. 2, No. 3, pp. 247–9, no date given.

3 For example, a medical law committee drawing up recommendations for withdrawing treatment from newborn babies with impairments, specifically excluded disabled adults or the parents of disabled children from the committee because 'the emotional discussion, which might have been likely, would have been very unhelpful and even counterproductive to the matter on hand', Prof Dr med. H.D. Hiersche in his introductory speech to the German Association of Medical Law on 'Limits on the Obligation to Treat Severely Handicapped Newborns', 27–29 June 1986.

4 A new screening test for Down's syndrome is recommended for all pregnant women on the grounds that the £88 test will reduce the cost per 'case' discovered (and, presumably, aborted) from the current £43,000 to £29,500. See *Pulse*, 25 May 1991.

   In an unpublished paper, a philosopher at Saarbrucken University in Germany used economic decision theory to quantify the value of life, including measuring which people should be subjected to involuntary euthanasia ('euthanasees'). Reported by Wilma Kobusch in a press statement; in *Gelenkirchen*, 5 November, 1991.

5 'Further Examples of Threats to Life', *Newsletter 13*; Disability Awareness in Action, January 1994.

References

Morris, J. (1994) Gender and Disability. In French, S. (ed.) *On Equal Terms: working with disabled people*. Oxford: Butterworth Heinemann.

Seale, C. and Addington-Hall, J. (1994) Euthanasia: why people want to die earlier. *Social Science and Medicine*, **39** (5), 647–54.

Union of the Physically Impaired Against Segregation (1976) *Fundamental Principles of Disability*. UPIAS.

United Nations Division for Economic and Social Information (1983) *World Programme of Action Concerning Disabled Persons*. United Nations.

> Liz Crow has, in this chapter, provided a powerful illustration of a recurring theme in this volume and the Learning from Each Other course – that of each of us having complex social identities. Our attempts to understand diversity and to theorise about experiences of marginalisation and oppression are more meaningful when they address the reality of our being more than any single aspect of our difference.

Chapter 12

Children's experiences of disability

Pointers to a social model of childhood disability

Clare Connors and Kirsten Stalker

This chapter reports findings from a two-year study exploring the lived experiences of 26 disabled children with a range of impairments aged 7–15. They experienced disability in four ways—in terms of impairment, difference, other people's behaviour towards them and material barriers. Most young people presented themselves as similar to non-disabled children: it is suggested they may have lacked a positive language with which to discuss difference. The chapter concludes by speculating why most of the children focused on 'sameness' rather than difference in their accounts and the implications of the findings for developing a social model of childhood disability.

Introduction

Disabled children have received little attention within the social model of disability: the extent to which it provides an adequate explanatory framework for their experiences has been little explored. Many studies about disabled children make reference to the social model, often in relation to identifying social or material barriers or in formulating recommendations for better services (Morris, 1998; Dowling and Dolan, 2001; Murray, 2002; Townsley *et al.*, 2004; Rabiee *et al.*, 2005). Few have focused specifically on children's perceptions and experiences of impairment and disability or explored the implications of these for theorizing childhood disability. Watson *et al.* (2000) and Kelly (2005), following Connors and Stalker (2003), are notable exceptions. Ali *et al.* (2001), in a critical review of the literature relating to black disabled children, concluded that the disability movement in Britain has neglected children's experiences.

[...] In order to understand general themes in children's lives it is necessary to pay attention to their narratives and personal experiences. Shakespeare and Watson (1998) pointed to the potential for drawing on insights from both the social model of disability and the sociology of childhood to explore disabled children's experiences. [...]

Study aims and methods

[...] The main aims of the study were to explore disabled children's understandings of disability and how they negotiate the experience of disability in their everyday lives. We asked the children to tell us about 'a typical day' at school and at the weekend, relationships with family and friends, their local neighbourhood, experiences at school, pastimes and interests, use of services and future aspirations. While open-ended questions were enough to launch some children on a blow-by-blow account of, for example, everything they had done the previous day, other youngsters, notably those with learning disabilities, needed the question broken up into more manageable chunks, such as: 'what time do you usually get up?; what do you like for breakfast?' We did not include direct questions about impairment in the children's interview schedules, nor did we think it appropriate to ask the children, in so many words, how they 'understood disability'. Rather, we preferred to wait and see what they had to say on these topics while telling us about their daily lives generally and in response to specific questions such as the following:

- Are there some things you are quite good at?
- Are there any things you find difficult to do?
- What's the best thing about school?
- What's the worst thing?
- Have you ever been bullied at school?
- Are there any things you need help to do?
- If you had a magic wand and you could wish for something to happen, what would you wish?

If individual children made little or no reference to impairment as the interview proceeded we raised the subject in follow-up questions, e.g. after the 'magic wand' question we might ask: 'what about your disability?; would you change anything about that?' This was easier with those who had physical or sensory impairments than those with learning disabilities (see Stalker and Connors, 2010, for an account of these children's views and experiences).
    [...]

Findings

The findings suggest that children experienced disability in four ways, in terms of impairment, difference, other people's reactions and material barriers.

Impairment

Much of what children talked about as 'disability' was impairment and the effects of impairment on their day-to-day living (although none used the word 'impairment'). The children's main source of information about the cause of their impairments was their parents. Parents told us they tended to use one of three explanations: the child was 'special', impairment was part of God's plan for the family or there had been an accident or illness around the time of birth. Several parents commented on their dread at being asked for explanations and it was notable that disabled children seemed to ask once and then let the subject drop; perhaps they were aware of the distress felt by parents. Generally, there seemed not to be much discussion within families about impairment. A number of children had never talked to their parents about it and in some families there was avoidance and/or silence about the subject. One sibling, a 13-year-old boy, reported that his mother had forbidden him to tell other people about his sister's impairment but rather to 'keep it in between the family'.

The disabled children tended to see impairment in medical terms—not surprisingly, given that most had a high level of contact with health services. Most had experienced multiple hospital admissions, operations and regular outpatient appointments, all of which might lead them to conclude that having an impairment linked them directly to healthcare professionals. A few had cheerful memories of being in hospital; for example one said she would give her doctor '20 out of 10' points for helping her, while another said his consultant was 'brilliant'. A 10-year-old boy with learning disabilities recalled an eye operation he had undergone aged five or six:

Researcher: What happened? Did you go into hospital on your own?

Child: My mum wasn't allowed to come in with me.

Researcher: Was she not?

Child: Into the theatre.

Researcher: Into the theatre. Was she allowed to be with you in the ward?

Child: Yes. Uh-huh.

Researcher: Good.

Child: What made me scared most was, there were these tongs, they were like that … with big bridges with lights on them, you know, and 'oh, oh, what are they for? What are they for?'

Researcher: Hmm. Hmm.

Child: And there were things all in my mouth.

> Researcher: Hmm. Hmm.
>
> Child: Then everybody was there.
>
> Researcher: Ah ha.
>
> Child: Then I went 'Mum!'
>
> Researcher: Hmm. So it's quite scary. Did it help?
>
> Child: Yeah.

However, none of the children appeared to view impairment as a 'tragedy', despite the close ties between the 'medical' and 'tragedy' models of disability (Hevey, 1993). They made no reference to feeling loss or having a sense of being hard done by.

Indeed, for some children it seemed that having an impairment was not a 'big deal' in their lives. When offered a 'magic wand' and asked if they would like to change anything about themselves or their lives, only three referred to their impairment: two said they would like to be able to walk and one wanted better vision. One girl with mobility difficulties compared herself favourably with other children: 'When I see people as they two are, I think "gosh" and I'm like glad I can walk and people see me and I walk like this'. When a boy aged nine was asked if he ever wished he didn't have to use a wheelchair, the reply was: 'That's it, I'm in a wheelchair so just get on with it … just get on with what you're doing'.

The children did tell us about what Thomas (1999) called 'impairment effects' (restrictions of activity which result from living with impairment, as opposed to restrictions caused by social or material barriers). They talked about repeated chest infections, tiring easily, being in pain, having difficulty completing schoolwork. At the same time, most seemed to have learned to manage, or at least put up with, these things. Most children appeared to have a practical, pragmatic attitude to their impairment. The majority appeared happy with themselves and were not looking for a 'cure'. However, there were some indications that a few of the younger children thought they would outgrow their impairment. The mother of a nine-year-old deaf boy said he thought he would grow into a hearing adult. (This child had no contact with deaf adults.) Only one younger child thought she would need support when she grew up, in contrast to most of the older ones, who recognized they would need support in some form or other.

Difference

Parents usually thought their children were aware of themselves as different from other children, but most of the children did not mention it. Instead, the majority focused on the ways their lives were similar to or the same as those of their peers. Most said they felt happy 'most of the time', had a sense of achievement through school or sports and saw themselves as good friends and helpful classmates. They were active beings with opportunities to mould at least some aspects of their lives. Most felt they had enough say in their lives, although some teenagers, like many youngsters of that age, were struggling with their parents about being allowed more independence. One girl said of her mother:

> She's got to understand that she can't rule my life any more … I just want to make up my own mind now because she's always deciding for me, like what's best for me and sometimes I get angry. She just doesn't realize that I'm grown up now but soon I'm going to be 14 and I won't be a wee girl any more.

When asked what they would be doing at their parents' age, the children revealed very similar aspirations to those of other youngsters, for example becoming a builder, soldier, fireman, vet, nurse or 'singer and dancer'.

Most problems the children identified were in the here and now: it was striking that on this subject their responses differed from their parents' accounts. Most parents were able to tell us about occasions where their child had been discriminated against, treated badly or faced some difficulty, but the children themselves painted a different picture of the issues which concerned them. Some, particularly in the older group, reported a high level of boredom; many of these young people attended special schools and so had few, if any, friends in their local communities. One teenager explained:

> It's like weird because people at my [segregated] school, they are not as much my friends as people here 'cos I don't know them that much. My friends past the years, they come to my house but not them. They've never even seen my house.

[...] Some schools with 'inclusive' policies seemed to take the view that difference should not even be acknowledged. We were not allowed to make contact with families through some schools because our research was about disabled children and they were not to be singled out (despite the fact that all the interviews were to take place in the family home). One danger of treating all children 'the same' is that rules and procedures designed for the majority do not always fit the minority. In an example from a mainstream school, one mother told us that her 14-year-old son, a wheelchair user, had been left alone in the school during fire drill:

> He was telling me the other day how they did the fire alarm and everybody was screaming out in the playground. Richard was still in the school and everybody was outside. He was saying 'Mum, I was really, really worried about what happens if there's a real fire.' No one came to his assistance at all.

Where difference was badly managed children could feel hurt and excluded, resulting in the 'barriers to being' that Thomas (1999) identified. One boy who attended an integrated unit within a mainstream school asked his mother what he had done 'wrong' to be placed in a 'special' class. Lack of information and explanation had led him to equate difference with badness or naughtiness.

Some special schools seemed to focus on difference in an unhelpful way, defining the children in terms of their impairment. At one school teachers apparently referred to pupils as 'wheelchairs' and 'walkers'. A wheelchair user at this school commented: 'It's sad because we're just the same. We just can't walk, that's all the difference'. Another pupil at this school told us: 'I'm happy being a cerebral palsy'. Despite her stated 'happiness', it seems unlikely that being publicly labelled in this way, and then apparently internalizing the definition, would help children develop a rounded sense of self. At the same time, a couple of children believed that needs relating to their impairment were better met in a special school than they would be in a mainstream school, with one deaf girl preferring to be:

> Child: Where there's signing, where everyone signs, all the teachers, all the children.
>
> Researcher: Why is that better than going to a school with hearing children?
>
> Child: Hearing children, no one signs. I don't understand them and they don't understand me.

Echoing findings made elsewhere (Davis and Watson, 2001; Skar and Tamm, 2001), there were several reports of children in mainstream schools feeling unhappy with their special needs assistants (SNAs), whose role is to facilitate inclusion. One older girl was very annoyed that at break times her SNA regularly took her to the younger children's playground when, understandably, she wanted to mix with young people of her own age. In another case a SNA always took a pupil into the nursery class at lunch times, because she (the SNA) was friendly with the nursery staff!

On the other hand, some schools responded to difference in a positive way. Many children had extra aids and equipment at school or were taken out of their classes for one-to-one tuition. Much of this support seemed to be well embedded in daily routines and not made into an issue. The mother of a boy attending mainstream school recounted:

> There was that time, remember, when … they'd asked a question in the big hall … It was 'does anybody in here think they are special?' and he put his hand up and said 'I am because I have cerebral palsy' and … he went out to the front and spoke about his disability to everybody.

It could be argued that encouraging children to see themselves as 'special' because they have an impairment is not a positive way forward. As indicated earlier in this paper in relation to different types of school, the word 'special' can be a euphemism (or justification) for segregated facilities. 'Special' might also be seen as a somewhat mawkish or sentimental way of portraying disabled children. However, some parents used this word to emphasize that their children were unique and valued individuals. Most worked hard to give the children the message that they were just as good as their brothers and sisters and any other children, that it was possible to be different but equal.

Reactions of other people

Nevertheless, children could be made to feel different and of lesser value by the unhelpful and sometimes hostile words and actions of others, whether people they knew or complete strangers. [...] We were told of incidents where people unknown to the child had acted insensitively, for example:

- staring;
- talking down, as if addressing a young child;
- inappropriate comments;
- inappropriate behaviour;
- overt sympathy.

Children who used wheelchairs seemed to be a particular target for the public at large. An older boy who had difficulty eating disliked going out to restaurants because he was stared at. He used a wheelchair and got annoyed when people bent down to talk to him as if he was 'small' or 'stupid': 'I don't mind if it's wee boys or wee girls that look at me but if it's adults … they should know. It's as if they've never seen a wheelchair before and they have, eh?'

A 13-year-old girl with learning disabilities described the harassment which she and her single mother had experienced from neighbours, including:

> The man next door came to our door and rattled the letter box and shouted 'come out you cows or I will get you'. So we called the police and then they did not believe us because I was a special needs.

Other children could also be cruel: almost half the disabled children had experienced bullying, either at school or in their local neighbourhood. One boy reported that he was 'made fun of' at school 'about nearly every day'. His mother reported he had once had a good day in school because no-one had called him 'blindie'. Although the children were very hurt by this kind of behaviour, a few took active steps to deal with it, reporting the bullying to parents or teachers. One girl faced up to the bullies herself and was not bothered by them again. A few were not above giving as good as they got, as this boy's response shows: 'No, I just bully them back. Or if they started kicking us, I'd kick them back'.

Material barriers

Thomas (1999) described 'barriers to doing' as restrictions of activity arising from social or physical factors. These caused significant difficulties in the children's lives. They included:

- lack of access to leisure facilities and clubs, especially for teenagers;
- transport difficulties;
- paucity of after-school activities;
- lack of support with communication.

One boy reported he had been unable to go to a mainstream high school with friends from primary school because parts of the building were not accessible to him. A 13- year-old boy who wanted to go shopping with his friends at the weekend found that his local Shopmobility scheme had no children's wheelchairs. A 14-year-old who wanted to attend an evening youth club at school was told it was not possible to arrange accessible transport at that time. It was suggested he remain in school after afternoon lessons ended until the club began. Understandably, he was not willing to wait around in school by himself for four hours, nor to attend the youth club wearing his school uniform.

There was less evidence of material barriers in the accounts given by children with learning disabilities. Some complained of boredom at weekends and during school holidays, sometimes linked to the fact that they attended a school outside their neighbourhood and lacked friends locally. Alternatively, they may have been less affected by, or aware of, the physical barriers affecting some of the children with physical and sensory impairments.

Discussion

So, children experienced disability in terms of impairment, difference, other people's behaviour and material barriers. Some had negative experiences of the way difference was handled at school, many encountered hurtful or hostile reactions from other people and many also came up against physical barriers which restricted their day-to-day lives. Despite all this, most of the children presented themselves as much the same as others, young people with fairly ordinary lives. They focused on sameness. Why?

There could be a number of explanations. First, it may be that some of the children felt they had to minimize or deny their difference. Youth culture and consumerism exert heavy pressures on young people to follow the crowd, keep up with others, not to stand out. Disabled youngsters are by no means immune to such pressures, albeit, as Hughes *et al.* (2005) argued, they may find themselves excluded from 'going with the flow'. [...] A significant number of children in our study were not encouraged to talk about impairment and disability at home or at school. These attitudes—or pressures—would tend to discourage children from talking about difference. It is notable that children at special schools tended to talk more openly about their impairments, although the schools themselves still seemed to be operating out of a medical model of disability.

Second, and taking a different tack, we could argue that the children in this study are self-directing agents, choosing to manage their day-to-day lives and experiences of disability in a matter of fact way. It is important to stress here that the children's (mostly positive) accounts of their lives differ significantly from earlier research findings about disabled children based on parents' or professionals' views, which tend to be considerably more negative (see Baldwin and Carlisle, 1994). Some of the older children were also active in responding to the hostile responses of other people, although there was less they could do about the structural barriers they came up against. They were also developing frameworks within which to understand the behaviours shown to them and, as active agents, chose not to be categorized by these responses. Impairment, and the resulting disability, was not seen as a defining feature of their identities [...] there were exceptions, like the girl who described herself as 'a cerebral palsy'.

However, we lean towards a third explanation. Perhaps the children were neither 'in denial' nor fully in command of resisting the various barriers they face. It may be that they did not have a language with which to discuss difference. We have already noted that they lacked contact with disabled adults—they did not have positive role models of disabled people nor opportunities to share stories about their lives with other disabled children. Without this framework it could be that children strove to be, or appear, the same as their non-disabled peers. If so, then there is a need for disabled children to have contact with organizations of disabled people and access to information and ideas about social models of disability. A counter-narrative is a critique of dominant public narratives constructed by people excluded from mainstream society to tell their own story (Thomas, 1999). The social model of disability is a counter-narrative (which has had considerable impact), but up to now children's narratives have played little part in its construction. Thus, there is a need for the social model to take children's experiences on board. How can it do this?

Our findings show that Thomas' social relational model of disability, which was developed from women's accounts of disability, can also inform our understandings of disabled children's experiences. First, despite the fact that the majority had relatively little information about the cause and, in some cases, nature of their impairments, impairment was a significant part of their daily experience. They reported various 'impairment effects'. In addition, our analysis showed some significant differences in the experiences and perceptions of those with learning disabilities compared with those with physical and sensory impairment. Second, there was evidence of 'barriers to doing' in the children's accounts, particularly those with physical or sensory impairments. They identified various material, structural and institutional barriers which restricted their activities.

Third, the young people told us about their experiences of being excluded or made to feel inferior by the comments and behaviour of others, sometimes thoughtless, sometimes deliberately hurtful. Some parents strove to give their disabled children positive messages about their value and worth and fought for them to have an ordinary life, for example to attend mainstream schools or be included in local activities, and some children received good support from teachers or other professionals. Nevertheless, they could be brought up against their difference, so to speak, in a negative way by other people's reactions, at both a personal and institutional level. In the children's accounts it was these incidents which upset them most, albeit some showed active resistance to, or rejection of, the labels or restrictions others sought to impose on them. Thus, in thinking about disabled childhoods, 'impairment effects', 'barriers to doing' and 'barriers to being' all seem to have a place. Our findings suggest that the last of these may have particular significance during the childhood years, when young people are going through important stages of identity formation which may lay the foundations of self-confidence and self-worth for years to come.

References

Ali, Z., Qulsom, F., Bywaters P., Wallace, L. and Singh, G. (2001) 'Disability, ethnicity and childhood: a critical review of research', *Disability & Society*, 16(7), 949–968.

Baldwin, S. and Carlisle, J. (1994) *Social support for disabled children and their families: a review of the literature* (Edinburgh, HMSO).

Connors, C. and Stalker, K. (2003) 'Barriers to "being"; the psycho-emotional dimension of disability in the lives of disabled children', paper presented at the conference *Disability Studies: Theory, Policy and Practice*, University of Lancaster, 4–6 September.

Davis, J. and Watson, N. (2001) 'Where are the children's experiences? Analysing social and cultural exclusion in "special" and "mainstream" schools', *Disability & Society*, 16(5), 671–687.

Dowling, M. and Dolan, L. (2001) 'Disabilities—inequalities and the social model', *Disability & Society*, 16(1), 21–36.

Finkelstein, V. (1996) 'Outside, inside out', *Coalition*, 1996(April), 30–36

Hevey, D. (1993) 'The tragedy principle: strategies for change in the representation of disabled people', in J. Swain, V. Finkelstein, S. French and M. Oliver (eds) *Disabling barriers—enabling environment* (London, Sage).

Hughes, B., Russell, R. and Paterson, K. (2005) 'Nothing to be had "off the peg": consumption, identity and the immobilization of young disabled people', *Disability & Society*, 20(1), 3–18.

Kelly, B. (2005) '"Chocolate … makes you autism": impairment, disability and childhood identities', *Disability & Society*, 20(3), 261–276.

Morris, J. (1998) *Still missing? Disabled children and the Children Act* (London, Who Cares? Trust).

Murray, P. (2002) *Hello! Are you listening? Disabled teenagers' experiences of access to inclusive leisure* (York, York Publishing Services).

Rabiee, P., Sloper, P. and Beresford, B. (2005) 'Doing research with children and young people who do not use speech to communicate', *Children and Society*, 19(5), 385–396.

Shakespeare, T. and Watson, N. (1998) 'Theoretical perspectives on research with disabled children', in
C. Robinson and K. Stalker (eds) *Growing up with disability* (London, Jessica Kingsley).

Skar, L. and Tamm, M. (2001) 'My assistant and I: disabled children's and adolescents' roles and relationships to their assistants', *Disability & Society*, 16(7), 917–931.

Stalker, K. and Connors, C. (2010) 'Children with learning disabilities talking about their everyday lives' in G Grant, P Ramcharan, M Flynn and M Richardson (eds) *Learning disability*, 2nd edition (Bucks: Open University Press).

Thomas, C. (1999) *Female forms: experiencing and understanding disability* (Buckingham: Open University Press).

Townsley, R., Abbott, D. and Watson, D. (2004) *Making a difference? Exploring the impact of multiagency working on disabled children with complex needs, their families and the professionals who support them* (Bristol: Policy Press).

Watson, N., Shakespeare, T., Cunningham–Burley, S., Barnes, C., Corker, M., Davis, J. and Priestley, M. (2000) *Life as a disabled child: a qualitative study of young people's experiences and perspectives: final report to the ESRC* (Edinburgh, University of Edinburgh Department of Nursing Studies).

This chapter argues that Thomas's (1999) social relational model of disability can help inform understandings of children's experiences, with 'barriers to being' having particular significance. It is early days and these ideas are no more than a potential starting point. The chapter clearly points out that there is a need for a two-way process in which disabled children have access to ideas and information about social models of disability, and social models of disability take account of their experiences and understandings. To facilitate this process we need to open up more space for conversations between disabled children, disability activists and researchers and their allies.

Chapter 13

Towards an affirmation model of disability

John Swain and Sally French

In this chapter John Swain and Sally French argue that a new model of disability is emerging within the literature by disabled people and within disability culture, expressed most clearly by the Disability Arts Movement. They call this the affirmation model; it is in direct opposition to the personal tragedy model and builds on the social model. The chapter and the model are positive affirmations of identity and of the life experience of being impaired and disabled.

'Proud, angry and strong'

The aim of this paper is to explore and trace the emergence of a model of disability which arises out of disability culture. For the purposes of the paper we call it *the affirmative model*. It is essentially a non-tragic view of disability and impairment which encompasses positive social identities, both individual and collective, for disabled people grounded in the benefits of life style and life experience of being impaired and disabled. This is succinctly expressed by the title of Johnny Crescendo's song, which is well known within British disability culture and has been often performed at disability arts events: *proud, angry and strong*. As argued here, this model is significant in theoretical terms, addressing the meaning of 'disability', but also more directly to disabled people themselves, in validating themselves and their experiences. It is significant, too, in understanding the 'disability divide', that is the divide between being disabled and being non-disabled. […]

Across the divide: existing models

The divide we are discussing here is not in the categorisation of people as disabled and non-disabled. Despite the evident personal, social and political reality of this conception of a divide, we believe it is problematic in a number of ways, two of which are particularly pertinent to this paper. Firstly, a division cannot be made on the grounds of impairment. The divide between disabled and non-disabled people is not that one group has impairments while the other does not. Indeed, many non-disabled people have impairments, such as short and long sight, and impairment cannot be equated with disability. Secondly, the divide between two groups cannot be sustained on the basis that one is oppressed while the other is not. Non-disabled people can be oppressed through poverty, racism, sexism and sexual preference, as indeed are many disabled people. Furthermore, oppressed people can also be oppressors. Disabled people, for instance, can be racist. Whatever definition of oppression is taken, it will apply to some non-disabled, as well as disabled, people.

The divide we are addressing is in perceptions of disability, in terms of the meaning it has in people's lives and social identity. Perceptions and the experiences on which they are founded vary considerably, not least as many people become disabled in later life having constructed understandings and lifestyles as non-disabled people. Nevertheless, there is a divide in perceptions which is most clearly related to a divide in experiences, being disabled or non-disabled.

The first question, then, is one of conceiving this divide in different models of disability. The opposition of the social model to an individual, particularly medical, model of disability is well established (Oliver 1996; Priestley 1999) and is clearly crucial to understanding the disability divide. The social model was born out of the experiences of disabled people, challenging the dominant individual models espoused by non-disabled people (French and Swain 1997). Nevertheless, it is our experience that many non-disabled people readily accept the social model, albeit superficially and at a basic conceptual level. Non-disabled people can generally accept that a wheelchair-user cannot enter a building because of steps (i.e. the person is disabled by barriers in an environment built for non-disabled people). Non-disabled people are much more threatened and challenged by the notion that a wheelchair-user could be pleased and proud to be the person he or she is.

The rejection of a tragic view and establishment of an affirmative model is far more problematic and not centrally addressed by the social model of disability. Essentially, the social model redefines 'the problem'. Disability is not caused by impairment or a function of the individual, but the oppression of people with impairments in a disabling society. The non-tragic view of disability, however, is not about 'the problem', but about disability as a positive personal and collective identity, and disabled people leading fulfilled and satisfying lives. Whilst the social model is certainly totally incompatible with the view that disability is a personal tragedy, it can be argued that the social model has not, in itself, underpinned a non-tragedy view. First, to be a member of an oppressed group within society does not necessarily engender a non-tragedy view. There is, for instance, nothing inherently non-tragic about being denied access to buildings. Secondly, the social model disassociates impairment from disability. It, thus, leaves the possibility that even in an ideal world of full civil rights and participative citizenship for disabled people, an impairment could be seen to be a personal tragedy. There is, for instance, nothing inherently non-tragic about having legs that cannot walk or feel.

In recent years a number of disabled people, particularly women, have sought to extend the social model of disability. Their major criticism has been the neglect of impairment (Morris 1991; Crow 1992; French 1993; Keith 1994; Abberley 1996; Crow 1996; Pinter 1996; Wendell 1996; Garland Thomson 1997; Hughes and Paterson 1997; Shakespeare and Watson 1997; Wendell 1997). However, it can be argued that any concentration on impairment will be counterproductive for disabled people. Shakespeare states:

> The achievement of the disability movement has been to break the link between our bodies and our social situation and to focus on the real cause of disability i.e. discrimination and prejudice. To mention biology, to admit pain, to confront our impairments has been to risk the oppressive seizing of evidence that disability is 'really' about physical limitations after all.
>
> (1992: 40)

Likewise, Oliver warns:

> There is a danger in emphasising the personal at the expense of the political because most of the world still thinks of disability as an individual, intensely personal problem. And many of those who once made a good living espousing this view would be only too glad to come out of the woodwork and say that they were right all along.
>
> (1996: 5)

Crow, in this volume, however, points out that 'an impairment such as pain or chronic illness may curtail an individual's activities so much that the restriction of the outside world becomes irrelevant' and that '... for many disabled people personal struggles relating to impairment will remain even when disabling barriers no longer exist'. The argument is basically, then, one of admitting that there may be a negative side to impairment and accounting for this by extending the social model.

It seems to us that this debate is limited in two major respects. First, it is notable that 'pain and chronic illness' are the recurring examples of impairments not addressed by the social model. This has distorted the debate. Pain and chronic illness are neither impairments nor restricted to the experiences of disabled people. Non-disabled people experience both pain and chronic illness. Indeed, in the pursuit of physical fitness, pain can be actively pursued by non-disabled people: 'no gain without pain'. Secondly, within this debate, impairment is regularly equated with personal tragedy. It is our contention that an affirmative model is developing out of individual and collective experiences of disabled people which directly confronts the personal tragedy model not only of disability but also of impairment.

Better dead than disabled?

The tragedy model is so dominant, so prevalent and so infused throughout media representations, language, cultural beliefs, research, policy and professional practice that we can only hope to cover a few illustrative examples. In terms of media representations, disabled characters (played by non-disabled actors) were featured in two major family films televised during the 1998 Christmas period when we were planning this paper.

The first was *A Christmas Carol*, which included two disabled characters. The best known is, of course, the pitiable and pathetic Tiny Tim whose tragedy of using a crutch is miraculously overcome at the end of the picture when he runs to meet the enlightened Scrooge. The other is a blind man, with both a dog and a white stick, who appears as a beggar. In the final scene, the humanised Scrooge can donate money in the proffered hat, for which the tragic figure of the cap-in-hand (handicapped) blind man is clearly grateful. The other film, again widely celebrated for the general sentiments it portrays, was *It's a Wonderful Life*. This features just one disabled character, Mr Potter, who is rich, evil, twisted, frustrated and in a wheelchair. No other explanation for his inhumanity, which includes theft, is offered other than his response to a life as a wheelchair user (despite the fact that he is the richest man in the town). It is the tragedy that has twisted him. The only other evil character, a minor character, in the film is the man who pushes the wheelchair. The tragedy, it seems, begets evil even by association.

Research can also clearly demonstrate the tragedy model. In a trial of a newly developed form of insulin, research subjects with diabetes were required to complete a questionnaire about '... you and your diabetes ... the way you feel and how diabetes affects your day to day life'. With each question was a choice of four answers ranging, basically, from 'very much' to 'not at all'. The first question set the scene: 'Do you look forward to the future?', with the implication that the tragedy of diabetes may negate any hope for the future. The 32 questions are peppered with words of tragedy, such as 'fear', 'edgy', 'worry' and 'difficult'. Some questions address psychological responses to the tragedy, such as: 'Do you throw things around if you get upset or lose your temper?', 'Do you get touchy or moody about diabetes?' and 'Do you hurt yourself or feel like hurting yourself when you get upset?' Two questions invoke the essence of the tragedy model: 'Do you even for a moment wish that you were dead?' and 'Do you wish that you had never been born?' Thus, the ultimate version of the tragedy model is that physical death is better than the social death of disability.

Perhaps the most intrusive, violating and invalidating experiences, for disabled people, emanate from the policies, practices and interventions, which are justified and rationalised by the personal tragedy view of disability and impairment. The tragedy is to be avoided, eradicated or non-disabled (normalised) by all possible means. Such are the negative presumptions held about impairment and disability, that the abortion of impaired foetuses is barely challenged. As Disability Awareness in Action (1997) states, there is considerable and growing pressure on mothers to undergo prenatal screening and to terminate pregnancies in which an impairment has been detected. The use of genetic technology in its different forms in so-called 'preventative' measures is, for many disabled people, an expression of the essence of the personal tragedy model, better dead than disabled. The erroneous idea that disabled people cannot be happy, or enjoy an adequate quality of life, lies at the heart of this response. The disabled person's problems are perceived to result from impairment, rather than the failure of society to meet that person's needs in terms of appropriate human help and accessibility. There is an assumption that disabled people want to be 'normal', although this is rarely voiced by disabled people themselves who know that disability is a major part of their identity. Disabled people are subjected to many disabling expectations, for example to be 'independent', 'normal', to 'adjust' and 'accept' their situation. It is these expectations that can cause unhappiness, rather than the impairment itself.

There are a number of different possible explanations of this tragedy view of disability. It is sometimes thought to reflect a deep irrational fear by non-disabled people of their own mortality (Shakespeare 1994). An alternative explanation, however, suggests that the tragedy perspective has a rational, cognitive basis constructed through experiences in disablist social contexts.

Fundamental to understanding non-disabled people's tragedy view of disability is the possibility of crossing the divide: 'there but for fortune go you or I'. Unlike the divide between people of different genders or different races, non-disabled people daily experience the possibility of becoming impaired and thus disabled (the causal link being integral to the tragedy model). Thus, so-called 'irrational fears' have a rational basis in a disablist society. To become visually impaired, for instance, may be a personal tragedy for a sighted person whose life is based around being sighted, who lacks knowledge of the experiences of people with visual impairments, whose identity is founded on being sighted, and who has been subjected to the personal tragedy model of visual impairment. This can be compounded, for non-disabled parents of disabled children, for instance, by beliefs about the benefits that non-disabled people have in education, work and relationships. Such beliefs speak to dominant social values that have a broader application than the disabled–non-disabled divide, particularly through the association of disability with dependence (Oliver 1993) and abnormality (Morris 1991). Thus, the personal tragedy view of impairment and disability is ingrained in the social identity of non-disabled people. Non-disabled identity, as other identities, has meaning in relation to and constructs the identity of others. To be non-disabled is to be 'not one of those'. The problem for disabled people is that the tragedy model of disability and impairment is not only applied by non-disabled people to themselves, it is extrapolated and applied to disabled people.

From this point of view, too, the adherence to a personal tragedy model by disabled people themselves also has a rational basis. For a non-disabled person whose life is constructed on the basis of being non-disabled, the onset of impairment and disability can be experienced as a tragedy, perhaps amplified if it is associated with the trauma of illness or accident. Even in affirming the social model, Oliver and Sapey state:

> Some disabled people do experience the onset of impairment as a personal tragedy which, while not invalidating the argument that they are being excluded from a range of activities by a disabling environment, does mean it would be inappropriate to deny that impairment can be experienced in this way.
>
> (1999: 26)

Furthermore, a personal tragedy view can have a rational basis for people with congenital impairments, living through the daily barrage from non-disabled people, experts, parents, and the media invalidating themselves and their experiences. Indeed, within the disabling context we have outlined here, the expression of an affirmative model by disabled people flies in the face of dominant values and ideologies. It is likely to be denied as unrealistic or a lack of 'acceptance', distorted as an expression of bravery or compensation, or simply ignored. The tragedy model is in itself disabling. It denies disabled people's experiences of a disabling society, their enjoyment of life, and their identity and self-awareness as disabled people.

Towards a positive individual identity

An affirmative model is developing in direct opposition to the personal tragedy view of disability and impairment. The writings and experiences of disabled people demonstrate that, far from being tragic, being impaired and disabled can have benefits. If, for example, a person has sufficient resources, the ability to give up paid employment, and pursue personal interests and hobbies, following an accident, may enhance that person's life. Similarly, disabled people sometimes find that they can escape class oppression, abuse or neglect by virtue of being disabled. We interviewed Martha, a Malaysian woman with a visual impairment. She was separated from a poor and neglectful family and sent to a special school at the age of five. She states:

> I got a better education than any of them (brothers and sisters) and much better health care too. We had regular inoculations and regular medical and dental checks.

She subsequently went to university and qualified as a teacher. Similarly, many visually disabled people became physiotherapists, by virtue of having their own 'special' college, at a time when their working-class origins would have prevented them entering other physiotherapy colleges. None of this is to deny, of course, that many disabled people who are educated in 'special' institutions receive an inferior education and may, in addition, be neglected and abused (Corker 1996).

A further way in which disability and impairment may be perceived as beneficial to some disabled people is that society's expectations and requirements are more difficult to satisfy and may, therefore, be avoided. A disabled man quoted by Shakespeare *et al.* said, 'I am never going to conform to society's requirements and I am thrilled because I am blissfully released from all that crap. That's the liberation of disfigurement' (1996: 81).

Young people (especially women) are frequently under pressure to form heterosexual relationships, to marry and have children (Bartlett 1994).

These expectations are not applied so readily to disabled people who may, indeed, be viewed as asexual. Although this has the potential to cause a great deal of anxiety and pain, some disabled people can see its advantages. Vasey states:

> We are not usually snapped up in the flower of youth for our domestic and child rearing skills, or for our decorative value, so we do not have to spend years disentangling ourselves from wearisome relationships as is the case with many non-disabled women.
>
> (1992: 74)

Though it is more difficult for disabled people to form sexual relationships, because of disabling barriers, when they do any limitations imposed by impairment may, paradoxically, lead to advantages. Shakespeare *et al.*, who interviewed disabled people about their sexuality and sexual relationships, state:

> Because disabled people were not able to make love in a straightforward manner, or in a conventional position, they were impelled to experiment and enjoyed a more interesting sexual life as a result.
>
> (1996: 106)

For some people who become disabled their lives change completely though not necessarily for the worse. A woman quoted by Morris states:

> As a result of becoming paralysed life has changed completely. Before my accident it seemed as if I was set to spend the rest of my life as a religious sister, but I was not solemnly professed so was not accepted back into the order. Instead I am now very happily married with a home of my own.
>
> (1989: 120)

The experience of being impaired may also give disabled people a heightened understanding of the oppressions other people endure. French found that most of the forty-five visually disabled physiotherapists she interviewed could find advantages to being visually impaired in their work. An important advantage was their perceived ability to understand and empathise with their patients and clients. One person said:

> The frustrations of disability are much the same inasmuch as it is a physical limitation on your life and you think, 'if only' … Having to put

up with that for so long, I know ever so well what patients mean when they mention those kinds of difficulties.

(French 1991: 1)

Others believed that their visual disability gave rise to a more balanced and equal relationship with their patients, that patients were less embarrassed (for example, about undressing) and that they enjoyed the extra physical contact the visually disabled physiotherapist was obliged to make. One person said:

Even as students when we had the Colles fracture class all round in a circle, they used to love us treating them because we had to go round and touch them. They preferred us to the sighted physios. I'm convinced that a lot of people think we are better.

(French 1991: 4)

As for non-disabled people, the quality of life of disabled people depends on whether they can achieve a lifestyle of their choice. This, in turn, depends on their personal resources, the resources within society and their own unique situation. The central assumption of the tragedy model is that disabled people want to be other than as they are, even though this would mean a rejection of identity and self. Nevertheless, the writings of disabled people demonstrate that being born with an impairment or becoming disabled in later life can give a perspective on life which is both interesting and affirmative and can be used positively. Essentially, impairment which is social death and invalidates disabled people in a non-disabled society, provides a social context for disabled people to transcend the constraints of non-disabled norms, roles and identity and affirm their experiences, values and identity. Phillipe explains:

I just can't imagine becoming hearing, I'd need a psychiatrist, I'd need a speech therapist, I'd need some new friends, I'd lose all my old friends, I'd lose my job. I wouldn't be here lecturing. It really hits hearing people that a deaf person doesn't want to become hearing. I am what I am!

(Shakespeare *et al*. 1996: 184)

Watson writes of Phil, a disabled participant in research he is conducting:

Phil sees his acceptance of his impairment as central to his sense of self and well-being...

(1998: 156)

Towards a positive collective identity

As a member of a poetry group of young disabled people, Georgina Sinclair wrote the following poem:

Coming Out

And with the passing of time
you realise you need to find
people with whom you can share.
There's no need to despair.
Your life can be your own
and there's no reason to condone
what passes for their care.
So, I'm coming out.
I've had enough
of passing and playing their game.
I'll hold my head up high.
I'm done with sighs
and shame.
        (Tyneside Disability Arts 1999: 35)

In his introduction to the anthology of poetry in which this poem is published, Colin Cameron writes:

> We are who we are as people with impairments, and might actually feel comfortable with our lives if it wasn't for all those interfering busybodies who feel that it is their responsibility to feel sorry for us, or to find cures for us, or to manage our lives for us, or to harry us in order to make us something we are not, i.e. 'normal'.
>
> (Tyneside Disability Arts 1999: 3)

The affirmation of positive identity is necessarily collective as well as individual. The growth of organisations of disabled people has been an expression not only of the strength of united struggle against oppression and discrimination, but also of group identity. Disabled identity, as non-disabled identity, has meaning in relation to and constructs the identity of others. To be disabled is to be 'not one of those'.

Group identity, through the development of the Disabled People's Movement, has underpinned the development of an affirmative model in a number of ways.

(1) The development of a social model of disability has re-defined 'disability' in terms of the barriers constructed in a disabling society rather than as a personal tragedy. Through group identity the discourse has shifted to the shared experience and understanding of barriers. 'Personal tragedy' has been reconceptualised as frustration and anger in the face of marginalisation and institutionalised discrimination.

(2) Simply being a member of a campaigning group developing a collective identity is, for some disabled people, a benefit of being disabled in its own right. It can feel exciting being part of a social movement which is bringing about tangible change.

(3) Frustration and anger are being collectively expressed. They are expressed through Disability Arts and campaigns of the Disabled People's Movement, rather than being seen as personal problems to be resolved, say, through counselling. The roots of Disability Arts lie in the politicising of disability issues. As Shakespeare *et al.* state:

> Drama, cabaret, writing and visual arts have been harnessed to challenge negative images, and build a sense of unity.
>
> (1996: 186)

The activities are so diverse it is difficult to talk in general terms. However, Vic Finkelstein, who was one of the founders of the London Disability Arts Forum (LDAF) in 1987, stated in his presentation at the launch that his hopes for the future were: 'disabled people presenting a clear and unashamed self-identity.' He went on to say that it was, 'essential for us to create our own public image, based upon free acceptance of our distinctive group identity' (Campbell and Oliver 1996). This development of identity has indeed been central to Disability Arts, challenging the values that underlie institutional discrimination. Through song lyrics, poetry, writing, drama, and so on, disabled people have celebrated difference and rejected the ideology of normality in which disabled people are devalued as 'abnormal'. They are creating images of strength and pride, the antithesis of dependency and helplessness.

(4) Through group identity it is recognised that just because there are benefits from being excluded from non-disabled society (which is capitalist, paternalistic and alienating) this does not mean that disabled people should be excluded. From this way of thinking, disabled people enjoy the benefits of being 'outsiders', but should not be pushed out, i.e. should have the right to be 'insiders' if they so wish.

(5) Finally, group identity has been, for some, a vehicle for revolutionary rather than revisionist visions of change, often under the flags of 'civil rights' and 'equal opportunities' (Shakespeare 1996). The inclusion of disabled people into the mainstream of society would involve the construction of a better society, with better workplaces, better physical environments, and better values including the celebration of differences. As Campbell and Oliver conclude in their history of the Disabled People's Movement:

> In building our own unique movement, we may be not only making our own history but also making a contribution to the history of humankind.
>
> (1996: 180)

Disabled people, encouraged by the Disabled People's Movement, including the Disability Arts Movement, are creating positive images of themselves and are demanding the right to be the way they are — to be equal, but different.

Towards an affirmative model of disability

[...] An affirmative model is being generated by disabled people through a rejection of the tragedy model, within which their experiences are denied, distorted or re-interpreted, and through building on the social model, within which disability has been redefined. The affirmative model directly challenges presumptions of personal tragedy and the determination of identity through the value-laden presumptions of non-disabled people. It signifies the rejection of presumptions of tragedy, alongside rejections of presumptions of dependency and abnormality. Whereas the social model is generated by disabled people's experiences within a disabling society, the affirmative model is born of disabled people's experiences as valid individuals, as determining their own lifestyles, culture and identity. The social model sites 'the problem' within society: the affirmative model directly challenges the notion that 'the problem' lies within the individual or impairment.

Embracing an affirmative model, disabled individuals assert a positive identity, not only in being disabled, but also being impaired. In affirming a positive identity of being impaired, disabled people are actively repudiating the dominant value of normality. The changes for individuals are not just a transforming of consciousness as to the meaning of 'disability', but an assertion of the value and validity of life as a person with an impairment.

The social model has empowered disabled people in taking control of support and services, the establishment of Centres for Integrated Living and the struggle for direct payment being clear expressions of this empowerment. The development of an affirmative model takes this fight squarely into the arena of medical intervention. Some impairments, such as diabetes, epilepsy and those involving pain, can respond to intervention. Just as the social model signified, for disabled people, ownership of the meaning of disability, so the affirmative model signifies ownership of impairment or, more broadly, the body. The control of intervention is paramount. This is an affirmation by disabled people of the right to control what is done to their bodies. It includes the right to know the basis on which decisions of medical intervention are made, the consequences of taking drugs (including side effects), the consequences of not taking drugs, and the alternatives. Disability Action North East states:

> Our movement should campaign for effective healthcare treatments that are under our control, treatments that are Holistic and see our differences not as Geneticists do (as 'defective traits') but as a *positive* sign of our human diversity.
>
> (1998: 3)

It has been argued that the greatest danger for disabled people in addressing impairment is political, with the possibility that impairment is seen to be 'the problem', as in the tragedy model. The danger is clearly apparent in the following quotation from a book entitled *An Introduction to Disability Studies*. Writing about the social model, Johnstone states:

> As an explanation it must somehow begin to incorporate, rather than stand in opposition to the medical/deficit model of disablement.
>
> (1998: 20)

Yet on the previous page he also recognises that

> The medical model encourages the simplistic view that disability is a personal tragedy for the individual concerned.
>
> (1998: 19)

Indeed, it is for this reason that the social model cannot 'incorporate' the medical model and for this reason, too, that the affirmative model is emerging to strengthen the opposition of the social model to the personal tragedy model. Oliver states:

This denial of the pain of impairment has not, in reality, been a denial at all. Rather it has been a pragmatic attempt to identify and address issues that can be changed through collective action rather than medical or other professional treatment.

(1996: 38)

The affirmative model, however, is not about the 'pain of impairment', but on the contrary the positive experiences and identity of disabled people from being impaired and disabled. The social model is collectively expressed, most obviously, through direct action and campaigns in the struggle of the powerless for power. The affirmative model again builds on this particularly through the development of the Disability Arts Movement within which disabled people collectively affirm their positive identity through visual arts, cabaret, song and, as in the following extract by Colin Cameron, poetry.

Sub Rosa

Fighting to establish self-respect …
Not the same, but different …
Not normal, but disabled …
Who wants to be normal anyway?
Not ashamed, with heads hanging,
Avoiding the constant gaze of those who assume
that sameness is something to be desired …
Nor victims
of other people's lack of imagination …
But proud and privileged to be who we are …
Exactly as we are.

(Tyneside Disability Arts 1998)

Rather than being politically threatening to disabled people, the affirmative model builds on and strengthens the Disabled People's Movement, not least by bringing disabled people, who would not otherwise engage in political action, into the Disability Arts Movement.

Finally, in terms of visions of the future, the affirmative model is building on the social model, through which disabled people envisage full participative citizenship and equal rights. Disabled people not only look towards a society without structural, environmental or attitudinal barriers, but also a society which celebrates difference and values people irrespective of race, sexual preference, gender, age or impairment.

In this paper, we have summarised an affirmative model and the social and historical context in which it is emerging. The broader significance of this view of disability and impairment has yet to be fully realised. We conclude by suggesting two directions for development. First, it is central to the concept of 'inclusion'. Policies, provision and practice, whether in community living or education, can only be inclusive through full recognition of disability culture and the affirmative model generated from the experiences of disabled people (Oliver and Barnes 1998). Secondly, an affirmative model also has a role to play in the development of a theory of disability. In his book on *Social Identity*, Jenkins (1996) writes of resistance as potent affirmation of group identity:

> Struggles for a different allocation of resources and resistance to categorisation are one and the same thing ... Whether or not there is an explicit call to arms in these terms, something that can be called self-assertion – or 'human spirit' – is at the core of resistance to domination ... It is as intrinsic, and as necessary, to that social life as the socialising tyranny of categorisation.
>
> (1996: 175)

As is so often the case, however, in relation to sociology generally and feminist theory, for instance, existing theory and concepts are rarely explicit in the validation of the experiences of disabled people and are often explicit in invalidation. Jenkins rarely mentions disability, and when he does the same old questions arise:

> Perhaps the most pertinent questions arise out of perceived, typically bodily, impairments: is the neonate to be acknowledged as acceptably human?
>
> (1996: 55)

Better dead than disabled? Quintessentially, the affirmative model is held by disabled people about disabled people. Its theoretical significance can also only be developed by disabled people who are 'proud, angry and strong' in resisting the tyranny of the personal tragedy model of disability and impairment.

References

Abberley, P. (1996) Work, Utopia and impairment. In L. Barton (ed.) *Disability and Society: emerging issues and insights*. London: Longman.

Bartlett, J. (1994) *Will You Be Mother? Women Who Choose to Say No*. London: Virago Press.

Campbell, J. and Oliver, M. (1996) *Disabling Politics: understanding our past, changing our future*. London: Routledge.

Corker, M. (1996) *Deaf Transitions: images and origins of deaf families, deaf communities and deaf identities*. London: Jessica Kingsley.

Crow, L. (1992) Renewing the social model of disability. *Coalition*, July, 5–9.

Crow, L. (1996) Including all our lives: renewing the social model of disability. In J. Morris (ed.) *Encounters with Strangers: feminism and disability*. London: Women's Press.

Disability Action North East (1998) *Fighting Back Against Eugenics and the New Oppressors*. Newcastle-upon-Tyne: Disability Action North East.

Disability Awareness in Action (1997) *Life, Death and Rights: bioethics and disabled people*. Special Supplement. London: Disability Awareness in Action.

French, S. (1991) The advantages of visual impairment: some physiotherapists' views. *New Beacon*, **75** (872), 1–6.

French, S. (1993) Disability, impairment or something in between? In J. Swain, V. Finkelstein, S. French and M. Oliver (eds) *Disabling Barriers – enabling environments*. London: Sage.

French, S. and Swain, J. (1997) It's time to take up the offensive. *Therapy Weekly*, **23** (34), 7.

Garland Thomson, R. (1997) Feminist theory, the body and the disabled figure. In J.L. Davis (ed.) *The Disability Studies Reader*. London: Routledge.

Hughes, B. and Paterson, K. (1997) The social model of disability and the disappearing body: towards a sociology of impairment. *Disability & Society*, **12** (3), 225–40.

Jenkins, R. (1996) *Social Identity*. London: Routledge.

Johnstone, D. (1998) *An Introduction to Disability Studies*. London: David Fulton.

Keith, L. (ed.) (1994) *Mustn't Grumble: writings by disabled women*. London: Women's Press.

Morris, J. (ed.) (1989) *Able Lives: women's experience of paralysis*. London: Women's Press.

Morris, J. (1991) *Pride Against Prejudice: transforming attitudes to disability*. London: Women's Press.

Oliver, M. (1993) Disability and dependency: a creation of industrial societies? In J. Swain, V. Finkelstein, S. French and M. Oliver (eds) *Disabling Barriers – enabling environments*. London: Sage.

Oliver, M. (1996) *Understanding Disability: from theory to practice*. Basingstoke: Macmillan.

Oliver, M. and Barnes, C. (1998) *Disabled People and Social Policy: from exclusion to inclusion*. Harlow: Longman.

Oliver, M. and Sapey, B. (1999) *Social Work with Disabled People*, 2nd edn. Basingstoke: Macmillan.

Pinter, R. (1996) Sick-but-fit or fit-but-sick? Ambiguity and identity at the workplace. In C. Barnes and G. Mercer (eds) *Exploring the Divide: illness and disability*. Leeds: Disability Press.

Priestley, M. (1999) *Disability Politics and Community Care*. London: Jessica Kingsley.

Shakespeare, T.W. (1992) A reply to Liz Crow. *Coalition*, September, 40.

Shakespeare, T.W. (1994) Cultural representation of disabled people: dustbins for disavowal? *Disability & Society*, **9**(3), 283–99.

Shakespeare, T.W. (1996) Disability, identity, difference. In C. Barnes and G. Mercer (eds) *Exploring the Divide: illness and disability*. Leeds: Disability Press.

Shakespeare, T., Gillespie-Sells, K. and Davies, D. (1996) *The Sexual Politics of Disability*. London: Cassell.

Shakespeare, T.W. and Watson, N. (1997) Defending the social model. *Disability & Society*, **12**(2), 293–300.

Tyneside Disability Arts (1998) *Sub Rosa: clandestine voices*. Wallsend: Tyneside Disability Arts.

Tyneside Disability Arts (1999) *Transgressions*. Wallsend: Tyneside Disability Arts.

Vasey, S. (1992) Disability culture: it's a way of life. In R. Rieser and M. Mason (eds) *Disability Equality in the Classroom: a human rights issue*. London: Disability Equality in Education.

Watson, N. (1998) Enabling identity: disability, self and citizenship. In T. Shakespeare (ed.) *The Disability Reader: social science perspectives*. London: Cassell.

Wendell, S. (1996) *The Rejected Body: feminist philosophical reflections on disability*. New York: Routledge.

Wendell, S. (1997) Towards a feminist theory of disability. In J.L. Davis (ed.) *The Disability Studies Reader*. London: Routledge.

Rhetoric about celebrating difference as a feature of participation and inclusion abounds. Through this discussion of the importance of affirming rather than denying who we are, this chapter may have helped to bring this notion to life. A culture in which we are visible, affirmed and valued is also one in which we are more likely to actively participate and to take the risks involved with being a learner.

Chapter 14

The news of inclusive education
A narrative analysis

Bruce Dorries and Beth Haller

The development of inclusive education has involved confrontations between parents and the state. In this chapter Bruce Dorries and Beth Haller analyse one confrontation that turned into a public debate concerning the best method of educating disabled children. They examine the way in which distinct narrative themes within the news media competed to persuade the public about the cost or benefits of inclusion.

[...][I]nclusive education is controversial. When inclusive education programmes were only directed at children with minor learning disabilities, such as slight hearing impairments, the issue was less controversial. However, parents of nondisabled children have long been concerned that children with more severe disabilities, such as autism, can be disruptive to their child's education. Others worry about finite educational resources, if large amounts may be needed for severely disabled children. Studies show that although approximately one third of children in the United States with special education needs receive an education in standard classrooms, few of these children have severe disabilities (Pae 1994). The controversy has grown as these severely disabled children and their families fight for inclusive education.

One high-profile case rocketed the topic of inclusive education to national media attention in the mid-1990s. Beginning in 1995, Hartmann v. Loudoun County Board of Education tested whether or not schools must include severely disabled children in regular classrooms. Because of their 3-year legal battle in northern Virginia, the Hartmanns and the inclusion movement became almost synonymous. Mark Hartmann, who is autistic, became a symbol in a national debate over whether, and how often, disabled youngsters should be educated alongside their non-disabled peers (Wilgoren and Pae 1994).

[...] This paper analyses four years of the extensive media coverage of the Hartmann story to provide a synopsis of the narratives that address the central issues of inclusion. Through the press, competing interests told their stories to the public, hoping to win the moral high ground and persuade others of the 'good reasons' that support their understanding of the costs or benefits of inclusion. Pedagogical issues concerning students with disabilities, who represent 11 per cent of the school population in the United States, raise complex questions of finance, ethics and academic standards. Varied state standards for the education of disabled children further complicate the discussion. Furthermore, as the inclusion debate continues, the diagnosis of disabled children steadily increases (Lewin 1997). [...]

Rather than being an evaluation of inclusive education, this study focuses only on news media narratives about inclusive education as a policy and its implications for the US education system.

The Hartmann case

[...] After moving from a suburb of Chicago in 1994, Roxana and Joseph Hartmann enrolled their 9-year-old son in second grade at Ashburn Elementary School in Loudoun County, VA. Officials of the northern Virginia school district reported that Mark hit, pinched, screeched and threw tantrums when placed in a standard classroom. Despite having reduced the class size and having an aide work individually with Mark, his behaviour made learning and classroom management problematic, according to school authorities. By the school year's end, officials concluded that the autistic youngster should be removed from a regular class and placed in a Leesburg school with four other autistic students in a 'mainstream' programme. In this type of 'mainstream' programme, the Leesburg school placed students with autism in regular classes only for music, art and gym classes. Mark's parents refused to accept this decision (Lewin 1997; Wilgoren 1994 a,b,c). They agreed that their son's experience at Ashburn had been a disaster:

> but they blamed the school system for not providing enough training to Mark's teacher and full-time instructional aide. They pointed to Mark's progress at an Illinois school, where he attended kindergarten and first grade, and they argued that it was crucial to Mark's social development that he go to school with his nondisabled friends.
>
> (Pae 1994: C1)

So began a lengthy battle 'that stands as a troubling example of how bitter placement disputes can become' (Lewin 1997: AI).

The Hartmanns believed the law supported their case. In line with historic American values of equal access to education by all, IDEA was created to guarantee disabled children the right to free and appropriate education in the least restrictive environment (US Department of Education 2000). [...] However, when Loudoun County did not receive the Hartmanns' approval to remove Mark from a regular classroom, the school district asked the State Supreme Court to appoint a hearing officer to decide Mark's academic future (Rosen and Jones 1994). The officer ruled that the boy's educational needs were not served by inclusion and gave school officials permission to transfer him to Ashburn. A spokesperson with the American Federation of Teachers indicated this was the first time any school district was allowed to remove a disabled child from classes since passage of IDEA (Rosen and Jones 1994). The Hartmanns appealed. [...]

Finally, the Hartmanns' attorney filed a petition with the US Supreme Court, arguing that Mark's case has significance for the nation (Abramson and Chadwick 1997a). Again the story made national news (Suarez 1997; Abramson and Chadwick 1997a,b), but the high court declined to act on the case (*Washington Post* 1998, 14 January). The Hartmanns, who spent more than $200,000 in legal fees arguing for inclusion for Mark (Lewin 1997), vowed to continue their struggle for the inclusive education movement (Lu 1998). [...]

The Hartmann v. Loudoun County Board of Education case focused national attention on the inclusive education issue, placing the narratives of competing points of view before the general public. Therefore, the narratives of this case merit closer critical analysis. Readers may notice one specific narrative is missing from the media coverage – that of Mark Hartmann's own stories told in his own voice. We can only speculate that some of the legal and ethical issues the media face may have caused them to avoid interviewing an autistic person who is not a legal adult. Media law specialists warn journalists that children cannot give legal consent to be interviewed; only their legal guardian can give the consent. Whatever the cause for 'exclusion' of Mark's voice in the coverage of the case, it suggests a significant issue in the discussion about inclusion and education in general: most media stories about any education issue fail to include the 'voices' of those most affected by the issue, children and teens. [...]

Narratives contain key themes that display humans' experiences, as well as their values. Through stories we explain our actions and beliefs, as well as lend meaning to our lives. The stories told in the Hartmann v. Loudoun tale illustrate the tellers' 'good reasons' for supporting inclusion or opposing the practice. In composing stories to explain their life/reality, the tellers make choices based on their 'good reasons'. [...]

This section presents brief narratives and the good reasons embedded in themes drawn from press coverage of the Hartmann v. Loudoun case. In an effort toward brevity, this paper examines eight themes that evolved from the inclusive education debate in the Hartmann case. Themes were embedded in the stories told by the actors in this social drama. They expressed 'something that people believe, accept as true and valid; it is a common assumption about the nature of their experience' (Spradley 1979: 186). [...]

The media stories came from a variety of sources, but most prominent were *The Roanoke Times*, *Richmond Times Dispatch*, *The New York Times*, *The Washington Post*, National Public Radio's (NPR) 'Morning Edition' and 'Talk of the Nation'. After achieving an understanding of the case, the social/moral arguments surrounding inclusion, and examining the narratives over time, the narrative themes began to reveal themselves. After common ideas and experiences were highlighted within the narratives, categories were created to characterise the narratives likely to increase readers' understanding of the moral arguments.

The themes are divided into those that support the Hartmanns for inclusion, and those that support the Loudoun School District or are against inclusion. (Four narrative themes each.) This division over-simplifies the nature of the public discussion about inclusion; there are more than two sides to this complex issue. However, this division provides a more concrete, linear way to discuss the narratives and themes. The themes found in narratives told by the Hartmanns' and inclusion supporters are explored below:

Narrative theme 1: Everyone wins with inclusive education

This narrative connects to an overarching theme imbedded within the IDEA legislation – that inclusive education benefits disabled children in the short run with better learning and, in the long run, with more employment and post-secondary educational opportunities. The benefit of inclusive education for non-disabled children is the ability to understand and cope with a more diverse society and people who are different from themselves.

For example, a *New York Times* analysis piece on inclusive education embraces the narrative of IDEA that it benefits all children, not just those with disabilities:

Many educators and parents believe that segregating children with disabilities is bad, both educationally and morally. They say such a policy undermines the development of both disabled children, by failing to give them a chance to develop the skills and relationships that they will need as adults, and other children, by preventing beneficial contact with the full range of people in their communities.

(Lewin 1997: 20)

Mark Hartmann's mother, Roxana, most often provides this 'everyone wins' narrative, in both her quotes to media and her *Roanoke Times* commentary on her son's case. In the following narrative from her commentary, she explains the benefits of inclusive education for all children:

... [Mark] has demonstrated that there are no long-term harmful effects on the classmates of a disabled child. In fact, full inclusion gives them an opportunity to embrace diversity and grow in compassion and understanding - honorable goals that will serve our children well through their lifetime. In sum, through inclusion, we can make our communities a better place for people with disabilities one child and one family at a time, if we work together. It's the best thing to do for our future together.

(Hartmann 1998: A7)

[...] Joseph Hartmann, Mark's father, presented this same narrative nationally when he was part of an NPR 'Morning Edition' story on inclusive education:

JOSEPH HARTMANN: He's becoming able to cope in society as society is, with his peers in the classroom. He knows when his teacher says: 'OK, class, everybody be quiet' that it is his job to be quiet. He knows when the teacher says: 'OK, class, it's time to go to lunch,' – 'OK, I've. got to get my lunch box and stand in line with everybody else and go on' ...
   If you have him in an autistic class, with three or four other autistic kids and they sit around and play with blocks all day, you don't take them out into the world except to visit.

(Abramson and Chadwick 1997b)

The news media also relied on prominent pro-inclusion sources, which made the narrative compelling. In articles about the broader inclusive education topic, such as the following *New York Times* article, Judith Heumann, an assistant secretary in the Office of Special Education and Rehabilitative Services at the US Department of Education, who is herself a wheelchair user, explains the 'everyone wins' narrative in a national community context:

> 'Education is academic, but it's also social, learning how to live in a community, learning about differences,' she said. 'I tell parents who are afraid to send a child with disabilities into a regular setting that overprotection does no service when that disabled child becomes an adult. If your child was out of Sight, out of mind, that doesn't change. People who might have become their friends in school won't know them.'

[...] The narrative takes on even more strength when adults with disabilities, who were the product of inclusive education, enter the discourse. The following was a letter to the editor in *The Roanoke Times*, written after a commentary disparaged the benefits of inclusive education:

> I have cerebral palsy and a hearing impairment. I spent most of my school years in 'regular' schools in Connecticut in the 1960s and 1970s, so I am a product of inclusion. I shudder to think what I would have become had I not been given the challenges and intellectual and social stimulation I received. It motivated me to get a good education and to try to make a difference in the world. The parents of children with disabilities in Montgomery County only want what I was given. These children are more likely to learn appropriate behavior if they are 'included' in regular classes. Able-bodied children learn about acceptance, tolerance and compassion toward those who are 'different', and perhaps something about 'the power of the human spirit'. Not all education is gained from books and facts. Holladay's misconceptions tell me we still have a long way to go toward understanding and accepting people with disabilities.
>
> (Vass-Gal 1998: A7)

[...]

Narrative theme 2: Inclusion is cheaper

This narrative appears in two ways. One implied theme is that society benefits in general from inclusive education because well-educated disabled children mean future contributing, tax-paying members of society, rather than tax burdens. However, typically, the narrative was more overt: inclusive education costs less than institutionalisation of severely disabled children.

Roxana Hartmann makes the argument that institutionalisation is expensive and has long-term costs for society

> But the commonwealth does support large institutions. A large chunk of your tax dollars are spent in institutions. It costs more than $80,000 per year to support a person in an institution, and it's getting more expensive all the time. By the year 2000, the national average will reach $113,000 per person in an institution. There are 189,000 Virginians with mental retardation alone – the greater majority housed in institutions. But why is this relevant to the education of a disabled child? We know from experiences of our sister states that it all begins with decisions focused on educating the disabled child. Early-intervention strategies and an inclusive education posture are proven as an effective approach to integrate our disabled citizens into the community with jobs that they can be trained for and normal home settings to live in. Community-based living and care works better than institutions, and costs far less.
>
> (Hartmann 1998: A7)

The message from the US Department of Education about IDEA is similar. It estimates that educating students in neighborhoods, who would previously have been institutionalised, saves $10,000 per child (US Department of Education 2000). Consistent with notions of American pragmatism, this narrative ties to capitalistic notions of 'the bottom line', in which citizens embrace policies that reduce taxes or give the most benefit for the least amount of tax dollars.

Narrative theme 3: Human rights should apply to everyone in a civilised society

Typically, this narrative is tied to every American's right to a free public education. The right to an education is presented as a human right available to all equally. Roxana Hartmann puts it succinctly:

> After contemplating this response, I have decided to review some facts that may be overshadowed by accusations (real or imagined) and that may not be obvious to a casual observer.

First of all, public education is the right of all children. The Individuals With Disabilities Act guarantees access for disabled students into the 'least restrictive environment.' The only measure is that the school must demonstrate that the disabled child is able to learn in the LRE with appropriate support, services and accommodations.

... In all our debates, we should remember that each and every child in our community, including the disabled, is a valued human being who has a basic right to opportunity – whether we are talking work, education, housing or access to public buildings. To consider it otherwise will take us back to the 1860s.

(Hartmann 1998: A7)

Several members of the local southwestern Virginia community continue the free and public education narrative in a number of letters to *The Roanoke Times*:

How does Holladay justify saying that his daughter has more of a right to an education than my brother? Holladay is concerned about students who 'can learn algebra and Spanish, children for whom the schools are intended, and whose futures will depend on what they learn now.' All children's futures are determined by what they learn. This is a public school system, and everyone has a right to an education.

(Greenberg 1998: A7)

... Public schools aren't for the learning elite. They are public schools, and by law must provide an appropriate education in the least restrictive environment for all children. There is no such thing as separate but equal.

(Eaton 1998: A7)

Although an explicit link is not made in the statements, the theme within these statements is reminiscent of the education reforms that African Americans fought for in the 1950s and 1960s to bring about integrated public education for black and white children. The inclusion movement puts forth the same notion, that separate but equal does not fit with American ideals.

Narrative theme 4: Inclusive education has proven itself

Specifically, this narrative tied into Mark Hartmann's success in an inclusive education environment before moving to Virginia and, broadly, the success of such programmes nationally and in Blacksburg, VA, where Mark Hartmann was placed early in the case. For example, Jamie Ruppman, an education consultant who works with disabled children, saw Mark's success back in Illinois destroying the case of Loudoun County. Educators from Illinois did testify that Mark was successful in their inclusion program before the family moved to Virginia (DeVaughn 1995a). As Roxana Hartmann explained:

> All you have to know about this case is that Mark was successfully included in Illinois and in Montgomery County. The only place he could not be successfully included was Loudoun County, and that's clearly because the school system did not have the commitment to do it.
>
> (Benning 1997)

Hartmann continued this argument by explaining why she chose to move to Montgomery County:

> [That county] is one of the few school districts in Virginia to honor and abide by IDEA – the law. Among other states, Virginia is ranked 46th in its support of people with disabilities and their families.
>
> (Hartmann 1998: A7)

Others made similar arguments:

> 'I have heard nothing negative about having this child stay,' the president of the Montgomery County Council of PTAs said. 'What I have heard is: Why did the school system take a negative stand against this child in the first place? From a parent standpoint, this woman did everything she could for her kid (in Loudoun County), then set out to find what she could for him somewhere else.' ... We need to show that it works so other school systems can try to do the same thing.
>
> (DeVaughn 1995b: AI)

The successful inclusive education program narrative is also connected specifically to Mark's educational growth. Roxana Hartmann says: 'He has blossomed in a very nurturing environment here with people who are dedicated and understand him and his disability. He'll stay here until he finishes school' (Lu 1998: AI). The Timmy Clemens case also bolsters the narrative of inclusive education 'proving itself':

> Four years ago, Timmy Clemens could not walk near a classroom without becoming so scared he couldn't enter the room. His autism required a full-time aide and much patient coaxing to get him through a day.

By his senior year last year, Timmy could walk to classes in Blacksburg High School on his own. With the help of his aide, Marc Eaton, and a special board that lists the alphabet and short words such as 'yes' and 'no', he did homework and took tests in courses such as algebra and honors history. Today, as a postgraduate, he works with an aide in a job at Blacksburg's Municipal Building.

'Some truly believe in it; some think it's a waste,' said Judy Clemens, Timmy's mother. But other people's opinions don't matter, she said, because she can see the improvements in her son.

I don't think inclusion is perfect. But I think it's going to get better and better, and I'm proud of Montgomery County.

(Applegate and Lu 1998: AI)

Although these narrative themes in the Hartmann case advanced the cause of inclusive education, many who opposed the Hartmann arguments and/or inclusion were included in media coverage or wrote commentaries against the issue. Their oppositional narratives suggested the following themes explored below:

Narrative theme 5: Not in my kid's school

This narrative presupposes that inclusive education will always have a disruptive effect on non-disabled children in the classes and therefore should not be allowed. It is based on some anecdotal reports that a few severely disabled children, such as those with autism, have been disruptive. However, there is also much anecdotal evidence of disruptive non-disabled children, which is rarely mentioned in anti-inclusion narratives. One parent, Steve Holladay, a Blacksburg, VA, parent, stated this narrative through his commentary piece in *The Roanoke Times*. The Virginia Tech professor claimed to quote his daughter, whose words were 'shocking':

Many of these children (inclusion students) are uncontrollable. They enter your classroom in the middle of a class, and it may take 15 minutes for their aide to return them to the classroom they are assigned to. They break into loud crying fits or other noise making episodes regularly, at unpredictable times and without apparent cause, bringing a halt to teaching until control is re-established.

They wander around the class while the teacher is trying to teach, sometimes selecting a student to sit with and engage in an up-close, face-to-face staring contest. They may unexpectedly slap you in the forehead when you walk by them in the hall ...

It cannot be denied that many of these children are extremely disruptive. And if they have been found to be too disruptive for normal classrooms in other school districts, why do we place them in our classrooms where our children have their only opportunity to learn many foundational concepts? Do they magically behave better here? ... Montgomery County has become an island that will accept highly disruptive children into our schools, children impaired to the point of being totally oblivious to the educational process going on around them, children incapable of learning in any way marginally related to the original intent of the school's programs, or to the expectations placed on other children in the classrooms.

(Holladay 1998: A7)

Other parents present this narrative of the disruptive effect of inclusive education. Even the mother of an autistic child wrote:

I am the mother of an autistic child, and I agree with Steve Holladay ... I do believe in mainstreaming, where the child is placed in a regular classroom for short periods of time and gradually works up to a full class period. With mainstreaming, 'normal' children get the education they deserve and need without disruption by our 'learning-challenged' children.

(Kingery 1998: A7)

A teacher continued the narrative of disruptive inclusion kids.

'Our biggest problem is putting up with emotionally disturbed kids when they are disruptive and distracting to other children,' she said. 'That's a waste of time and that's where we're losing ground.'

Hall, [a] language arts teacher, also resents having to design different tests and notes and other material for some students and fears it inevitably watered down the lesson for all students.

(Applegate and Lu 1998: AI)

Narrative theme 6: Protect the sensitive 'normal' students

Those who question inclusion also argued that it may be traumatic for non-disabled children to be in the presence of severely disabled children:

Beyond lost education, what effect might this have on the sensitive child who isn't yet ready to experience this type of behavior and instability?

I am sincerely sympathetic for Ms. Hartmann and her situation, and very thankful that my own children are healthy. I further admire her obvious determination to provide what she believes to be the best growing and learning environment possible for her son. However, she and others who move here to take advantage of our inclusion policy seem to have little concern about the effect their children may have on other children in the classrooms.

... Does Ms. Hartmann care about the boy or girl who sits in front of the inclusion child during the uncontrollable screaming fit? What about the child whose personal space is invaded by stares or inappropriate touching? Or my own daughter, who receives a stunning slap on the forehead out of the blue? ...

(Holladay 1998: A7)

Narrative theme 7: School is about academics

In contrast with the inclusive education argument that it benefits children in many more ways than just academics, those opposed to the practice argue schools are to provide an education in reading, writing, arithmetic, etc. The attorney for Loudoun County illustrates this narrative in her comments to NPR's Morning Edition:

KATHLEEN MAYFOUD, ATTORNEY FOR LOUDOUN COUNTY, VIRGINIA, SCHOOLS: Socialization is part of that, but academic and educational instruction is obviously the primary responsibility. So, Loudoun would have had to totally overlook the educational requirements in favor of a minor goal.

(Abramson and Chadwick 1997b)

Holladay ties the idea of a proper learning environment with this narrative and argues that inclusive education is its antithesis.

Doesn't it seem obvious that loss of teaching time to disruptive or ongoing distractive behavior isn't conducive to learning?

Similar to Ms. Hartmann, we (the other parents) are also determined to provide our children the best possible learning environment. As an educator myself, I don't like our inclusion policy. I would never tolerate such disruption in my classrooms unless, as has become the case in Montgomery County, I was mandated to do so by law.

I truly do care about Mark. However, I care more about his classmates who can learn algebra and Spanish, children for whom the schools were intended, and whose futures will ultimately depend on what they learn now.

(Holladay 1998: A7)

Narrative theme 8: Attendance is not the same as integration

This narrative questions definitions of inclusive education. It also re-interprets various aspects of inclusive education as having a negative effect. For example, Richard Schattman, a Vermont principal who believes in inclusion, explains how inclusion, when poorly implemented, gives those opposed to inclusive education fodder to urge for its dismantling.

> 'A student can be more isolated and segregated in a normal classroom than in special education,' Mr Schattman said. 'Inclusion isn't about placing the kid. It's about making the placement successful both for the kid and for the rest of the class. And it's not easy. You need small classes, lots of planning time, and staff that believes in it.'
>
> Some special education experts worry that the inclusion movement may lead to dumping children with special needs into classes where they will be ignored or taunted, and eliminating the special services and support that they receive in settings intended just for them.
>
> 'It has not been demonstrated that regular classrooms, even fortified regular classrooms using the best practices can accommodate all children all the time,' said Douglas Fuchs, a professor of special education at Vanderbilt University. 'The full inclusionists honestly believe that creating a situation in which teachers individualize instruction for each student is a terrific goal we should all dedicate our lives to. So we should kick away the crutch of special education. But that's a high stakes game, and I'm not sure it's realistic.'
>
> Nor are all parents and advocates for children with disabilities convinced that it is the correct goal.

(Lewin 1997: 20)

This narrative supports those opposed to inclusion by noting that it may not be the right accommodation for every disabled child. This type of theme turns inclusive education on itself, i.e. because it may not be appropriate for all disabled children, maybe it should not be used at all. *The New York Times* story above continued this narrative by explaining that because of disruptive, abusive and violent children, Vermont, the premier state for successful inclusive education, is placing such children in separate settings (Lewin 1997).

Conclusions and discussion

As noted in this analysis, narrative themes were divided into those that support the Hartmanns/inclusive education and those that do not. This reflects a problem that is imbedded within the debate itself, by creating a division that oversimplifies the nature of inclusive education. The public discussion about this case reflects standard news coverage of a controversial issue – 'either-or' dichotomy, debate rather than discussion (Tannen 1998). When the news narratives follow lines of 'yes' or 'no' about inclusive education, they miss an opportunity to critically assess the issue for all children in US public school systems. When the focus is on a two-sided debate, rather than a multifaceted discussion, the news media are also more likely to drop coverage of the topic if one side of the debate tires of presenting their narratives.

[...] Although this paper touched on just a few of the prominent themes about inclusive education in the news, we believe the themes offered in this paper dominate the discussion. Furthermore, we conclude that even though some parents of nondisabled children are vehemently opposed to inclusive education, it was the more numerous and more vocal parents of severely disabled children, educators and proponents of IDEA who set the tone of the debate and framed inclusion as a workable approach to educate disabled children. We conclude that though the Hartmanns lost their case against Loudoun County, the narratives they inspired actually won in the court of public opinion.

It has taken almost 25 years for pro-inclusion narratives to take hold. As programmes in Montgomery County, VA, Illinois and Vermont show, school districts need not only well-trained faculty and well-financed programmes to succeed, but public support as well. For example, when parent Steve Holladay wrote to criticize inclusive education in Montgomery County, VA, his criticism was met with seven letters to the editor positively endorsing inclusive education. In the pro-inclusion environment of Montgomery County, VA, the local newspaper, *The Roanoke Times*, seemed to present the proponents' narratives wholeheartedly. Even when the Hartmanns lost their case, the newspaper published a family-provided colour photo of Mark Hartmann on its front page (Lu 1998). In the photo, Mark Hartmann, wearing T-shirt and shorts, grins broadly as a picture-perfect 'average' kid. The image alone provides a 'good reason' that Mark should be in a regular classroom because he is presented visually as a 'regular kid'. Earlier, the newspaper published a large two-page spread on inclusive education in the county, providing a location for thoughtful discussion of the issue and primarily 'good reasons' for inclusive education.

Some opponents of inclusive education fear the public and policymakers may be swayed by an underlying message of pity for the 'poor, little disabled children'. The conservative *National Journal* feared during the re-authorisation of IDEA in 1997 that:

> Overhaul of the Individuals with Disabilities Education Act is tailor made for policy decision by anecdote. The facts and figures are sparse and conflicting; the horror stories are stark and vivid. And the interest groups are well organized, disciplined and loaded with heart-tuggers or spine-chillers, depending on their legislative goal. In the past, organizations representing the disabled could count on their substantial political clout in Congress. 'Politicians are terrified of them – that they'll trot out people in wheelchairs,' a lobbyist for an education organization said enviously. 'It's very easy for a Member to feel virtuous voting for their issues.'
>
> (Stanfield 1995)

[...] These themes/stories in support of inclusion are consistent with American values of equality – the country has determined that schools cannot be separate and truly *equal*. Furthermore, the effects of inclusion, while perhaps detrimental to a few students, largely have promising effects for both students with and without disabilities. [...] While many of the stories against inclusion suggest pragmatic or traditional bases for educational policy readers of the narratives are likely to find the rationality of the pro-inclusion arguments more consistent with US history and culture. For example, the 1960s civil rights movement, which successfully dismantled separate but unequal educational systems for blacks and whites, suggests the type of ideal conduct to which Fisher refers. The civil rights movement forced the United States to acknowledge once again the central narrative of its founding – that all citizens are created equal and deserve equal opportunities in all aspects of US society, including education.

[...] After the loss of her son's case, Roxana Hartmann said she will continue to lead national discourse about inclusive education:

> 'This is the end, but it's not going to stop me from talking about inclusion,' Roxana said. 'No, if anything, it's made me more of a believer

than ever' ... 'This is not about winners and losers; this is about schools doing the right thing for the children,' she explained.

(Lu 1998: 1A)

Widespread media coverage of Hartmann's narrative and those of other supporters of inclusion should also prove to help make others believers in the movement's aims.

References

Abramson, L. and Chadwick, A. (1997a) Disabilities. *Morning Edition*, 6 November (transcript # 97110611-210).

Abramson, L. and Chadwick, A. (1997b) 'Mark Hartmann: Part II', *Morning Edition*, 7 November (transcript # 971101709-210).

Applegate, L. and Lu, K. (1998) 'Seeking best place to learn', *Roanoke Times*, 1 February, p. AI.

Benning, V. (1997) 'Court backs decision to remove autistic boy from regular class', *Washington Post*, 10 July, p. D1.

DeVaughn, M. (1995a) 'Autistic pupil not welcome', *Roanoke Times and World News*, p. AI.

DeVaughn, M. (1995b) 'Judge hears from autistic boy's mom, school board', *Roanoke Times and World News*, 17 February, p. B 1.

Eaton, M. (1998) 'Inclusion can help all students' [Letter to the Editor], *Roanoke Times*, p. A7.

Greenberg, L. (1998) 'Everyone has a right to go to public schools' [Letter to the Editor], *Roanoke Times*, p. A7.

Hartmann, R. (1998) 'My son's right to an education doesn't hurt others', *Roanoke Times*, 16 February, p. A7.

Holladay, S. (1998) 'Learning-challenged kids shouldn't be in regular classrooms', *Roanoke Times*, 7 February, p. A7.

Kingery, D. (1998) 'Mainstreaming can be done gradually' [Letter to the Editor], *Roanoke Times*, p. A7.

Lewin, T. (1997) 'Where all doors are open for disabled students', *New York Times*, 28 December, p. AI.

Lu, K. (1998) 'Autistic pupil loses fight to be "included"', *Roanoke Times*, 14 January, p. 1A.

Pae, P. (1994) 'Loudoun can take autistic boy out of regular class', *Washington Post*, December 16, p. Cl.

Rosen, M. and Jones, R. (1994) 'Odd child out', *People*, 17 October, p. 113.

Spradley, J. (1979) *The Ethnographic Interview*, New York: Holt, Rinehart & Winston.

Stanfield, R. (1995) 'Tales out of school', *National Journal*, 2733–4.

Suarez, R. (1997) 'Inclusion', *Talk of the Nation*, 17 November (transcript # 97111701-211).

Tannen, D. (1998) *The Argument Culture*, New York: Random House.

US Department of Education (2000) Overview of IDEA, http://www.ed.gov/offices/OSERSIIDEA/

Vass-Gal, S. (1998) 'Parent's worries reflect misconceptions' [Letter to the Editor], *Roanoke Times*, p. A7.

Washington Post (1998) 'Loudoun disability case won't be heard', 14 January, p . B3.

Wilgoren, D. (1994a) 'Loudoun wants autistic boy out of class', *Washington Post*, 16 August, p. B1.

Wilgoren, D. (1994b) 'Mother says regular school is crucial for autistic boy', *Washington Post*, 28 October, p. B3.

Wilgoren, D. (1994c) 'Ruling due on boy's schooling', *Washington Post,* 8 December, p.VI, Virginia Weekly section.

Wilgoren, D. and Pae, P. (1994) 'As Loudon goes, so may other schools', *Washington Post*, 28 August, p. BI.

The narrative analysis contained in this chapter clearly identifies the way in which the meaning of inclusion is being contested. The competing narratives carry with them different 'truths' about what inclusion is and the values underpinning it. By illuminating these narratives Dorries and Haller provide a thought-provoking tool for analysing 'the inclusion debate' and also a means for reflecting on one's own beliefs.

Chapter 15

Guardians of tradition

Presentations of inclusion in three introductory special education textbooks

Nancy Rice

Textbooks contain information. They also contain attitudes, beliefs and values that are conveyed covertly through a variety of mechanisms such as the use of language, the choice of topic, the focus on certain aspects of an issue, the simultaneous omission of other aspects, and other strategies. This chapter analyses discussions of inclusion and 'full' inclusion in three bestselling textbooks in the US college market. The chapter highlights the responsibility of teacher educators: (1) to analyze their course material for ideological underpinnings; (2) to teach future educators to develop a critical consciousness; (3) to model how to consider issues from a range of perspectives; and (4) to provide opportunities for future teachers to develop the habit of listening to the viewpoints of disabled people and their families.

[...]

Professional socialization into special education

Part of the socialization into any profession is understanding and adopting the vocabulary and practices of that profession. Along the way, values and perspectives are also conveyed. Becoming socialized into a profession means:

> adopting a system of language, thought and action that becomes standard and customary within the social order ... In professions such as special education there is a tendency to adopt an orthodoxy as vital to the identity and purpose of the profession ... Unity, coherence, direction

and political power are achieved through the continued proliferation of orthodox writings and the conforming inculcation of the professional ranks into the institutional order.

(Danforth, 2004, p. 449)

One medium through which the 'orthodox writings' are communicated to those new to the field is through textbooks. Introductory special education textbooks are an important tool in the professional education of teachers. According to a report published by the Center for Education Information 200,545 students graduated from teacher preparation programmes at Institutes of Higher Education in the US in 1998 (Feistritzer, 1999). During fiscal year 1999, sales of introductory special education textbooks were estimated at 94,135 (Monument Information Resources, 2000). This figure accounts for the sale of new textbooks and does not include those bought used, both at college bookstores and from on-line booksellers. One estimate is that used books account for approximately 40 per cent of all textbooks purchased in a given year (Monument Information Resources, 2000). [...]

Why study textbooks?

Textbooks are purveyors of what is implicitly understood to be legitimate material for a particular area of study. They signify constructions of reality and ways of selecting, organizing and prioritizing knowledge. Textbooks provide selected access to ideas, information and practices that are interpreted by students as natural, fixed and inevitable. Much of the information that textbooks convey to students involves cultural and professional values. Symbolic representations in textbooks are often used to confer legitimacy on particular groups, while the silencing or omission of other perspectives may have the opposite effects for those groups (Sleeter and Grant, 1991). Textbooks are one mechanism by which ideological positions in a field of study can be conveyed. [...]

Discussions of inclusion in the texts

The discussions surrounding inclusive education, where 'opposing camps appear to be arguing past each other' (Gallagher, 2001, p. 638), have crystallized into a seemingly straightforward presentation in the textbooks. The structure of arguments and ideological strategies used in favour of maintaining the current system are: (1) omitting a central element of the concept of inclusion: restructuring; (2) holding inclusion to a higher level of scrutiny; (3) constructing a profession that appears unified in maintaining the current system; (4) 'radicalizing' proponents of inclusive education; (5) interpreting and presenting empirical data selectively; (6) elevating empiricism over ethics; (7) presenting a medical versus a social model of disability; and (8) presenting a limited definition of inclusion. It should be noted that there is some overlap; that is, some quotes from the textbooks could fit within several of the just-named categories. In the next section, I look more closely at each of the formulations of these arguments.

Omitting a key concept in defining inclusion: restructuring

In defining inclusion and full inclusion, textbooks in this study did not present the aspect of restructuring that proponents have argued would be necessary for successful inclusion. The omission of this central piece of the definition has a ripple effect throughout the authors' treatment of the topic. That is, there are several aspects of the authors' definitions that depend on this omission in that these aspects would not be relevant if restructuring was part of the discussion. This section looks at the structure of the following presentations and arguments: (1) 'one size fits all'; (2) the current organization of general education classrooms; and (3) positing no alternatives to the current structure.

'One size fits all'

Textbook presentations

In two textbooks descriptions, 'full' inclusion is presented as being a 'one size fits all' policy:

> [Recent legislation] reaffirms the belief that a continuum of services be available to children and youth with disabilities and their families, and the law does not suggest that a single service delivery option (such as only the general education class) should be the only alternative.
>
> (Smith, 2001, p. 47)

> [E]mpirical evidence is scant and … what is available does not support any one service delivery option.
>
> (Hallahan and Kauffman, 2003, p. 55)

Analysis

These presentations suggest that 'full' inclusion means that all students would receive the same services. There is no mention of the restructuring of the dual educational systems (nominalization; passivization). The continuum of placements, which offers a variety of placement options that can meet individual student needs, is presented as the antidote to inclusion. Readers are presented with an either–or proposition: one must choose between either the current system, which offers the option to meet student needs, or a system where all students are put into general education without individualized supports.

   Implicit in the 'one size fits all' presentation is the idea that individualized planning and instruction cannot occur in general education classrooms (eternalization; standardization). Taylor (1988, p. 17) wrote:

> The LRE principle confuses segregation on the one hand with intensity of services *on the other*. ... [These] are separate dimensions. Brown *et al.* (1983) write: '... any developmentally meaningful skill, attitude, or experience that can be developed or offered in a segregated school can also be developed or offered in a chronological age appropriate regular school'.

The notion that individualization cannot occur in a general education setting equates location or setting with the service to be provided. [...]

Arguing that general education classrooms are not designed for specialized instruction

Textbook presentations

Many parents of children with disabilities [...] have resisted [the placement of their children in regular classes], thinking the regular classroom does not offer the intense, individualized education their children need (Heward, 2000, p. 68).

   Unfortunately, teachers in general education classrooms often find it difficult to provide enough intensive instruction, even with 'supports' intended to help students survive the general education curriculum. The current structure of resource room programmes, in which teachers have high case loads and cannot provide the instruction students need, is a setup for failure (Hallahan and Kauffman, 2003, p. 55). [...]

Analysis

Implicit in these statements is the notion that inclusive education is seen as an 'add-on' in the general education classroom, rather than a restructuring of the dual systems. Classrooms as currently structured are viewed as *the* standard (standardization); the only viable option. Consideration of locating intensive instruction in the restructured general education classroom is not presented as an option (externalization). Using 'many parents' and 'teachers of general education' conveys the impression of two united groups that oppose any change in the current structure (unification).

Positing no alternatives to the current system

Textbook presentation

> In a synthesis of over two dozen surveys of general educators' views on integrating students with disabilities into their classes, only about half thought that integration could provide some benefits (Scruggs & Mastropieri, 1996). Furthermore, only about one-fourth to one-third thought they had sufficient time, skills, training, and resources for working with students with disabilities.
>
> (Hallahan and Kauffman, 2003, pp. 53–54)

Analysis

These are important findings. The central challenge presented by inclusion is the notion that we must re-think general education. To present these issues as problems without suggesting solutions (e.g. restructuring) naturalizes general education, itself a social and historical artefact (naturalization, externalization, standardization) (Brantlinger, 1997).

'It might not work'

Textbook presentation

> We know that simply placing a child with disabilities in a regular classroom does not mean that the child will learn and behave appropriately or be socially accepted by children without disabilities [nominalization; legitimation; standardization; eternalization].
>
> (Heward, 2000, p. 69)

Analysis

Proponents of inclusion do not argue that placement *is* enough. Their focus on restructuring the dual systems is an acknowledgement that merely changing the location of services would not necessarily result in substantive changes in the expectations and instruction of students who currently do not have access to the general education curriculum.

Presentations of 'full' inclusion as a 'one size fits all' policy, arguing that general education is not prepared to handle students with disabilities, and not providing a vision of alternatives to the current structure all hinge on the omission of restructuring and school reform as central to inclusion. Without restructuring as part of the discussion, 'full' inclusion as presented by these authors could indeed seem like a risky proposition.

Restructuring and school reform are aspects of successful inclusive schools. To presume that what exists necessarily creates the future is to posit no alternative to reproducing the current system. Allowing for the possibility of change is an important part of creating inclusive schools and society.

Holding 'full' inclusion to a higher level of scrutiny

Textbook presentations

In two textbooks, discussions of inclusive education are introduced by the following headings:

Premises of full inclusion
(Hallahan and Kauffman, 2003, p. 45)

Arguments against full inclusion
(Hallahan and Kauffman, 2003, p. 51)

'Arguments for and against full inclusion'
(Heward, 2000, p. 69)

Analysis

In these presentations, the central issue to be debated is 'full' inclusion. Readers are presented with four premises that the authors argue are the basis of 'full' inclusion: '1. Labeling people is harmful; 2. Special education pull-out programs have been ineffective; 3. People with disabilities should be viewed as a minority group; 4. Ethics are more important than empirical evidence' (Hallahan and Kauffman, 2003, p. 45).

Each of these *premises* (not *arguments* in favour of 'full' inclusion) is challenged in turn. For example, the authors discuss: (1) instances in which labels are useful (p. 46); (2) research that shows the mixed results of pull-out programmes (p. 47); (3) the difficulty of people with disabilities [in joining] forces on specific issues due to their 'heterogeneous population' (p. 50); and (4) their view that empirical data are more important than ethics (pp. 50–51). The authors then present six arguments against 'full inclusion'. [...]

Heward's (2000) text similarly looks at arguments on 'both sides'. The presentations appear fair and seem to represent the views of both inclusion advocates and critics. For instance, Heward reproduced Taylor's (1988) seven-point critique of the least restrictive environment principle. As an example, one of the points is that the continuum of placements 'legitimates restrictive environments'. That is, if one environment is less restrictive, then there must be others that are 'more restrictive'. However, after presenting this critique of one of the bedrock principles of the current structure, Heward wrote: 'Most special educators, however, are not in favor of eliminating the LRE concept and dismantling the continuum of alternative placements' (p. 71). He also included a two page color insert titled, 'Inclusion versus Full Inclusion'. The four bolded sub-headings read: 'What is Inclusion?; What is Full Inclusion?; Many Children, Many Needs; and Why the Full Inclusion Movement Will Not Succeed' (pp. 72–73).

These presentations are the primary definitions and examples of 'full' inclusion in these textbooks. If one were to look in the table of contents or the index for 'full inclusion', s/he would be directed to these pages. The presentations centre 'full' inclusion as the issue that must be proven. Meanwhile, the current structure is exempt from examination, presumed effective and beyond the need for scrutiny or discussion (naturalization, externalization, standardization). Pre-service teachers are not exposed to critiques of or alternatives to the current system.

Constructing a profession that appears unified in maintaining the current system

Textbook presentations

One rationale that has been advanced for maintaining the system as it presently operates is that the majority of professionals prefer it:

> Most special educators ... are not in favor of eliminating the LRE concept and dismantling the continuum of alternative placements.
>
> (Heward, 2000, p. 71)

> General educators, special educators, and parents are largely satisfied with and see the continuing need for the continuum of alternative placements.
>
> (Hallahan and Kauffman, 2003, p. 51)

> Defenders of the full continuum point out that, for the most part, teachers, parents, and students are satisfied with the degree of integration into general education now experienced by children with disabilities and see the needs to maintain it.
>
> (Hallahan and Kauffman, 2003, p. 51)

> Repeated polls, surveys, and interviews have indicated that the vast majority of parents of students with disabilities, as well as students themselves, were satisfied with the special education system and placement options.
>
> (Hallahan and Kauffman, 2003, p. 51)

> The attitudes of many general educators toward including students with disabilities in regular classes have been less than enthusiastic. ... Although some critics blame teachers for their unwillingness to accommodate more students with disabilities, many agree that their hesitation to do so is justified.
>
> (Hallahan and Kauffman, 2003, pp. 54–55)

Analysis

The use of terms such as 'most educators', 'for the most part', 'largely satisfied', 'majority' and 'many agree' rhetorically constructs a profession that is largely unified in its perspective on educational policy. Thompson (1990) described this strategy as *unification*. Presented as an 'argument' against inclusion, the desires and opinions of teachers are privileged over their legal responsibility to provide the most integrated environment possible for all students. The preferences of educators are positioned as a legitimate rationale for disregarding the rights of students with disabilities to be educated with their non-labelled peers. As Gallagher (2001, p. 650) noted, 'What are advanced as reasons look a great deal more like rationalizations'.

Radicalizing proponents of inclusive education

Textbook presentations

> Critics of full inclusion claim that the idea of full inclusion is being championed by only a few radical special educators.
>
> > (Hallahan and Kauffman, 2003, p. 52)

> Fuchs and Fuchs (1994) … are concerned that reform in special education is being 'radicalized' by a minority who want to do away with all special education placements in favor of full inclusion.
>
> > (Heward, 2000, p. 74)

Analysis

Thompson (1990) viewed *fragmentation* as the opposite side of the unification coin. The goal of fragmentation is to discredit 'those individuals and groups that might be capable of mounting an effective challenge to dominant groups' (p. 65). Positioning proponents of 'full' inclusion as radical and outside of the mainstream is an attempt to harm the reputation and credibility of those individuals, thus weakening their impact.

Interpreting and presenting empirical data selectively

Textbook presentations

Smith (2001) included the perspectives of students in her text. She presented interpretations of three studies which, she suggested, show that students prefer special education to general education settings. She wrote, 'Children with learning disabilities preferred pull-out programs because they thought they received special assistance and could work in a quieter setting' (Klingner *et al.*, 1998, p. 61).

   In their text, Hallahan and Kauffman (2003) also cited the Klingner *et al.* (1998) study as evidence for maintaining the continuum of placements:

> Many students themselves say they prefer pull-out to in-class services, which may be interpreted to support the preservation of a full continuum of placement options.
>
> > (Klinger [*sic*] *et al.*, 1998, p. 51)

Analysis

Klingner *et al.* (1998) cited 32 fourth to sixth graders, 16 with a label of learning disabilities and 16 without, and they were asked about their experiences, both with a resource room (pull–out) model and an inclusive model (where the learning disabilities teacher co-taught from 30–90 minutes per day in the general classroom). In response to the question, 'Which do you like best, pull-out or inclusion?' eight of the students with a label of learning disabled preferred pull-out, six preferred inclusion and two responded 'both ways'. Two students reportedly preferred pull out because 'there were less people' in a resource room; two students said they could concentrate better; and one student's preference related to the fact that 'they test you to see what you most need help with' (Klingner *et al.*, 1998, p. 153).

The six students who preferred the inclusion arrangement said that in the general education class they 'learned more and worked harder' and 'could get more help'. They also gave these reasons: 'So I don't miss anything'; 'You don't waste time going somewhere'; and 'In Ms. M's class we played games and in a normal class we don't' (p. 153).

Presentations of this study by textbook authors did not mention the strengths of the inclusive settings that students articulated (nominalization). In addition, the groups are presented as representing larger numbers than a group of eight children: 'children with learning disabilities'; 'many students' (unification; universalization). Percentages of students who responded in favour of pull-out versus inclusion, a standard way of reporting research results, were also omitted (passivization). The results of this study as presented in these textbooks are designed to elicit support to maintain the current structures of education (naturalization; reification). [...]

Elevating empiricism over ethics

Textbook presentation

In their textbook, Hallahan and Kauffman (2003, p. 54) wrote:

> Some professionals see as folly the disregard of empirical evidence espoused by some proponents of full inclusion (Fuchs & Fuchs, 1991; Kauffman, 1989, 1999; Kauffman & Hallahan, 1997). These professionals believe that ethical actions are always of the utmost importance. They assert, however, that decisions about what is ethical should be informed by research. In the case of mainstreaming, they think it is important to have as much data as possible on its advantages and disadvantages and how best to implement it before deciding if and how it should be put into practice. Some critics maintain that full-inclusion proponents have gone too far in championing their cause, that they have resorted to rhetoric rather than reason. These critics assert that backers of full

inclusion have traded in their credentials as scientific researchers in favor of becoming advocates and lobbyists.

Analysis

In this passage, the authors present a web of statements which, particularly for those new to the field, might be difficult to unravel. First, they include proponents as uninterested in research (expurgation of the other). The plethora of research into the experiences of students and teachers in various instructional arrangements, parent perspectives, effective instructional practices, methods of administration in inclusive buildings, and collaboration among professionals contradicts this claim.

Next, referring to themselves and those who agree with them as professionals, they position science over ethics (standardization; scientism). Ethics can be informed by research, they argue, but not vice versa. This implies that research is both superior to ethics as well as somehow value-neutral (fallacy of objectivity; moral neutrality). Such statements draw on the cultural authority of science to bolster support for current practice and to weaken support for a position presumably backed only by ethics, rhetoric, emotionalism and advocacy (scientism; fallacy of objectivity; moral neutrality). Such statements allow the future teacher – and the field – to hide behind 'science' when taking a position that could limit life chances for students with disabilities.

Those who hold a view different from these authors are implicated as 'political' – advocates and lobbyists (expurgation of the other). An additional implication is that, as 'scientists' themselves, these authors are objective and thus outside of a political arena; 'beyond' advocating for a particular position (fallacy of objectivity; moral neutrality). However, the authors' citation of themselves to support the discrediting of others belies their own advocacy.

Presenting a medical versus a social model of disability

Textbook presentation

Hallahan and Kauffman (2003, p. 54) wrote:

> Many critics of full inclusion … argue that for [racial and ethnic minorities and women], separation from the mainstream cannot be defended on educational grounds, but for students with disabilities, separation can. Students with disabilities are sometimes placed in special

classes or resource rooms to accommodate their educational needs better. Placement in separate educational environments is inherently unequal, these critics maintain, when it is done for factors irrelevant to learning (e.g. skin color), but such placements may result in equality when done for instructionally relevant reasons (e.g. student's ability to learn, difficulty of material being presented, preparation of the teacher).

Analysis

The meaning that disability is given is not a fixed 'truth' but is interpreted differently in different historical periods and in different cultures. British social theorists have made an important distinction between impairment and disability (Oliver, 1990), where the former is, for example, an inability to walk while the latter is an inability to access a building due to the lack of a ramp. In the same vein, individuals with labels of more severe disabilities have shown that their ability to communicate is dependent upon context, thereby challenging the notion that the disability lies within the individual (Marcus and Shevin, 1997; Rubin *et al.*, 2001).

When disability is located within the individual, defined as 'the medical model' of disability, the structure of the environment is taken to be neutral and natural, not in need of modification. When one takes the approach that the environment creates the disability, 'the social model', the focus shifts to analysing societal structures and practices that are disabling.

In the education context, professional constructions of disability point to typological thinking (Gelb, 1997). According to typological thinking, the notion that *this* group of exceptional learners is different – cannot handle abstract thought or literacy, for instance – translates into material practices, including a different curriculum, different teaching methods and a different educational setting.

Confusing impairment with disability allows the lens to be trained on individuals rather than on environments and structures that may be problematic (eternalization). The focus is on how to improve, remediate and fix the child rather than on how the curriculum, the schedule, the instructional delivery, the educational activities and the physical and social environments might be adjusted to help students function optimally.

When the meaning of disability-as-individual-deficit circulates as a central truth about certain groups of people, it has material effects on those individuals. Such a construction perpetuates the false notion that the general education setting has no responsibility to accommodate diverse learners (standardization; nominalization). Further, it supports and reinforces the implicit notion that students with labels can learn only and/or best in segregating settings (narrativization; externalization). In an inclusive setting, students with disability labels prompt a question not about placement, but about resources and accommodations: what does this student need to learn the most and function best a given setting with her peers?

Omission of a broader context for understanding inclusion

Textbook authors discuss 'full' inclusion versus a continuum of placements as though the only issue at stake is where a child spends his or her school day. While this is clearly central to the construct of inclusion, a variety of other dimensions have been advanced. For instance, many have argued that inclusion is a social justice issue having to do with equity, access and opportunity for students with disabilities (e.g. Biklen, 1992; Rizvi and Lingard, 1995). Others view it as having to do with the politics of recognition (e.g. Armstrong *et al.*, 2000; Corbett and Slee, 2000). For instance, Corbett and Slee see inclusion as a 'political and social struggle to enable the valuing of difference and identity' (p. 134). Others remind us that the goal of inclusion is to create welcoming contexts for *all* students in schools (e.g. Lipsky and Gartner, 1996).

Brantlinger (2003) argued that special education textbooks present a view of special education as 'the peaceable kingdom'. The political challenges in the field are omitted in order to create the perception of a conflict-free profession that is steadily moving forward. In contrast, Ware (2004) highlighted the on-going nature of the struggle to create inclusive schools and societies. The work required to inch toward the ideal of inclusion is difficult; this is all too often concealed. Moving toward more inclusive schools is anything but uncontested and apolitical. Future teachers should be exposed to both the challenges and the complexities of inclusive education, as it will likely impact both their career and the lives of the students they work with. This framework will also position students to better understand the need for their continued professional development in improving instruction, but also in areas such as teacher leadership and strategies for school reform.

Discussions of 'full' inclusion in the textbooks in this study tended to be narrow. Having a socio-political context within which to consider inclusive education would shift the discussion from one that centres primarily on location to one that looks at the politics and possibilities of teachers' roles in providing opportunities for students with disabilities in schools and society.

Conclusion and recommendations

Because it is impossible to be 'outside of ideology', it is impossible not to write from a particular ideological position. Textbook authors are no exception. Regardless of the narrative and rhetorical strategies authors use in their writing to appear objective, their values, beliefs and preferences are nonetheless present. Through introductory textbooks, future teachers are exposed to particular ideas and certain ways of looking at those ideas; at the same time, alternative views are omitted. The rhetoric, the exclusions, the confusing representations, the authority of 'science' presented by 'experts' in a professional field, carried through the cultural authority of textbooks, are likely to go unchallenged by newcomers to the field. [...]

An alternative discourse would be one that situates special education within a context of equity and social justice; another would be change and possibility; a third would be to take the perspective of an individual with a disability. Special education is a field with multiple perspectives on how to educate students, where to educate students, the goals of special education, research methods in the field, and who should be considered when 'doing' research and writing policy. On any given issue, people with disabilities, their parents, and educational and medical 'experts' are likely to have different perspectives. Being able to understand and articulate the views of others, particularly when they may differ from one's own ideological positioning, is an important discourse for future special educators to acquire. [...]

The field of special education has entered a new era, where multiple goals for the field, a variety of research methodologies, instructional philosophies and approaches all fit under the 'special education' umbrella. It is more important than ever that we provide future teachers with the means by which they can talk with others who hold viewpoints different from our own (Danforth, 2004). Being able to listen to and understand the viewpoints of others – particularly people with disabilities and their parents, who are most directly affected by teachers' beliefs, decisions and actions – should be a central goal of the socialization of special education teachers.

References

Armstrong, F., Armstrong, D. and Barton, L. (2000) 'Introduction: What is this book about?', in F. Armstrong, D. Armstrong and L. Barton (eds) *Inclusive education: policy, contexts and comparative perspectives* (London, David Fulton), 1–11.

Biklen, D. (1992) *Schooling without labels* (New York, Teachers College Press).

Brantlinger, E. (1997) 'Using ideology: cases of nonrecognition of the politics of research and practice in special education', *Review of Educational Research*, 67, 425–459.

Brantlinger, E. (2003) 'The big glossies: how textbooks structure (special) education', paper presented at the Annual Meeting of Disability Studies in Education, Chicago, IL.

Corbett, J. and Slee, R. (2000) 'An international conversation on inclusive education', in: F. Armstrong, D. Armstrong and L. Barton (eds) *Inclusive education: policy, contexts and comparative perspectives* (London, David Fulton), 133–146.

Danforth, S. (2004) 'The "postmodern" heresy in special education: a sociological analysis', *Mental Retardation*, 42, 445–459.

Feistritzer, E. (1999) *The making of a teacher: a report on teacher preparation in the U.S.* (Washington, DC, Center for Education Information).

Fuchs, D. and Fuchs, L. (1994) 'Inclusive schools movement and the radicalization of special education reform', *Exceptional Children*, 60, 294–309.

Gallagher, D. J. (2001) 'Neutrality as a moral standpoints, conceptual confusion and the full inclusion debate', *Disability and Society*, 15, 637–654.

Gelb, S. (1997) 'The problem of typological thinking in mental retardation', *Mental Retardation*, 35, 448–457.

Hallahan, D. and Kauffman, J. (2003) *Exceptional learners*, 9th edn (Boston, MA, Allyn & Bacon).

Heward, W. (2000) *Exceptional children*, 6th edn (Columbus, OH, Merrill).

Kauffman, J. (1989) 'The regular education initiative as Reagan–Bush education policy: a trickle-down theory of education of the hard-to-teach', *Journal of Special Education*, 23, 256–278.

Kauffman, J. (1999) 'Commentary: today's special education and its messages for tomorrow', *Journal of Special Education*, 32, 244–254.

Klingner, J., Vaughn, S., Schumm, J., Cohen, P. and Forgan, J. (1998) 'Inclusion or pull-out? Which do students prefer?', *Journal of Learning Disabilities*, 31, 148–158.

Lipsky, D. K. and Gartner, A. (1996) 'Inclusion, school restructuring, and the remaking of American society', *Harvard Educational Review*, 66, 752–796.

Marcus, E. and Shevin, M. (1997) 'Sorting it out under fire: our journey', in D. Biklen and D. Cardinal (eds) *Contested words, contested science* (New York, Teachers College Press).

Monument Information Resources (2000) *College textbook national market report* (Princeton, NJ, Monument Information Resources).

Oliver, M. (1990) *The politics of disablement: a sociological approach* (New York, St Martin's).

Rizvi, F. and Lingard, B. (1995) 'Disability, education and the discourses of justice', in Christensen and F. Rizvi (eds) *Disability and the dilemmas of education and justice* (Philadelphia, PA, Open University Press), 1–26.

Rubin, S., Biklen, D., Kasa-Hendrickson, C., Kluth, P., Cardinal, D. and Broderick, A. (2001) 'Independence, participation, and the meaning of intellectual ability', *Disability and Society*, 16, 415–429.

Sleeter, C. and Grant, C. (1991) 'Race, class, gender, and disability in current textbooks', in: M. Apple and L. Christian-Smith (eds) *The politics of the textbook* (New York, Routledge).

Smith, D. (2001) *Introduction to special education*, 4th edn (Boston, MA, Allyn & Bacon).

Taylor, S. (1988) 'Caught in the continuum: a critical analysis of the principle of least restrictive environment', *Journal for the Association for Persons with Severe Handicaps*, 13, 41–53.

Thompson, J. (1990) *Ideology and modern culture: critical social theory in the era of mass communication* (Stanford, CA, Stanford University Press).

Ware, L. P. (2004) 'Introduction', in L. P. Ware (ed.) *Ideology and the politics of (in)exclusion* (New York, Peter Lang), 1–8.

This chapter alerts us to the fact that through repeated presentations in textbooks such as the ones analyzed in this study, and reinforcement through additional readings, course lectures (using publisher's overheads and PowerPoint presentations), websites, tests and classroom presentations, students are likely to acquire a discourse of special education that would reproduce traditional views of the field. This discourse often maintains the current system or status quo around ideas of inclusion and this chapter works as a counter-story to challenge and empower readers to be more aware of how textbooks are positioning them to believe certain, seemingly closed, ideas and understanding of inclusion that are essentially challengeable. The chapter also highlights how educators can 'argue with the text' in class, to demonstrate for future teachers how a mainstream perspective on a particular issue can be challenged.

Chapter 16

Transcending transculturalism?

Race, ethnicity and health-care

Lorraine Culley

This chapter challenges us to reflect on our ways of thinking and working which fix ethnicity as a specific set of cultural properties. It raises a critical culturalist approach to difference and healthcare practice, which includes a consideration of racism. The relevance of a critical culturalist approach is not restricted to healthcare. Rather, it is a process we all should consider and think about engaging in.

Race, racism and ethnicity

There is considerable confusion in popular, political and administrative discourse around the use of the terms race and ethnic group, with the two often being used interchangeably (Bradby 1995; Fenton 1999). Things are no better in social research, where there are different usages expressing varying theoretical, epistemological, political and legal standpoints (Malik 1996). A key analytic distinction is usually drawn between the idea of 'race' as signifying the division of humankind into discrete groups, marked by immutable biological characteristics and the term 'ethnic', which is used to denote differences associated with culture, learning and socialisation.

Modern genetics has discredited the science of races because it proved impossible to sustain any single classificatory system, given that the degree of variation within postulated races came to be recognised as greater than the variation between them (Fenton 1999). However, the *idea* of race is clearly still of considerable social and political significance (Miles 1989; Brah 1992). Race may not be real, but *racism* is. Evidence abounds of the persistence of ideas about racial categories in everyday discourse and their very real effects in many forms of racist exclusion (Goldberg 1993). Racism should not be restricted to forms of exclusionary practices based on the notion of biological difference. Goldberg (1993) articulates racism as a set of postulates, images and practices that serve to differentiate, exclude and dominate, and which can use all kinds of signifiers or markers. In Goldberg's anti-essentialist and anti-reductionist approach, racism is not a homogenous phenomenon but seen as taking many forms (racisms) in different contexts.

Understanding the process of racialisation (the way in which ideas about race are mapped onto particular groups or populations in specific contexts) and the operation of many forms of racism may be crucial to understanding some of the apparent differences in the health status of minority ethnic groups. This is because racisms may adversely affect health and well-being in many ways (Karlsen and Nazroo 2002, 2004). First, there is the possibility of direct physical or psychological violence against those who are perceived as 'Other'. Second, racism may be embedded in exclusionary practices in, for example, employment, housing, education and immigration law, adversely affecting the socioeconomic circumstances of racialised groups, and thus impacting on their health. Third, there is growing evidence to suggest that there is a direct impact on health, as unhealthy symptoms such as high blood pressure may be a clinical response to racial harassment (Krieger 1990, 2003). Fourth, racism in health service delivery may adversely affect health. This effect may occur through the actions of individuals or through institutional practices, which have the effect of denying access to services or providing inadequate care (Parekh 2000).

Racism and nursing

Discussions of racism rarely feature in nursing discourse (Shaha 1998). As Porter and Barbee (2004) have argued, while cultural diversity is accepted, racism is euphemised, denied or negated. [...] Nursing discourse constructs the nurse as a caring professional, who, in a colour-blind (and class-blind) way, treats people who are ill from various microlevel causes (Barbee 1993). There is a denial that nursing is embedded in unequal relations of power that structure interactions between nurses and their patients (and also interactions among nurses). The discursive construction 'nurse' 'assumes a magnanimity supposedly permitting nurses to transcend whatever racial and class biases constrain ordinary people's interactions with "others"' (Harrison 1994, 93). Where racism *is* addressed within nursing, it tends to be equated with individual acts deriving from (irrational) prejudice that, it is usually argued, can be eliminated by an appropriate dose of education (Mulholland 1995; Culley 1996).

Generally speaking, nurses are much happier in the domain of 'culture' than racism (Barbee 1993; Culley 1996, 1997). An exploration of the 'sensitive care of the culturally different client' and the research needed to realise this practice is preferred to the theorisation of individual and institutional racist practices and their effects on clients and colleagues. As culture rather than racism is the proper concern of nursing, the concept of *ethnicity* is invoked, albeit often in a form which is divested of connotations of hierarchy and dominance. In the discourse of health and nursing the notion of ethnicity has become the most common way of constructing a racialised subject. There is little recognition, however, that ethnicity is a contestable and contested concept.

Ethnicity: a contested concept

There is no single, universal concept of ethnicity. It is a term that appears in a variety of theoretical traditions (Jenkins 1997) and constitutes what Anthias and Yuval-Davis (1992) have called a 'contested concept'. Within nursing discourse ethnicity is conceived of in ways that are similar to the classical anthropological model of ethnicity as culture, and ethnic groups as largely static collectivities or 'tribes' characterised by common cultural attributes or shared origins (Bromley 1989). In this example of essentialist discourse, ethnic groups are constructed as essentially cultural groups, marked out by their common cultural heritage, homogeneity and distinctiveness vis-à-vis other ethnic groups (Rattansi 1992; Mulholland 1995). Essentialism in this context can be thought of as 'the process by which particular groups come to be described in terms of fundamental, immutable characteristics, inherent within an individual or social group which determine their nature and the manner in which that nature is expressed' (May 1999, 34). As May (paraphrasing Werbner 1997) adds, in this process, 'the relational and fluid aspects of identity formation are ignored and the group itself comes to be valorised as subject, as autonomous and separate, impervious to context and to processes of internal as well as external differentiation' (34).

This essentialist notion of ethnicity can be seen to operate in two arenas of health discourse. First, cultural differences are called upon to 'explain' ethnic differences in health status and health behaviours. Second, gaining knowledge of 'other' cultures is regarded as the appropriate professional response to an ethnically diverse population. While this can be seen across all health professional disciplines (see, for example, Qureshi 1994 in relation to medical discourse), it is particularly evident in nursing, where one of the major responses to 'meeting the needs of minority ethnic groups' has been the development of cultural factfiles, checklists and guides. These play a key role in the notion of transcultural care.

Transculturalism

The view that there are distinct cultures which 'interact' with each other is implicit in the very notion of transculturalism (Dobson 1991). [...] Recent contributions to transculturalist discourse in the British context have taken a more critical turn, insisting that we need to understand how wider social, political and economic factors may affect the lives of minority ethnic groups (Le Var 1998; Papadopoulos, Tilki and Taylor 1998). While an explicit insistence on the recognition of wider social processes represents a considerable advance on conventional transculturalism, the notion of ethnicity as culture remains implicit in this project. The idea of cultural boundedness remains fundamental to transculturalism. It is still an issue of 'us' learning about 'them', but now the constituents of the 'Other' are viewed in less individualistic ways. It is still predicated on the idea of cultural groups, with a relatively stable identity and with cultural 'needs' – about which we must learn and to which we must 'respond' empathetically. There is a coexistence of the insistence on the importance of class, gender and generation, with a concept of ethnic groups as relatively fixed and uncomplicated cultural groups with defined sets of health beliefs and (consequent) sets of health behaviours. This apparent contradiction remains largely unproblematised.

The impact of such culturalist thinking on practice is manifested in the repeatedly expressed desire of a range of healthcare practitioners for information on the 'cultural needs' (for example dietary 'needs' and prayer 'needs') of clients (Narayanasamy 2003; Cortis 2004). In this quest for cultural knowledge, transculturalism can itself be seen as contributing to a racialising agenda. 'The manufactured need to know about and construct categories of difference justifies the reproduction of the white liberal imaginings about the beliefs and practices of non-dominant groups' (Gustafson 2005, 12).

[...]

The negative effects of a concept of ethnicity as shared culture on theorising the relationship between ethnicity and health have been discussed at length elsewhere (Ahmad 1993, 1996). Ahmad charts the way in which professional discourses in health–care construct and reinforce cultural differences as the source of health problems. Cultures, defined in rigid and static terms, come to be classified as 'alien' and people are defined as more or less 'other'. The impact on health–care has been to perpetuate a deficit approach to cultural difference; to engender negative stereotyping of minority ethnic clients; to render 'white' ethnicity invisible; to fail to see the significance of racisms and, ultimately, to encourage a limited form of professional practice (Gerrish, Husband and Mackenzie 1996; Gunaratnam 1997; Culley 2000, 2001).

Rethinking ethnicity

The need to challenge this approach to ethnicity, however, does not mean we must cast aside any attempt to understand a relationship between ethnicity and health. A number of critiques of the classical notion of ethnicity within social theory have revitalised debates around ethnicity and have led to alternative formulations that are potentially helpful to health-care practice.

Ethnicity as a social process

One of the earliest challenges to the notion of ethnicity as culture came from the social anthropologist Frederik Barth, who argued that ethnicity should not be thought of as an organisational form (as if it were an object to be studied) but as a social process (Barth 1969). For Barth, ethnicity is about the relationship between groups rather than the content of those groups. […] 'Barth emphasizes that ethnic identity is generated, confirmed or transformed in the course of interaction and transaction between decision-making strategizing individuals' (Jenkins 1997, 12). Rather than seeing ethnicity as defined by culture, and ethnic groups as cultural groups, culture and identity are part of the building blocks of ethnicity as a social construction. This is summarised in Barth's famous vessel analogy. Ethnic categories are the vessels of culture but it is the ethnic boundary that defines the group and not the 'cultural stuff' that it encloses.

Joanne Nagel has more recently reformulated Barth's vessel analogy in constructing the analogy of the shopping cart (trolley). Ethnic boundary construction determines the shape of the shopping cart (size, number of wheels), and 'ethnic culture' is composed of the things we put into the cart such as music, dress, religion, beliefs, symbols and customs. Culture is not a shopping cart that comes to us already loaded with a set of goods; rather, we construct culture by picking and choosing items from the shelves of the past and the present. Cultures change, 'they are borrowed, blended, rediscovered and reinterpreted' (Nagel 1994, 162).

Within this discourse ethnicity is rooted in social interaction and ethnic identity is mutable and situational. As the individual moves through daily life, ethnic identity can change according to variations in the audiences encountered. […] Jenkins (1994) also importantly argues that ethnicity is not *simply* a matter of personal choice. External discourses play an important part in the understanding of what it means to be a member of an ethnic group (Karlsen 2004). While there is a degree of agency, there are also external forces shaping ethnic boundaries. Boundaries are also constructed by outside agents and organisations, so that one's ethnic identity is influenced by the views held by others about oneself.

[…] External forces such as immigration policies, census and other ethnic categories, ethnically linked resource policies and legislation are very significant. Individual choices are circumscribed by the ethnic categories available at a particular time and place. Jenkins argues that some individuals and groups are in a position of power whereby they are able to impose a characterisation on others in ways that affect their social experience in significant respects (Jenkins 1997). Ethnic identities are externalised in social interaction and internalised in personal self-identification and, as such, are subject to change, redefinition and contestation. Health discourses are themselves involved in constructing ethnic categories and racialised identities. This is perhaps most clearly seen in the role of medicine in the construction of 'scientific racism', which served to legitimate slavery in the nineteenth century, the eugenics movements of the early twentieth century and the racial policies of the Nazi state (Krieger 1987; Muller-Hill 1988).

Ethnicity is not merely symbolic; it is also materially constituted in structures of power and wealth. […] There are some societies (and some times) in which ethnic boundaries have monumental effects and there are others where ethnic categories play a relatively minor part or where their importance varies from context to context. For some, ethnic identity is of little import. Fenton (1999) theorises this in terms of a double contextualisation of ethnicity:

> Ethnicity as a social phenomenon is embedded in social, political and economic structures which form an important element of both the way ethnicity is expressed and the social importance it assumes. At the same time ethnicity as an element of individual consciousness and action varies in intensity and import depending on the context of action.

(21)

Postmodernism, identity and ethnicity

Postmodernism also offers us some interesting insights in theorising ethnicity, radically challenging the concept of ethnic groups that underpins transcultural theory. Postmodernism sees the world as fragmentary, discontinuous and often chaotic – the neat rational models of science and progress are displaced. [...] Culture is constantly made and re-made – ever changing, fluid and shifting.

Cultural hybridity is an important concept in postmodernist work on theorising ethnicity. [...] Hybridity refers to the fact that not only do ethnicities change over time, their development cannot be understood as being separate or self-contained. 'New ethnicities' are hybrids – the ever-changing products of complex processes of social change and the continual juxtapositioning of traditions and cultural practices in a global era. [...] Jenkins (1997) makes the point that historical and ethnographic records demonstrate that the world has always been ethnically hybrid: 'Cultural and ethnic diversity (pluralism) is nothing new. The secure hermetically bounded group is an imaginative, somewhat romanticised retrospect' (38).

[...]

Critical culturalism

May (1999) argues that we need to seek an alternative to the essentialism of classical anthropological concepts of ethnicity while acknowledging and explaining why, at the collective level, ethnicity remains a very durable and powerful force. At the same time we need to recognise, as Jenkins and others argue, that power relations are involved in the process of ethnic ascription. Identity choices are structured by a number of constraints and historical determinations. [...] A critical (multi)culturalism means adopting a reflexive position that recognises cultural differences, situates these within a wider nexus of power relations and accommodates an ongoing process of cultural reconstruction (see May 1999, 28–33).

Thinking about ethnicity in more complex and critical ways than transculturalism offers, leads us to a construction of ethnicity that goes beyond the idea of bounded cultural groups. [...] We cannot thus talk of ethnic groups as fixed and uncomplicated entities and so we cannot talk simply of interethnic or *trans*-ethnic relations. Ethnicity is contextual. At the level of the individual, its importance varies according to the context. At the same time, ethnic identity is overlaid with gender, age, socioeconomic and professional identities, each of which may be more or less significant in any specific context, at any specific moment: 'We are all ethnic, yet our ethnicity does not define us. We all need our ethnic identity to be respected, yet we cannot be adequately understood solely in terms of our ethnicity' (Gerrish, Husband and Mackenzie 1996, 19).

Yet black people in particular are often defined (by others) primarily in terms of their supposed ethnicity. Ethnicity is commonly associated with 'non-whiteness'. We rarely see 'white' people as constituted by an ethnic identity (Frankenberg 1993). For many in nursing, the 'ethnic' is still the 'Other', making the ethnicity of the dominant group so hegemonic that it is not perceived as ethnicity at all. The silence on the construction of 'white' ethnicities marks a major omission in health research (Smaje 1996). The need to deconstruct the category 'white' is especially important in understanding the potential health experiences of many less visible minorities (McLaren and Torres 1999).

The implications for health-care

There is no easy answer to the question of what might represent good health-care practice in the context of a critical culturalist discourse. [...] Despite claims to view the subject as simultaneously defined by multiple aspects of difference, performing 'culturally competent care' still attends to individual behaviour rather than the systemic practices (such as racism, sexism and homophobia) that organise that behaviour (Gustafson 2005).

It is argued here that a failure to understand ethnic identification as a complex and dynamic process has led, in the nursing context, to an approach that may limit professional practice rather than liberate it from ethnocentricity. Transcultural nursing has not really recognised the need to come to terms with the implications of the anti-essentialist critique of ethnicity. In contrast to a crude transculturalism there are those who (rightly) insist on the relevance of racism, of the importance of class, gender and age differences within ethnic groups – but at the same time in the very notion of *trans*-culture have in reality maintained the idea of consistent and coherent cultural groups with defined sets of beliefs and health behaviours. There are understandable reasons for this stance. We will still resort to the factfile or something like it because it is comfortable and it seems like a useful tool. It seems to offer us certainty in work which is in fact very uncertain (Gunaratnam 1997, 2001).

As Gunaratnam (1997) has argued, the factfile approach to ethnic identity is relatively simple to understand and can be programmatically applied – people can quickly learn the 'right thing to do'. It gives us a platform to move forward – something concrete to be doing. But as Gunaratnam has shown in her excellent research on palliative care – this approach can stifle good practice. It turns the addressing of need into a task rather than a process issue – factfiles fit well into the idea of task-based competencies. As a practice, the use of cultural checklists can result in bypassing the need to engage with the knowledge that underpins the experience and the personal choice of users. It can limit professional intervention and make it more difficult for professionals to support the choices of users. It gives rise to professional anxieties about 'getting it right' and channels practice into safe and unimaginative areas (Gunaratnam 1997).

[…]

However, abandoning the notion of fixed and homogeneous 'cultures' does not mean rejecting cultural processes as one set of influences on health and health behaviours or rejecting the importance of ethnic identification in specific contexts (Kelleher 1996; Kelleher and Leavey 2004). It means that we cannot 'read off' health status, health beliefs and behaviours from an individual's designated ethnic status. While an uncritical culturalism can be an obstacle to improving health–care, it should be possible to explore in a critical way how ethnicity as structure and as identity (Karlsen and Nazroo 2002) may be significant for clients in any specific context, and how practitioners and policy makers need to respond to this (Bradby 2003). To do this nursing and other healthcare discourses need to overcome their 'structural blindness' and to seek ways of bringing issues of ethnicity, gender and class (and their intersections) to the forefront of the research agenda. […]

The central question is how to take ethnicity seriously in a way that does not entail its reification as a set of fixed cultural properties and how to work with this approach in practice [   ] To begin the process of evaluating and changing practice there are several suggestions that could be proposed as a first step. First, we need to *think in terms of complexity and fluidity*. We need to develop ways of avoiding essentialist assumptions about patients and clients from 'minority groups' and actively seek understandings that might be relevant to our healthcare practice. We need to ascertain rather than assume that certain preferences and practices are of significance to users (Henley and Schott 1999). At the same time we need to be aware of the power relations inherent in the social and political context in which professional–client interactions occur, which themselves organise the range of decision-making options available to patients (Gustafson 2005, 151). We need to be in a position to respond to cultural change, hybridity and fluidity. We need to recognise that ethnicity may be important in some contexts but that we cannot define people solely in terms of their ethnicity. Ethnicity informs individual (and group) identities in culturally and historically specific ways (Bradby 2003).

Second, we need to think about difference, between 'groups' and *within* them. We need to recognise the importance of other identities or locations in structures of class, gender and generation, for example, and how these mediate encounters with health practitioners. We need an approach to educating healthcare workers that does not assume that there is a 'common cultural need' to learn about. Rather, there are heterogeneous groups with diverse social aspirations and interests and there are systemic processes that prevent fair treatment and equitable access.

Third, this paper has reiterated the untenable status of race as a biological entity. It has argued that a critical understanding of culture and ethnicity as overlapping social processes needs to be developed in healthcare discourse and that healthcare encounters are mediated by other important social signifiers. However, a desire to understand and theorise ethnicity does not require a rejection of the implications of *racisms* and *racialisation*: far from it. While rejecting the idea of race as a biological/genetic reality we need to understand the potentially devastating effects of racisms. We must develop an awareness of the ways in which racialisation can be enmeshed in health discourse and extend the research agenda to include a consideration of racisms, which might impact on clients (and colleagues). As we have seen, transculturalism tends to construct racism as interpersonal prejudice or discrimination arising from ethnocentrism, which can be erased by 're-education' (Nairn *et al.* 2004). In opposition to this, it is argued that we need to pay attention to the differential exclusion which is the 'deep structure' of racism, and the many forms that this can take in different historical places (Goldberg 1993). It is important to remember that when we meet clients they may well have been subjected to a variety of racisms, both individual and institutional, which may impact on their health status, their access to health-care, their feelings about using health services and their subsequent interactions with health-care providers. As hooks (1991) reminds us, the politics of 'difference' should not be separated from the politics of racism.

References

Ahmad, W. ed. 1993. *'Race' and health in contemporary Britain*. Buckingham: Open University Press.

Ahmad, W. 1996. The trouble with culture. In *Researching cultural differences in health*, eds Kelleher, D. and Hillier, S. 190–219. London: Routledge.

Anthias, F. and Yuval-Davis, N. 1992. *Racialized boundaries*. London: Routledge.

Barbee, E. 1993. 'Racism in US nursing'. *Medical Anthropology Quarterly* 7: 346–62.

Barth, F. ed. 1969. *Ethnic groups and boundaries: The social organisation of cultural difference*. London: Allen & Unwin.

Bradby, H. 1995. 'Ethnicity: Not a black and white issue. A research note'. *Sociology of Health and Illness* 17: 405–17.

Bradby, H. 2003. 'Describing ethnicity in health research'. *Ethnicity and Health* 8: 5–13.

Brah, A. 1992. 'Difference, diversity and differentiation'. In *Race, culture and difference*, eds Donald, J. and Rattansi, A. 126–45. London: Sage.

Bromley, Y. 1989. 'The theory of ethnos and ethnic processes in Soviet social science'. *Comparative Studies in Society and Social Science* 31: 425–38.

Cortis, D. 2004. 'Meeting the needs of minority ethnic patients'. *Journal of Advanced Nursing* 48: 51–8.

Culley, L. 1996. 'A critique of multiculturalism in health care: The challenge for nurse education'. *Journal of Advanced Nursing* 23: 564–70.

Culley, L. 1997. 'Ethnicity, health and sociology in the nursing curriculum'. *Social Sciences in Health* 3: 28–40.

Culley, L. 2000. 'Working with diversity: Beyond the factfile'. In *Changing practice in health and social care*, eds Davies, C., Finlay, L. and Bullman, A. 131–42. London: Sage in association with the Open University.

Culley, L. 2001. 'Nursing, culture and competence'. In *Ethnicity and nursing practice*, eds Culley, L. and Dyson, S. 109–27. Basingstoke: Palgrave.

Dobson, S. 1991. *Transcultural nursing: A contemporary imperative*. London: Scutari.

Donnelly, T. 2002. 'Representing "Others": Avoiding the reproduction of unequal social relations in research'. *Nurse Researcher* 9: 57–67.

Fenton, S. 1999. *Ethnicity: Racism, class and culture*. London: Macmillan.

Frankenberg, R. 1993. *White women, race matters: The social construction of whiteness* . Minneapolis: University of Minnesota Press.

Gerrish, K., Husband, C. and Mackenzie, J. 1996. *Nursing for a multi-ethnic society*. Buckingham: Open University Press.

Goldberg, D.T. 1993. *Racist culture*. Oxford: Blackwell.

Gunaratnam, Y. 1997. 'Culture is not enough: A critique of multi-culturalism in palliative care'. In *Death, gender and ethnicity*, eds Field, D., Hockey, J. and Small, N. 166–86. London: Routledge.

Gunaratnam, Y. 2001. 'Ethnicity and palliative care'. In *Ethnicity and nursing practice*, eds Culley, L.A. and Dyson, S. 169–85. Basingstoke: Palgrave.

Gustafson, D. 2005. 'Transcultural nursing theory from a critical cultural perspective'. *Advances in Nursing Science* 28: 2–16.

Harrison, E.V. 1994. 'Racial and gender inequalities in health and health-care'. *Medical Anthropology Quarterly* 8: 90–5.

Henley, A. and Schott, J. 1999. *Culture, religion and patient care*. London: Age Concern.

Hooks, B. 1991. *Yearning: Race, gender and cultural politics*. London: Turnaround.

Jenkins, R. 1994. 'Rethinking ethnicity: Identity, categorization and power'. *Ethnic and Racial Studies* 17: 197–223.

Jenkins, R. 1997. *Rethinking ethnicity*. London: Sage.

Karlsen, S. 2004. '"Black like Beckham"? Moving beyond definitions of ethnicity based on skin colour and ancestry'. *Ethnicity and Health* 9: 107–37.

Karlsen, S. and Nazroo, J. 2002. 'Relation between racial discrimination, social class and health among ethnic minority groups'. *American Journal of Public Health* 92: 624–31.

Karlsen, S. and Nazroo, Y. 2004. 'Fear of racism and health'. *Journal of Epidemiology and Community Health* 58: 1017–18.

Kelleher, D. 1996. 'A defence of the use of the terms "ethnicity" and "culture"'. In *Researching cultural differences in health*, eds Kelleher, D. and Hillier, S. 69–90. London: Routledge.

Kelleher, D. and Leavey, G. eds. 2004. *Identity and health*. London: Routledge.

Krieger, N. 1987. 'Shades of difference: Theoretical underpinnings of the medical controversy on black/white differences in the United States 1830–1870'. *International Journal of Health Services* 17: 259–78.

Krieger, N. 1990. 'Racial and gender discrimination: Risk factors for high blood pressure?' *Social Science and Medicine* 30: 1273–81.

Krieger, N. 2003. 'Does racism harm health? Did child abuse exist before 1962? On explicit questions, critical science, and current controversies: An ecosocial perspective'. *American Journal of Public Health* 93: 194–9.

Le Var, R. 1998. 'Improving educational preparation for transcultural health care'. *Nurse Education Today* 18: 519– 33.

Malik, K. 1996. *The meaning of race*. Basingstoke: Macmillan.

May, S. ed. 1999. 'Critical multiculturalism and cultural difference: Avoiding essentialism'. In *Critical multiculturalism*, ed. May, S. 11–41. London: Falmer Press.

McLaren, P. and Torres, R. 1999. 'Racism and multicultural education: Rethinking "race" and "whiteness" in late capitalism'. In *Critical multiculturalism*, ed. May, S. 42–76. London: Falmer Press.

Miles, R. 1989. *Racism*. London: Routledge.

Mulholland, J. 1995. 'Nursing, humanism and transcultural theory: The "bracketing out" of reality'. *Journal of Advanced Nursing* 22: 442–9.

Muller-Hill, B. 1988. *Murderous science*. Oxford: Oxford University Press.

Nagel, J. 1994. 'Constructing ethnicity: Creating and recreating ethnic identity and culture'. *Social Problems* 41: 152–76.

Nairn, S., Hardy, C., Parumal, L. and Williams, G. 2004. 'Multicultural or anti-racist teaching in nurse education: A critical appraisal'. *Nurse Education Today* 24: 188–95.

Narayanasamy, A. 2003. 'Transcultural care. Transcultural nursing: How do nurses respond to cultural needs?' *British Journal of Nursing* 12: 185–94.

Papadopoulos, I., Tilki, M. and Taylor, G. 1998. *Transcultural care: A guide for health care professionals*. Salisbury: Quay Books.

Parekh, B. 2000. *The future of multi-ethnic Britain*. London: Profile Books.

Porter, C. and Barbee, E. 2004. 'Race and racism in nursing research: Past, present and future'. *Annual Review of Nursing Research* 22: 9–37.

Qureshi, B. 1994. *Transcultural medicine: Dealing with patients from different cultures*. Boston, MA: Kluwer Academic Publishers.

Ramsden, I. 1992. *Kawa whakaruruhau: Guidelines for nursing and midwifery education*. Wellington: Nursing Council of New Zealand.

Rattansi, A. 1992. 'Changing the subject? Racism, culture and education'. In *Race, culture and difference*, eds Donald, J. and Rattansi, A. 11–48. London: Sage in association with the Open University.

Shaha, M. 1998. 'Racism and its implications in ethicalmoral reasoning in nursing practice: A tentative approach to a largely unexplored topic'. *Nursing Ethics* 5: 139–46.

Smaje, C. 1996. 'The ethnic patterning of health: New directions for theory and research'. *Sociology of Health and Illness* 18: 139–71.

Werbner, P. 1997. 'Essentialising essentialism; essentialising silence: Ambivalence and multiplicity in the constructions of racism and ethnicity'. In *Debating cultural hybridity: Multicultural identities and the politics of antiracsim*, eds Werbner, P. and Modood, T. 226–54. London: Zed Books.

Lorraine Culley highlights a key challenge for all those seeking equality, participation and inclusion. How do we respond to individual and collective difference without fixing it within a category whilst at the same time recognising that people experience life within categories into which they have been fixed? Ongoing reflection upon our` own ways of thinking and being – and upon the systems within which we work – is the starting point for resolving the issues that arise for such a question.

Chapter 17

Countering the Attention Deficit Hyperactivity Disorder epidemic

A question of ethics?

Linda J. Graham

In Australia in 2007, a media skirmish erupted after a respected District Court judge claimed that doctors were creating violent juvenile offenders by prescribing Ritalin to young children identified as having ADHD. This chapter is written in the context of a policy in Queensland which required a medical diagnosis of impairment for disability support eligibility. Within the UK, the paediatrician may not be involved, but the educational psychologist or general practitioner is very likely to be. Linda Graham's personal interest and subsequent research in this field began when her daughter was diagnosed with ADHD. She subsequently realised that her daughter met many other diagnostic criteria for other labels, but neither ADHD nor any other diagnosis provided any clear way to proceed at school.

Attention Deficit Hyperactivity Disorder, or ADHD as it is now commonly known, never lacks for attention in the Australian media. The most recent frenzy to dominate arose when a New South Wales District Court judge, Paul Conlon, accused doctors of creating a generation of violent children who are now coming before the courts (Fife-Yeomans, 2007). He argued that their kneejerk response to challenging or 'naughty' behaviour was to prescribe Ritalin, the long-term effects of which are still unknown – although Conlon stated that his own research indicates that children medicated with Ritalin mature into violent young people predisposed to drug addiction. In response, the vice-president for the Australian Medical Association argued that we should blame the disorder for violent young offenders, not the treatment. Claiming that 'ADHD is associated with significant issues, including problems with the law and delinquency, drug use, family breakdown and school failure', Dr Choong-Siew Yong said that we should not 'blame Ritalin or any ADHD medications, because these are actually improving the situation' (McLean, 2007, p. 1).

Curiously, unlike psychiatrist Michael Glicksman (1997), Yong seems oblivious to the chicken and egg scenario often associated with ADHD; i.e. is ADHD the cause of these problems or do social problems manifest in behaviours that come to be diagnosed as ADHD? Leaving questions of chickens, eggs and causality aside, I wish to concentrate on where this current media storm leaves us. […] Unless taken to the next level, all Judge Conlon's comments will succeed in doing is to create yet another media stir. The accusation that doctors are creating violent young offenders by prescribing psychostimulant medication is guaranteed to get the media's attention, which […] can be very difficult for the rest of us to do. But what does that actually achieve, and does 'slamming' (Australian Associated Press, 2007a) doctors help anyone in the long run? Actually, it doesn't. What it does do is prematurely foreclose the debate. Here I would like to try to ram a hole through that closure in two ways. First, I will explain how media frenzies such as the one I describe simply (re)invent and (re)secure the medical construct. Second, and perhaps more importantly, I consider what the rest of us – especially those of us who work and live with children who can be described in these ways – can do to circumvent this.

(Re)inventing ADHD

Media storms kick up a lot of dust but fail to ask the right questions. In the end, we are no further towards a solution for the children, parents and teachers at the centre of all the fuss. Indeed, the popular response to Judge Conlon's comments has so far been the same as every other media storm; i.e. Is ADHD over-diagnosed? Are we over prescribing Ritalin? Are doctors to blame? If critically analysed, however, Judge Conlon's comments could lead us to ask more important questions, like: Is the current approach to children who can be described in these ways the best that we can do? But first, I wish to argue that the question 'Is ADHD over-diagnosed?' obscures a more important question; that is, what exactly *is* ADHD?

'Attention Deficit Hyperactivity Disorder' is a *label* (one of many, including Minimal Brain Damage and Hyperkinetic Reaction of Childhood) that the medical domain has coined to both group and describe certain challenging behaviours exhibited by children and young people. I am not disputing the existence of these behaviours nor the ability of doctors (or anyone else) to observe them. My contention is that the problem with 'ADHD' occurs once these behaviours have been observed and the medical label assigned. The path that opens up to children who have been diagnosed with ADHD is a highly medicalised one where the child, their family and their teachers are encouraged to view them as defective – as not completely whole or incompletely formed. Stimulant medication is viewed as a medical prosthesis that can band-aid that gap, until such time as the child either matures or 'learns' the correct ways to behave. However, given that 6 per cent of young children aged between zero and four years in care have been prescribed stimulant medications (Commission for Children and Young People and Child Guardian, 2006), is it not fair to ask whether the fault lies with our expectations and that perhaps these should be subject to inquiry?

Getting back to the perennial question, 'Is ADHD *over*-diagnosed?' my objection to this is that when it is being asked, two assumptions have already been made. The first is that an accurate diagnosis of something is possible, despite the co-location of ADHD on a grey diagnostic continuum with a myriad of other similar 'disorders'. The second is that the medical model (i.e. that certain behaviours could/should be grouped in a certain way, assigned a label and treated medically with stimulant medication) is the only and best response available. When we make these assumptions, as a general community, we then fail to ask questions like: Should certain childhood behaviours be 'diagnosed' at all? What else can we do? More fundamentally: Is it time to review the way we respond to fidgety, distractible, impulsive children? And finally, has the medical model failed these children? Judge Conlon's comments suggest that it has.

Stating that he was 'starting to lose count of [the number of] offenders coming before the courts who were diagnosed at a very young age with ADHD for which they were "medicated"' (Australian Associated Press, 2007b, p. 1), Judge Conlon is actually raising a very important point – one that has been missed in the media furore. His observations suggest that the current approach does not work – although I realise that one has to specify what the aim is to determine whether something works. If the aim is to get a very active child to sit still in a classroom or an impulsive child to remember to put their hand up, then one could argue that the medical response and stimulant medication does the job. If the aim is to get a child from Kindergarten to Year 12 with their dignity and enthusiasm for life and learning intact, then I think it is fair to say that Judge Conlon is witnessing the failure of the medical model to achieve this for a growing number of young people.

In the moment a child is labelled with ADHD, some paths close down and others open up. Despite media claims that a diagnosis of ADHD is a medical excuse for bad behaviour (Shanahan, 2004; Devine, 2006), the ADHD road is not what some might believe it to be. A diagnosis of ADHD does not result in compassion and understanding. More often than not, children who are diagnosed with ADHD (and their parents) meet attitudes tainted by suspicion and contempt (Carpenter and Austin, 2007). Furthermore, they often experience institutional discrimination and social rejection (see Neophytou, 2004). Recent research in education shows just how debilitating these early years experiences can be to children's self-esteem and self-worth (see Exley, 2005) but also that these are not mediated by medication – indeed, the child's 'need' for medication serves to reinforce to the child that they are defective and 'bad'. And so the spiral begins … but this is also when and where it can be circumvented.

Circumventing ADHD

ADHD is characterised by controversy. Indeed, the most enduring question in relation to ADHD is: does it or does it not exist? This is highly problematic because the doubt surrounding the ADHD diagnostic category functions as a red herring forestalling any real progress. […]

What this means from an educational perspective is that for teachers dealing with children who can be described in these ways there is little support available – other than a diagnosis of ADHD and a prescription for stimulant medication. Research shows, however, that these are the kind of students that teachers feel most ill equipped to teach inclusively (Fields, 2006). Public schools and teachers are critically over-stretched and the result, in the state of Queensland (Australia) at least, is that children who present a problem to the system end up in paediatricians' offices. Whether they come out with a diagnosis of ADHD or Autistic Spectrum Disorder can have huge impact on the child's experiences at school, influencing how the child is perceived and the ways in which they are supported (or not, as the case may be).

Describing a child's behaviour as hyperactive, impulsive and distractible (or those popular terms we have all heard before, like fidgety, feral and hyper!) can actually precipitate their journey down the ADHD road – precluding other, perhaps more beneficial, avenues. Disturbingly, greater numbers of very young children are becoming medicated and treated for ADHD. How these children become characterised by their teachers in the early years has enormous influence on how they are perceived by subsequent teachers and the professionals they encounter along the way. The mere suggestion of 'attentional' difficulties is enough to raise the ADHD spectre and once certain words are written in a child's file, those words will continue to colour how that child's abilities and difficulties are viewed (Graham, 2007). One thing that teachers and parents can do to change course is resist categorising children in behavioural terms, as such terms link directly to the diagnostic triad for ADHD and other disruptive behaviour disorder categories. Instead of using behavioural characteristics to describe problems in the schooling context, educators can make an ethical choice and switch the lens we apply by (re)focusing on pedagogical needs. For example, rather than describing a child as 'distractible' and leaving it there, educators and administrators have an ethical responsibility to: (1) acknowledge that this particular student needs redirection more often than other students; (2) make adjustments to their teaching programmes in response to that need; while (3) also advocating at the school and district level for adequate resourcing to enable individual class teachers to achieve this.

Many children who end up with a diagnosis of ADHD and stimulant medication have significant learning difficulties for which there are only educational answers. But if we keep describing these difficulties in behavioural terms, these children are unlikely to get the support they require and educational departments can continue to deny that these children have a legitimate claim to meaningful educational support structures. Using pedagogical descriptors switches the focus away from individual deficit towards teaching and learning and forces educational systems to respond to the needs of challenging students *and* those of the teachers trying to teach them.

References

Australian Associated Press (AAP) (2007a) 'Judge Slams Number of ADHD Prescriptions', Sydney: AAP Bulletins. 26 April.

Australian Associated Press (2007b) 'Labor Calls on Govt to Act after Explosion of ADHD Pills', *Australian Associated Press General News.* Source: Factiva, Canberra. 26 April, p. 1.

Carpenter, L. and Austin, H. (2007) 'Silenced, Silence, Silent: motherhood in the margins', *Qualitative Inquiry.*

Commission for Children and Young People and Child Guardian (CCYPCG) (2006) 'Views of Children and Young People in Care: Queensland 2006', Brisbane: CCYPCG.

Devine, M. (2006) 'Quality Parenting Takes Quantity Time', *Sydney Morning Herald*, 8 June, pp. 1–2.

Exley, B. (2005) 'The Behaviour "Crisis": young children's mis/understandings of the identities of ADHD', Sydney: Australian Association for Research in Education. http://www.aare.edu.au/05pap/exl05566.pdf (accessed on 3 June 2010).

Fields, B. (2006) 'Beyond Disabilities: broadening the view of special needs and the inclusive education challenges facing primary teachers', *Australian Association for Research in Education*, Adelaide, 26–30 November. http://www.aare.edu.au/06pap/fie06330.pdf (accessed on 3 June 2010).

Fife-Yeomans, J. (2007) 'The Ritalin Generation: top judge condemns the ADHD explosion – exclusive', *Daily Telegraph*, Sydney, 26 April, pp. 1, 4.

Glicksman, M. (1997) 'Social Issues at the Root of Child Disorder', *The Australian*, 8 December, p. 11.

Graham, L. (2007) 'Speaking of "Disorderly" Objects: a poetics of pedagogical discourse', *Discourse*, 28(1), pp. 1–20. http://dx.doi.org/10.1080/01596300601073044 (accessed on 3 June 2010).

McLean, T. (2007) 'Blame ADHD, not Ritalin: doctors', *Australian Associated Press General News*, 26 April, p. 1.

Neophytou, K. (2004) 'ADHD, a Social Construct?' Master of Social Science (by research), Australian Catholic University, Melbourne.

Shanahan, A. (2004) 'Jumping on the Victim Bandwagon', *Sunday Telegraph*, Sydney, 30 May, p. 4.

This chapter highlights the role we all have to play in the ways in which we talk and think about children and young people. We need to avoid practices and ways of thinking which lead to the diagnosis and medication of young children when they cannot meet our expectations of learning and behaviour. We also need to be encouraging and supporting each other to seek out creative solutions to the difficulties such situations create, drawing on the everyday classroom practices which are already at hand and within our control.

Part 4

Looking from within

The experience of inclusion

Chapter 18

Inclusion in mainstream classrooms

Experiences of deaf pupils

Joy Jarvis, Alessandra Iantaffi and Indra Sinka

Joy Jarvis, Alessandra Iantaffi and Indra Sinka discuss what deaf children think about their school-experiences and the issues that they see as important. The diversity of experiences and attitudes presented in this chapter reveal the existence of both significant barriers to inclusion and also successful examples.

(The British Deaf Association has very strong objections regarding the widespread placement of individual children in local mainstream [schools].

(British Deaf Association 1996: 7))

This statement, from a major organisation representing Deaf[1] people in the UK, goes against the international and national move towards inclusive education. Currently over 85 per cent of deaf pupils in the United Kingdom are educated in mainstream schools (Lynas *et al.* 1997). Why are some Deaf adults against this practice and do the experiences of deaf pupils in mainstream classrooms reflect these concerns?

Cultural issues

The arguments against placing deaf pupils in mainstream classrooms, particularly against placing them individually in their local schools, fall into two categories: issues of culture and issues of access, and we examine the former first. The cultural issues are in relation to the Deaf community and the understanding of deafness, not as a disability, but as a difference. The main aspect of this cultural difference is the use of a different language: British Sign Language (BSL). The right of deaf children to be part of this culture, to have a deaf peer group, to have Deaf adult role models and to use BSL as a first language is advocated by many Deaf people (British Deaf Association 1996).

Through membership of this community, it is argued, children will develop self-esteem and a strong first language and can thrive in a context where their access to communication and understanding about the world is not limited by their difficulty in understanding and/or producing spoken English. This then gives them a position of strength from which to operate in the wider, hearing community.

Deaf culture is nourished by Deaf clubs and community activities and by Deaf families. It is also developed in specialist schools for deaf children, although these are now fewer in number than in the past (Eatough 2000). One argument is that as most deaf children are born to hearing parents it is only when they are with Deaf adults and peers that they can access this culture and that this takes place most easily in special schools. A group of adults who attended mainstream schools and have subsequently formed the 'Deaf Ex-Mainstreamers Group' felt that attending 'hearing' schools meant that they did not develop an understanding of the Deaf community and its language and culture and were thus excluded from this. 'Deaf ex-mainstreamers are made to feel excluded from the Deaf community because their behaviour is different from other Deaf people…' (DEX 1996: 5).

Access issues

It could be argued that as most deaf children are born to hearing parents and have hearing siblings and peers, then it is important that they can be part of the hearing community and culture. The issue of access is important here; to what extent can one be a full participant in a community if one has problems understanding its language? Most deaf children will have some difficulties understanding spoken language. Many will be able to achieve good comprehension and use of spoken English by using hearing aids, cochlear implants, radio systems, speech reading or a form of sign supported English. Most of these children are currently in mainstream schools where Deaf writers, such as Paddy Ladd (1991), argue that they may see themselves as inferior hearing people, unable to understand everything that is going on, misunderstanding information and jokes and feeling isolated from hearing children. One deaf secondary-aged pupil expressed this feeling of difference when she responded to a questionnaire about integration for the National Deaf Children's Society. She explains, 'At a hearing school you always have to work towards being the same as the others, but you will always be different so you never get there …' (NDCS 1990: 19).

For a minority of deaf children British Sign Language will be the language they are using to communicate and to learn at school. This implies either that teachers are delivering the curriculum in BSL or that it is being interpreted for them by support staff. It also implies that there is a deaf signing peer group to interact with, or that hearing children in this context are fluent sign language users. In practice, if BSL users are not attending special schools, then they are likely to be in a resourced school where there is a group of deaf pupils and where communication support workers interpret what the teacher is saying. In this case much of their teaching is indirect and is delivered by someone who may not be a specialist in a particular subject area. This raises the question of equal access to the curriculum.

Academic inclusion for deaf pupils in a mainstream school can be inhibited by lack of deaf awareness, teaching that is not related to pupils' preferred learning styles, inappropriate support and low expectations (Monkman and Baskind 1998; Powers *et al.* 1999). In many cases the deaf child's level of English is below that of hearing classmates, which can lead both to children failing to understand key aspects of the curriculum and to teachers and other adults providing inappropriate support for language development (Hopwood and Gallaway 1998). The need for many deaf pupils to have support with their English and, for BSL users, their development of sign language, can conflict with full access to the curriculum. If pupils are withdrawn for additional work then they are unable to attend all mainstream classes. A slower pace of communication due to interpretation may limit participation within the classroom. Difficulties with group work and classroom discussion arise owing to the rapid pace of conversation, deaf pupils being unable to understand individuals' contributions and having difficulties in hearing when there is background noise (Stinson and Antia 1999). In general deaf children perform less well academically than hearing pupils (Powers *et al.* 1998), although a minority of deaf pupils show good academic achievement (Lewis 1996). Factors supporting academic achievement would seem to be: high expectations of what deaf pupils can achieve, the involvement of specialist staff and the incorporation of their skills into mainstream practice, appropriate support for staff and pupils, team working by all involved and specific strategies to ensure classroom participation by deaf pupils (Stinson and Liu 1999).

Access to social interaction is seen to be particularly problematic for deaf pupils in mainstream schools. Communication difficulties between deaf and hearing children can leave a deaf pupil isolated (Baldwin 1994; Jarvis 2002). Problems of loneliness and frustration seem likely if a child is the only deaf pupil in a setting (Gregory *et al.* 1995). Difficulties with communicating on an equal footing, misunderstanding information, missing jokes and being unable to understand in group settings can lead to low self-esteem. Baldwin (1994: 165) argues that 'full inclusion denies.the deaf child access to an environment that addresses his/her unique social and emotional needs.'

Identifying pupils' experiences

So far, the potential negative aspects of inclusion have been outlined, but what do those deaf pupils currently being educated in mainstream schools really think of their school experience? Taking into account the views of the pupils themselves is vital if successful inclusion is to be achieved and children have a right to be consulted about their education (DfES 2001). A research project by The University of Hertfordshire and the Royal National Institute for Deaf People (UH/RNID 2002) interviewed 61 deaf pupils and 22 hearing pupils being educated in mainstream secondary schools in England. Both Deaf and hearing researchers were involved in the process of data collection. The project aims were: to document and disseminate deaf pupils' experiences of inclusion and to identify barriers and factors facilitating the effective inclusion of deaf pupils into mainstream schools.

The deaf pupils covered an even spread across the range of hearing losses, from moderate to severe to profound, including pupils who had received a cochlear implant. Figure 18.1 shows the numbers of pupils according to communication mode used during interviews and degree of hearing loss.

The research team visited 25 schools, in 16 different educational authorities. Fifteen schools had specialist provision for deaf pupils, such as hearing impaired units; seven schools had no specialist provision beside the

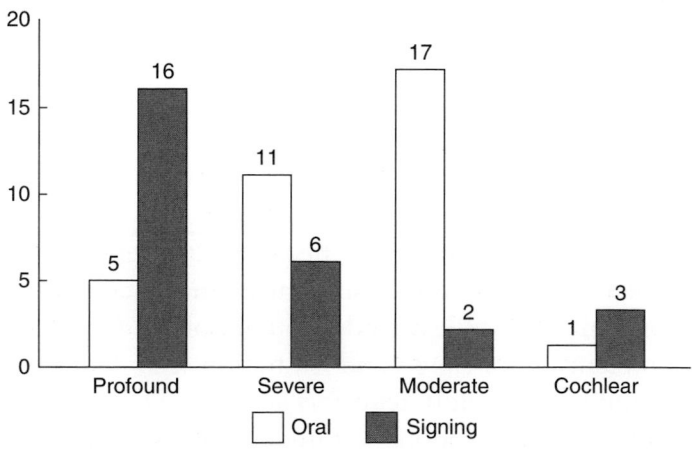

Figure 18.1 Communication mode and level of deafness.

peripatetic services of a teacher of the deaf and three schools had special educational needs bases but no dedicated provision for deaf pupils.

Both individual interviews and focus group discussions were carried out. A variety of methods ensured that the pupils had an opportunity to express their views in detail and in the manner that best suited them. These included the use of mindmaps, which children could draw, write or ask the researcher to write under their dictation; brainstorm exercises; question and answer scenarios; role-playing and the exploration of metaphors. This approach generated a wealth of qualitative data and its analysis identified the following key themes: identity, pupils' views on deafness, school ethos, staff roles, academic inclusion, social inclusion. The rest of the chapter outlines these themes and highlights their implications for policy and practice.

Pupils' views on being deaf in a hearing school

Identity was an issue that emerged spontaneously from the pupils' comments about themselves and their hearing peers. This issue was closely related to that of the school ethos. Some pupils were very confident about deafness as being part of their identity, while others saw it as something to hide. Similarly, in some schools the profile of deafness was high, with the use of visual images of deaf people, such as posters, issues related to deafness as part of the curriculum – for example, looking at hearing aids when studying sound – and identification of the special needs of deaf people within the school environment. In other schools the deaf pupil became invisible under an 'all children are special' blanket philosophy, where the particular issues raised by deafness may not have been identified and therefore addressed. The pupils quoted hereon are all deaf unless noted otherwise. The findings can be studied in more detail in the UH/RNID (2002) report.

Identity

The deaf pupils were asked to choose the terminology they would normally use to describe themselves, which led to discussions around whether they would willingly disclose their hearing status to others. Some of the pupils felt that, if they could 'pass' as hearing, then they would and that they would only disclose their hearing loss on a need-to-know basis. The following quote from a Year 8 pupil with a moderate hearing loss exemplifies this stance:

> I tend not to tell people I'm deaf unless they find out … and when they asked me I'd go 'yeah, I am', but I wouldn't tell them.

Another Year 8 pupil with a profound hearing loss had similar views:

> I wouldn't unless they needed to know – if they spoke really quietly or didn't look at me and I needed to.

Most of the deaf pupils interviewed chose to label themselves as either partially hearing or partially deaf, but overall the replies spanned a range of terms including hearing, hard of hearing, a little bit deaf, Deaf and profoundly deaf. Different labels were used by different individuals and their choices were not necessarily related to their degree of hearing loss. For example a pupil with a moderate loss might readily identify as deaf, whilst other pupils with severe or profound losses might see themselves as hearing or partially hearing. Some also felt that there were disadvantages in being identified as being deaf as they might be teased, bullied or just treated differently:

> I prefer sometimes people not to know 'cause some people tend to act strangely … They kind of talk overdramatically and say H–E–L–L–O and it's easier if they just talked normally. I just say, 'Please don't do that. I prefer it if you talk normally. I'm not stupid.'
>
> (Year 8 pupil, severe hearing loss)

One Year 9 pupil with a cochlear implant pointed out that posters displayed in school, promoting good communication with deaf people, might be the cause of some hearing people's behaviour.

> There's actually a couple of posters about, telling people to, like, t–a–l–k l–i–k–e t–h–i–s and I don't really like it when people do that.

Other pupils felt that it could help with communication if people understood that they were deaf and that other people would notice anyway.

> Don't pretend there's not a problem, there is. Well, it's not a problem but you have to explain to people, otherwise they don't understand and that causes a big problem.
>
> (Year 8 pupil, moderate hearing loss)

Interestingly, some hearing pupils commented quite emphatically about the need of deaf pupils to have deaf peers as a means of feeling more secure in their identity.

> If it's only one person in the entire school who has a hearing aid, that person is like, left out. He or she might say things like 'Oh why am I the only one? Why am I like this?' It's like they start to get upset about who they are because they are the only one that needs a hearing aid.
>
> (Year 9, hearing pupil)

> Because you want to talk to someone who is deaf … you want someone who knows what you're going through, how you're feeling … It's alright for us because there's lots of hearing people…
>
> (Year 8, hearing pupil)

Most deaf pupils also said that they liked having other deaf pupils in the school as they could communicate more easily with them and it meant that there was someone else with similar experiences. Nevertheless, they also liked having hearing pupils in the school as this could lead to understanding each other's worlds and to wider experiences.

> We can talk about things, we're the same. Like. In my primary school, people didn't really understand and it's much easier to talk to my friends who are hearing impaired …
>
> (Year 7 pupil, severe hearing loss)

> It is good that it is mixed here, you can have more friends. Deaf pupils can teach hearing to sign and hearing pupils can teach deaf to speak. It will help for the future when you work with hearing or go out with hearing friends.
>
> (Year 8 pupil, profound hearing loss)

School ethos

The majority of pupils spoke positively about their school and mentioned particular arrangements made for them, such as counselling or structured peer support (these were often open to hearing students as well). They also noted activities designed to encourage deaf and hearing pupils to communicate and socialise together, such as sign language clubs, open to all pupils, and deaf awareness sessions for hearing pupils. The acknowledgement of the particular needs of deaf pupils was usually seen as positive.

> I like the way they can arrange stuff like this to happen, so, like, they don't just treat me like, 'oh, I'm another person.' They don't just say, 'oh,

you're deaf,' whatever, 'you can carry on.' They actually say you can
come up here and you can talk to someone about it. I'm treated a bit
more than other people are, which I don't think it's very fair but it's still
quite good for me. They're just not acknowledging me like another
person, they get to arrange other things for me and stuff. Good special
needs arrangements.

(Year 7 pupil, moderate hearing loss)

Some pupils, however, reported negative experiences and found themselves
excluded from activities hearing pupils were undertaking. This raises the
question as to the extent to which the needs of deaf pupils are considered in
the initial planning for school activities.

I couldn't go [on the school trip] because the man might give us
instructions like how far to go [in the water] and without my hearing aids
on I wouldn't understand it.

(Year 7 pupil, moderate hearing loss)

Deaf awareness, of both staff and hearing pupils, is a key aspect of
inclusion. This includes awareness of the particular communication needs
of deaf people and therefore using appropriate strategies and equipment
such as radio hearing aids. It also means being sensitive to the desire of
many pupils not to be overtly identified as needing special treatment. The
level of deaf awareness varied between schools involved in the project and
within the schools themselves and it significantly affected the pupils'
experiences.

It's really embarrassing 'cause sometimes teachers tend to go, 'Oh
can you be quiet. We've got deaf children in the class!' and how
you should be quiet and how you shouldn't be noisy otherwise
they won't be able to hear and everything. And you're like 'Why
did you do that? You've just embarrassed me so much, why did you
have to?'

(Year 8 pupil, moderate hearing loss)

Everybody used to pull them out [hearing aids connected to radio aid].
This teacher even pulled them out and he never said sorry or anything.
He thought it was a stereo and it wasn't.

(Year 7 pupil, profound hearing loss)

Pupils' access to the curriculum and staff roles

Access to the curriculum is facilitated by a variety of people: the mainstream teacher, teachers of the deaf working within the classroom or withdrawing the pupil for separate tuition, support staff and peers. Pupils expressed a range of perceptions in relation to curriculum access, ranging from very poor to very good. Some pupils highlighted the need for more support in mainstream lessons and felt that they were otherwise unable to access them. Many pupils found that mainstream teachers in particular used inappropriate teaching styles, such as talking when moving around the room or facing the blackboard, talking quickly and without using any form of visual aid and allowing noise levels to rise so that deaf pupils found it uncomfortable.

> I like the way teachers always make sure that you've understood things.
> (Year 7 pupil, severe hearing loss)

> I would tell [a new pupil] that school is horrible and pointless. People will mess about and they would need more support at school.
> (Year 9 pupil, profound hearing loss)

> I prefer teachers here, at the Unit, than the mainstream teachers. Here they help me to understand the meaning. The mainstream teachers don't, they talk way too fast.
> (Year 7 pupil, profound hearing loss)

> This teacher is always angry and shouting in my radio aids. When he shouts my radio aid is hurting me.
> (Year 7 pupil, profound hearing loss)

The role of support staff was seen as to aid deaf pupils' communication with mainstream teachers, help them to understand their work and ensure that they stay on task. Deaf pupils appreciated that support staff facilitated communication with mainstream teachers, encouraged them with their work and were there when they needed them. But they also commented on how support staff might over-explain things and be intrusive by over-helping or by interjecting in the deaf pupils' social interactions with hearing pupils. Of course, the balance between giving adequate, but not too much, support can be difficult to achieve and it requires particular skills and knowledge. Below are some of the comments that pupils voiced on this topic.

> This school is very helpful, I got a communicator help me do some work. They help me with the subjects I don't understand.
>
> (Year 9 pupil, moderate hearing loss)

> If I'm stuck, like on a question, she helps me out and gives me a little example of it. If I'm struggling she's there.
>
> (Year 7 pupil, moderate hearing loss)

> Some of them always help me so they can annoy you because you don't want them to help you a lot.
>
> (Year 8 pupil, profound hearing loss)

> At school, helpers, in lessons, keep prodding me and asking me if I'm alright, that sort of thing, they try to do my work for me! I mean, I think if the LSAs get bored, they just try to help me; they don't like sitting there with nothing to do. The teachers, they've got a whole class so they tend to leave me alone but the LSAs are trying to help just me so I don't get a lot of peace.
>
> (Year 9 pupil, profound hearing loss)

> Sometimes when I stop writing realising that I have made a mistake, she would leap to the rescue, asking if I wanted any help. Often I said no but she would push me aside and take my work to check. I wish I could conjure up something that would freeze her at least for a few minutes!
>
> (Year 8 pupil, profound hearing loss)

Pupils' social inclusion

Having friends and being part of a group was, for most of the pupils, the most significant aspect of school and what they commented on the most. The following quote by a Year 8 pupil with a moderate hearing loss exemplifies the feelings shared by the vast majority of the pupils interviewed:

> It's my mates that make me go through school. If I'm having a bad day, it's friends who talk to me about what I can do. Friends are the best thing.
>
> (Year 8 pupil, moderate hearing loss)

The deaf pupils in the project had a range of experiences, both positive and negative, regarding social inclusion. The key factor seemed to be the ability to communicate, which required strategies to be used by both deaf and hearing pupils, and above all, the willingness to use these strategies.

> With a group of hearing people talking I feel left out. One girl signs for me but the others wouldn't wait and carry on talking. They say I talk like a baby.
>
> (Year 7 pupil, profound hearing loss)

> Sometimes when they say a joke and we don't hear it and they all start laughing and then they don't say the joke again. I do fake laughs. Sometimes I pretend I understand and then, to my best friend maybe, I might go and say, 'I didn't quite get that joke.'
>
> (Year 7 pupil, severe hearing loss)

> Here lots of people are hearing and don't want to speak to deaf people. Here lots of hearing people just say, 'I don't know what he's saying.'
>
> (Year 8 pupil, profound hearing loss)

> It was hard because they didn't understand us at first but, after a while, they got used to how we talk and it was a lot easier.
>
> (Year 9 pupil, profound hearing loss)

> No problem. I like both deaf and hearing. I have made lots of new friends and they're being very nice. I like sitting with them and it's nice to make new friends.
>
> (Year 7 pupil, moderate hearing loss)

> They don't treat us like outcasts, they just treat us with respect and that's fine.
>
> (Year 8 pupil, profound hearing loss)

Because friendship was such a vital part of their school lives, the pupils felt that being able to work alongside their friends enhanced the quality of lessons and made them more fun, as well as helping them with their work. Friends were therefore seen as a resource, which could facilitate academic, as well as social, inclusion. Unfortunately teachers often had a different opinion on the matter and separated groups of friends in lessons in order to reduce distractions.

> I can work better when I'm around friends.
>
> (Year 9 pupil, profound hearing loss)

> You actually can make more friends [working in a group]. You're basically working and then you know what people are doing, their ideas and that.
>
> (Year 7 pupil, moderate hearing loss)

> Hearing classmates are not nice and I don't feel right. It would be better if I had my deaf friend with me. The teacher said she had to separate us. I was angry inside.
>
> (Year 9 pupil, profound hearing loss)

> They [teachers] give you seating plans, which is bad because you can't sit with your friends.
>
> (Year 7 pupil, severe hearing loss)

Pupils were asked about social activities both within and outside school and their responses revealed that, as well as valuing individual friendships, most of them took part in a range of sports and social clubs. These activities encouraged further the socialisation of deaf and hearing pupils.

Conclusions

There is no easy answer to the question of whether inclusion in mainstream schools is the right educational choice for deaf pupils. However, one of the pivotal elements that should not be overlooked is what deaf pupils themselves think and feel. This research highlights that while for some pupils mainstream placement might be the best solution, for others it may not be so. The following two quotes, both from pupils with profound hearing loss who prefer signing as a mode of communication, illustrate the opposite poles of a continuum of experiences within the field of mainstream education for deaf pupils.

> I'm not interested in school. Lots of people, hearing, they group all together and I'm left out.
>
> (Year 8 pupil)

> I wish all schools mixed deaf and hearing. My mom thinks about that I should go to my brother's and sister's school but no, they're all hearing. There are so many hearing schools and few deaf and hearing mixing very few, and we need many schools that are a mixture of deaf and hearing, ideally I would like every school!
>
> (Year 7 pupil)

If inclusion in mainstream schools for deaf pupils is to be successful, services, schools and teachers need to think carefully about the resources, strategies and training necessary for all involved. An issue that requires careful consideration is whether the deaf pupil will be included individually in a school with no dedicated specialist provision and no deaf peers or adult role models available, as such an arrangement could have a significant impact on his/her sense of identity. Solutions to these issues are already being sought and trialled by some services. For example, one education authority has established an e-mail network of deaf pupils, who are placed in different mainstream schools, in order to foster peer support, while another brings hearing aid users from different schools together for discussion of mutual concerns (Moore *et al.* 1999). Access to D/deaf adults, in relation to developing a sense of personal identity, also needs planning and consideration. Deaf pupils have needs, which are specific to the fact that they have a hearing loss and these must be addressed rather than glossed over. Therefore, mainstream teachers will need support in developing, adopting and maintaining the use of relevant strategies that, while facilitating the inclusion of the deaf child, respect the child's desire to be seen as being 'normal' by his or her peers. New and supply teachers, as well as students and trainees, in particular, need to be provided with appropriate information so that deaf pupils' education is not disrupted by staff changes. Support staff also need to be aware of the boundaries of their roles and need to receive adequate training to develop the skills required in order to provide effective support for both mainstream staff and pupils.

Our research project revealed that deaf pupils linked the success or failure of their educational experiences to their experiences of friendship within their schools. These experiences, however, were not just personal and, as such, separate from school life. In fact, those deaf pupils interviewed who expressed positive views on friendship were located in school environments that celebrated diversity and where deafness had a high profile amongst both staff and student bodies.

Currently in the UK there is no clear conception of what inclusion means and it is often associated merely with placing a deaf child in a mainstream context (Powers 2002). For some children inclusion in a wider sense would best be supported by placement in a specialist provision. If mainstream placement is the preferred option then the range of issues discussed in this chapter must be considered if the experience and the outcomes are to be positive for all concerned.

References

Baldwin, S. (1994) Full inclusion: reality versus idealism. *American Annals of the Deaf*, Selected Topics of Interest, 1994: *Full Inclusion*, **139**, 147–71.

British Deaf Association (1996) *The Right to be Equal*. London: BDA.

Deaf Ex-Mainstreamers Group (1996) *Mainstreaming Issues for Professionals Working with Deaf Children*. Barnsley: DEX.

DfES (2001) *Special Educational Needs Code Of Practice*. London: DfES.

Eatough, M. (2000) Raw data from the BATOD survey England January 1998. *British Association of Teachers of the Deaf Magazine*, (May), 1–8.

Gregory, S., Bishop, J. and Sheldon, L. (1995) *Deaf Young People and their Families*. Cambridge: Cambridge University Press.

Hopwood, V. and Gallaway, C. (1999) Evaluating the linguistic experience of a deaf child in a mainstream class: a case study. *Deafness and Education International*, **3**(3), 172–87.

Jarvis, J. (2002) Exclusion by Inclusion? Issues for deaf pupils and their mainstream teachers. *Education 3–13*, **30**(2), 47–51.

Ladd, P. (1991) Making plans for Nigel: the erosion of identity by mainstreaming. In Taylor, G. and Bishop, J. (eds) *Being Deaf: the experience of deafness*. London: The Open University.

Lewis, S. (1996) The reading achievement of a group of severely and profoundly hearing-impaired school leavers educated within a natural aural approach. *Journal of the British Association of Teachers of the Deaf*, **20**, 1–7.

Lynas, W., Lewis, S. and Hopwood, V. (1997) Supporting the education of deaf children in mainstream schools. *Deafness and Education*, **21**(2), 41–5.

Monkman, H. and Baskind, S. (1998) Are assistants effectively supporting hearing–impaired children in mainstream schools? *Deafness and Education*, **22**(1), 15–22.

Moore, M., Dash, J. and Bristow, L. (1999) A social skills programme with primary aged isolated hearing aid users. *Deafness and Education International*, **1**(1), 10–24.

National Deaf Children's Society (1990) *Deaf Young People's Views on Integration: a survey report*. London: NDCS.

Powers, S. (2002) From concepts to practice in deaf education: A United Kingdom perspective on inclusion. *Journal of Deaf Studies and Deaf Education*, **7**(3), 230–43.

Powers, S., Gregory, S. and Thoutenhoofd, E. (1998) *The Educational Achievements of Deaf Children*. London: DfEE.

Powers, S., Gregory, S., Lynas, W., McCracken, W., Watson, L., Boulton, A. and Harris, D. (1999) *A Review of Good Practice in Deaf Education*. London: RNID.

Stinson, M. and Liu, Y. (1999) Participation of deaf and hard-of-hearing students in classes with hearing students. *Journal of Deaf Studies and Deaf Education*, **4**(3), 191–202.

Stinson, M. and Antia, S. (1999) Considerations in educating deaf and hard of hearing students in inclusive settings. *Journal of Deaf Studies and Deaf Education*, **4**(3), 163–75.

University of Hertfordshire/Royal National Institute for Deaf People (2002) *Inclusion: what deaf pupils think*. London: RNID.

Note

1 NB Here Deaf with a capital D refers to people who identify themselves as members of the Deaf community. A lower case d in deaf indicates a person with a hearing loss

This chapter most valuably places students' views at the foreground of the discussion. Once again we see that we can learn from each other and that deaf students have particular experiences that need to inform our understanding of inclusive outcomes as well as intentions.

Chapter 19

Voices on

Teachers and teaching assistants talk about inclusion

Pat Sikes, Hazel Lawson and Maureen Parker

This chapter emphasises the need to engage with the voice of practitioners about their understandings and ways of enacting inclusion. The authors choose to read these lengthy extracts when presenting at conferences. They recognise that performance of such articulations helps an audience to 'hear' the tensions and resistances between systemic and personal elements in their understanding of inclusion. Listening to others – however uncomfortable that can sometimes be – is essential if we wish to identify barriers and opportunities in seeking equality, participation and inclusion.

Introduction

In this paper we […] explore what teachers and teaching assistants working in mainstream schools in the UK had to say about inclusion in order to better inform initial and in-service professional understanding and development aimed at facilitating socially just pedagogies. […]

Towards inclusion: a global project?

[…]Over the years, changing notions and values have led to the widening of educational provision and experience, so that now, for instance, throughout the world, more and more girls go to school, as do increasing numbers of 'poor' and 'disabled' children.

In relatively recent times, the education and schooling, particularly in mainstream institutions, of those considered to have some form of special need and/or disability has come under the inclusion spotlight to the extent that the word has almost come to be synonymous with those so identified. […] Despite this international usage of 'inclusive', 'inclusion' and 'integration' it would seem that neither the words themselves, nor the concepts they denote and which underpin them (e.g. social justice, equity, equal opportunities, or, specifically, the 'social model' of disablement; Oliver, 1990, 1996) are commonly understood. This lack of shared definition is problematic, not least because it can be exploited in various ways by different factions and interest groups. [...] As Armstrong (2005) points out, the implications of there not being a common discourse are far-reaching since, 'different usages reflect the contested nature, not simply of inclusive education as a policy but of wider political contestations across the post-colonial political landscape' (p. 1). This contestation, we suggest, is both extant and problematic through all levels of social life, since it seems that understandings are not shared between, within and across individuals, groups (e.g. school departments, professional groups within schools), and larger collectives (e.g. local areas, countries, nation states).

Inclusion in England: a shared endeavour?

Inclusion has been firmly on the English educational agenda since 1997 although the rhetoric and discourse by which it has been promoted and articulated in governmental policy and publications could be described as somewhat vague. [...] This vagueness has translated into practice, as Avramidis *et al.* (2002) note when they comment that, '*inclusion* is a bewildering concept which can have a variety of interpretations and applications' (p. 158). It has also, as Thomas and Loxley (2001) suggest, become something of a cliché that has been 'evacuated of meaning' (Benjamin, 2002; also Azzopardi, 2005).

Inclusion in practice?: our research

But what does inclusion mean to the people working in schools who are charged with enacting it? Surely their views are of paramount significance in that they shape the 'inclusion experience' of the community in which they work. And why, at any time, do they make their particular interpretations?
[...]
We embarked upon research which took an auto/biographical and narrative approach to investigate how teachers and teaching assistants working in mainstream schools make sense of, interpret and perform 'inclusion'. [...] We made three visits to one primary and one secondary school located in small, quiet seaside towns in the south-west of England, chosen because they had no special inclusion brief or expertise. Conversations were held with teachers and teaching assistants who

volunteered to talk and who were invited both to discuss what inclusion meant to them and to share stories about inclusive practice, both positive and negative, from their personal experiences. [...]

We were not surprised that each account was unique and idiosyncratic, reflecting the complexities, dilemmas, constraints and possibilities that variously impact on all and any lives. In every case it was possible to make an interpretation that pointed to a tension between the systemic and personal elements (or, in other terms, the structural and agentic; Giddens, 1984), the political and the personal in individual understandings and experiences of inclusion. We found that the concept of inclusion was variously defined and often seemed to accord with at least some aspects of government, local authority or institutional rhetoric and discourse. Peoples' own *stories* about inclusive practice, however, frequently focused on the human and personal aspects of day to day involvement with individual pupils (the therapeutic discourse of 'care and support' referred to by Avramidis *et al.*, 2002) within the context of specific institutions. Rhetoric and 'reality' were tenuously, if at all, linked.

Performative performance approach

[...] In this paper we have chosen to present extracts from six of our conversations with the intention of re-presenting what our informants said in a way which retains/depicts/conveys an impression of at least some of the texture, complexity, messiness and emotionality that was there in the original saying (Wolcott, 2002). In our conference performances we have treated the transcriptions as we would a playscript, taking it in turns to present/speak the words of individual informants. [...] because we believe that a verbal rendition creates a different relationship with words and has a special potential to encourage an audience to engage with and hear in an immediate and intimate fashion—providing the audience is 'hearing' which is a point worth making, particularly with regard to a piece that deals with inclusion. We feel that such verbalization contributes to analysis in that: 'performance becomes the vehicle by which we travel to the worlds of Subjects and enter domains of intersubjectivity that problematize who is "us" and who is "them", (Madison, 1998, p. 282), forcing an engagement that has an experiential element as well as a distanced one, which can add a further dimension to criticality.

[...]

Researchers generally have to make editorial and creative decisions about what to include in their research accounts, which means omissions usually have to be made, not least in order to meet time and word limits. Inclusions and omissions inevitably result in a particular slant, in one specific story, rather than another, being told. We wanted to show what we felt was an inclusive range of perspectives, reflecting and representing the range of stories that we were told. We take no responsibility for what may be seen as the 'omissions' made by the people who spoke with us and would suggest that these may relate to folks' working definitions and understandings of 'inclusion'. Thus, out of the 60 people we spoke with, no one mentioned inclusion of lesbian, gay and bisexual students and teachers, only two people referred to inclusion as relating to gender and there were only three passing references to ethnicity. We should also note that there were no Black or Asian teachers in either of the schools we visited.

Given the centrality of the concern as it arose in our conversations, we have sought to give some insights into interactions between personal agency and biography and structural influence and to illustrate what we have called the 'Yes Buts' of inclusion: 'Yes, inclusion is a good thing. But the money for doing it properly isn't there'. 'Yes,   inclusion is a good thing. But the curriculum we have to teach is inappropriate'. 'Yes, inclusion is a good thing. But the teachers don't have the training to deal with kids with the variety of special needs'. 'Yes, inclusion may be a good goal. But what about the rest of the class?' So we have chosen to re-present the stories told by:

> *Sally*, a teaching assistant in a primary school – because she herself had a child who had been in danger of inclusion and this had, inevitably, coloured her own perspectives.
>
> *Timothy*, a teacher in a secondary school – because he talked about finance and the National Curriculum as structural barriers to inclusion.
>
> *Louise*, a teaching assistant in a primary school – because she spoke about the impact of inclusion on all the children in a class.
>
> *Theresa*, a teacher in a secondary school – because she voiced extreme opinions that other people may well share but wouldn't necessarily feel able to express; because she articulated the view that including children with special needs teaches other kids compassion; because she suggested that inclusion does not provide the specialist help and environment that some youngsters need.
>
> *Rose*, a teaching assistant in a primary school – because she reflected on how different teachers have different approaches to inclusion; because, as a teaching assistant, she questioned her 'right' to have a view on inclusion.

Ruth, a teacher in a primary school – because her words illustrated the tension between rhetoric and reality.

Within the extracts we have chosen there is minimal editing and what there is is mainly of the order of removing our own responses. Other than that, the accounts are, more or less, direct transcriptions. We want to emphasize that informants were fully aware that their words would be used in any accounts we might write and were content that this should be so. Pseudonyms have been used.

Sally

My thoughts will never change on inclusion. I'm a teaching assistant and I work with six-year-old autistic twins that have got speech problems and one of them is dyspraxic, so I will never change my opinions about inclusion. Definitely not. I think that sometimes we've got to be very careful because, obviously, with some of the children, it may be some of their problems are too extreme to be included in a mainstream school. Sometimes there could be a question mark when you think, maybe they shouldn't be here, but at the end of the day where else do they go if they can't go in here? So, you know they have a right to be educated so if you haven't got special schools then they come in here, and we do the best that we can. But I think that if you've got a child that's probably a little bit testing you need to have somebody that really is trained up so they can actually work with that child and support it to the best of the ability.

We've got a big year 5 group that have got special needs and they've all got different issues. We're having to look at them now and the transition man down at the secondary school said to me 'Well it might be that some of them will have to be channelled off into a different school where their needs will be met better'. Well to me, they have the right to go to their local secondary school so I'm determined that they're going to be included down there as part of their … you know … as part of their natural progression. Why should they have a special school? You know they're not that bad. They're still here – they haven't been excluded from here … you know [...]

It's children's education that's at stake and if we don't get it right from day one, it jeopardises their secondary education and I feel that's not a nice way to go. I've got a son who's normal, but he was labelled quite early as a, you know, a cocky git and teachers don't like it and yeah he didn't have very good memories of secondary school. And you sort of think when you go through it with a child. He was re-tracked – that's a system where parents become involved. David had an allocated teacher, which we eventually had to change because she didn't particularly like him and we changed to a man and this man turned my son around completely. It's about spending time with the parents, talking to the parents, how we can help at home and things like that. And my husband is a man that works away a lot so it just made him realise that he needed to come in a bit more and become more a part of his education and what we did with him. And it just made David realise as well. And he had to get books signed to say he'd been in lessons and how he'd been in lessons. It just makes you realise that behaviour doesn't actually work. You get more praise and you actually achieve more if you're good. He's an apprentice mechanic now. And I had a teacher tell me that he would end up in prison. So when I've somebody like that to work with, yes I become bolshy because I feel no way is any teacher going to speak to a child like that and get away with it and then say he's going to end up in prison and I've got a son that's in his fourth year of an apprenticeship, so yeah he's done OK.

Timothy

I'm a head of year and I see inclusion as a way of keeping children involved who would be otherwise lost to the system in a sense, and trying to find suitable courses that will keep them interested – which requires money – and capitation's been chopped for that, effectively. So we haven't got the facilities I don't think to operate certain courses that can keep them and maintain the interest of some of these youngsters who become disaffected and give us problems and the National Curriculum doesn't necessarily have the same relevance to some of them.

I think that's probably the way most staff would see inclusion, we try to keep all the youngsters motivated, regardless of where they feature in terms of their ability and I think the biggest problem is really finding a curriculum that suits all and I don't think it's available with the funding that we've currently got – I'm taking youngsters into year 10 at the moment, where we're trying to offer extra courses for those who find languages difficult and have really got no hope of continuing on any level, so we're looking for alternatives, but which we wouldn't normally have outside the lesser academically demanding courses, so we're mainly offering courses as day-out courses that we can fund, but where's that money to come from? I don't think it's readily available within the budget, for the sort of numbers which it could be useful to, that's the thing.

Louise

To me it [inclusion] just means everybody, give everybody a fair chance including, you know, physically handicapped. But I do have a problem with it.

I mean I have been a teaching assistant for fifteen years and I have watched things change very gradually, and I really do feel that a lot of the class – basically because we are trying to include children who have all sorts of different problems, you know whether it is their own backgrounds, whether it's because they're emotionally disturbed. You know it's not their fault, I just think that there are lots and lots of other children suffering because of it. I mean I have been in a class, a year 2 class here with someone with emotional, you know he ended up being excluded, but before he was excluded we tried everything to include him and so many of the other children suffered. You know he would punch and kick and disrupt the class, and there was very little we could do. He isn't meant to be here and now he isn't, but how many children have suffered while we were going through all that, you know? I do find it all very difficult, so I'm not totally for it.

Well it's good for the school isn't it because they will take anybody from anywhere really. And it helps with money you know. And if you've got a policy whereby you have enough spaces where you can take people.

I mean we've had a lot of children that have come in from other schools. But it is constantly changing the dynamics of this school. You know, you get a nice little class and then you get someone that has problems somewhere else and really they create problems here. I think that just perhaps I am being old fashioned. It didn't used to be like this, that's all.

Theresa

When I heard you were interested in hearing people's thoughts on inclusion I really wanted to take the opportunity to come and tell you mine. I teach drama here now three times a week, lower school drama. I used to work in a Special School in London, the first school that I taught in – it was deemed delicate but that might mean they'd had an asthma attack once before. And there were some seriously ill children but often there were children who couldn't actually integrate within mainstream education; of course there were some children who even 20 years ago we were trying to integrate and it seemed like a good idea, but it's just gone too far in my view.

There's one child here – I'm probably not allowed to mention names. This poor child, Sean, one of seven, is completely mad, he's violent. We're putting him in a failing situation. It's such a shame for these kids, yes we shouldn't put handicapped people in institutions and think they don't have brains, but I think it's just so wrong to have these children I think. It's almost like you put everybody into a school and, 'let's just see how they cope'. And the devastation it causes to the rest of that class and their education. And in the case of this one particular kid, he's not going to make it. And the time of the staff that's taken up. He just reminds me of the children in the Special School who you know, any sort of change was difficult, you know, all those things that special needs children find very hard to cope with. And in drama you have to work in groups and pairs and listen and co-operate, he can't do that. He needs to be in a smaller environment where there is much more one-to-one where people can help him. So we are putting these children in a failing situation.

Now there's another student here, Dan, who's a bit of a wooden top, you know he's a bit strange. And the kids know that he's handicapped and that's different. You know what I'm saying, it's different to 'off the wall' children; who are constantly just failing, every single lesson is a failing experience for them. It's just there, all day everyday. It's pretty sad, I think anyway. Inclusion is good for some things. It's quite interesting because the kids, with Dan in particular, in drama, show compassion. And even though he may say things that are a bit naïve and innocent and sweet, I think that in many ways, does help the children develop, it brings out a side of compassion in them. But when it's a child like Sean who is a behavioural nightmare and off the wall, there's something seriously wrong with this child.

We've got a child in year 8 who's unbelievably immature, Rachel, she has a mental age of about seven or eight. Unbelievably immature in her social ways – socially she's about seven or eight and she's a bit strange. The other day one of the big tough boys laughed at her when she was showing her piece and of course she looks up nervously because she knows somebody's going to ridicule her. He was sitting next to me and I just said to him, 'you know that's really sad to pick on somebody like Rachel isn't it?' and he said, 'yeah miss it is actually'. I then said, 'you know, laugh at somebody of your own standing, but to laugh at Rachel, that makes you a bit sad doesn't it' – and he said, 'yeah miss'. So that sort of inclusion is good and it's good for the rest of the class. It's not that I'm not against it – but it's all like it's gone from huge amounts of special schools and isolation – you know if you go back to Victorian times, just appalling, awful, to throwing them all in.

A child like Sean is going to get naughtier and naughtier because he's failing and he's never going to get anywhere. And then when he comes out he's not going to hold a positive experience of school – which if he'd been put in a small integrated group with heavy support, in the right setting with the right curriculum for a Special Needs child, then he would get something out of it. We were doing engines in cars yesterday in drama and being racing machines. Everyone was being a part within the machine, we had a crash and everybody had to roll over everybody, but Sean can't be part of the group – he can't work *with* people and so in the end I said, 'we can't have people lying on their backs in the middle of drama Sean – you either join in or you go and stand outside of the classroom' so he said, 'I don't care, I don't like drama anyway'. And you know it's pathetic, his little eyes looking in, it's almost like the whole of his life he's got this glass screen and he's looking in through the screen, desperately wanting and trying to join in, but can't – and putting him in a school like this is not going to help him at all – it's tragic.

I went to a convent school in Oxford; it was an all girls' school. I'm 47 so that's quite a long time, but there was nothing like wheelchair access, rights of people who, you know, not at all, no. Any sort of handicap or anything was pushed under the carpet. At my school there wasn't anybody who had any sort of handicap, other than somebody who might have a sharp temper or something like that, no. In those days more were excluded and put into various boxes, it wasn't necessarily the right thing.

Rose

I'm a classroom assistant. Well actually I often associate it [inclusion] with bad behaviour and keeping children in school, but I'm sure it also means less able students staying in the class and staying with the rest of the class to be taught, so that they are not identified perhaps, or made to feel different. Some teachers think it is very important to keep children in at all times and others if they've got a less able group, they like them to be withdrawn from time to time with a classroom assistant to do some different work.

I think it depends. I mean, teachers seem to interpret it differently, they have different ideas of what it means and it is a bit of a grey area really. Some teachers feel that they will let a group go out with a teaching assistant because they think that's effective, but they're sort of a bit, they know it's not really approved of that, well senior management really like everybody to stay in the classroom. But it seems to me – I've never really got to the bottom of it, I suppose I've never asked, so nobody is actually saying 'you must'. It is left to individual teachers how they're going to organise their groups or whatever so I, personally I can see, because I've worked with two teachers and one teacher has asked me to withdraw a group and I have seen how effective that is. Just a few sessions a week doing some very basic work. They actually have caught up very well, and I have worked with a teacher who always wants me in the room with the children.

I suppose I don't have to have a view because I feel, you know I come here and a teacher tells me what to do so it doesn't matter what my view is, so I don't bother thinking about it may be. I wouldn't dream of saying anything. Oh no I wouldn't think it my place to say, oh no I couldn't do that.

Ruth

To me it is a very, very nice idea, inclusion but unfortunately teachers aren't given the training or backup or support to include children properly. I think it is all a very, very, very nice idea but the money and the support and everything isn't there to cope with it.

I mean I understand quite a lot about children with autism but I have never had to deal with a boy like the one I have in my class at the moment. So it's not that I don't know something about it and what do to but when you get one as extreme as this one I really don't know what to do and so although he's in my class and he has been assessed by psychologists and all the various things like that there's ... it's then like well you've got to get on with it – you've just got to deal with him. And I sort of wonder, well how? What do I do? You know, he sits there and some days he writes nothing, growls and makes noises, and I keep saying this and saying it and saying it and it's like nobody's listening and you know I don't know whether to push on and try and keep on trying to make him do something National Curriculum, or give him a completely different programme. You know I want someone to say to me this is what he needs and then I can do it but it's, it's just really difficult knowing what to do. At the end of the day he's going to move up to year 6, he's going to move up into secondary school and he's going to end up in a special school or he's going to end up in massive trouble or whatever. He's a very disturbed boy as well I think, with other things. Everyone just thinks that you can cope with it. You're an experienced teacher, you can cope with it. It makes me feel quite angry really. Quite angry. Yeah, quite angry because you do try to do the best that you can but you know I'm not trained in those things. I'm not trained specifically in some of these very, very major problems. Yes, it's nice that people have faith in me, but there is only so much that you can do.

Performative meanings of inclusion

[…]
Whilst policy, structure, and culture might shape the broader social and institutional contexts in which teachers and teaching assistants operate, it is their personal interpretations and understandings, their day-to-day

enactments, how they perform inclusion, their *agency* which determines how the policy is formulated and reformulated in practice. [...] Underpinning our study is the belief that, methodologically, the study of the stories that people tell about aspects of their lives can generate fruitful insights not only in relation to the lives and topics being investigated, but also about the wider context in which those lives and topics are lived out. Also, that performance allows access to the ways in which lives are lived and negotiated in a performative manner.

Thus, in this research, the personal views and stories told about inclusion inform us about the reality of inclusion on the ground and illuminate 'the ambiguities of policy as practice'. There were frequently 'contradictory elements within their own thinking' (Croll and Moses, 2000), ambiguities *in* practice and performance perhaps; they expressed support for the principle of inclusion while, at the same time, qualifying this – *Yes But*.

Croll and Moses observe: 'At one level, inclusion as an educational ideal has the 'moral high ground', but at the day-to-day level of the thinking that informs education policy its position is much less secure.' (p. 2) In our conversations with teachers and teaching assistants a tension was clearly evident between an educational ideal, perhaps, and the day-to-day living and performance of inclusion; between an espousal of government and local (local authority and school) rhetoric and their subjective experiences, their woven unique realities (Broadfoot, 2002); between systemic and personal elements in their perceptions and understandings of inclusion. Thus in the stories re-presented here the systemic elements, for example, of the organization of special and mainstream schooling, transition between phases, withdrawal groups, curriculum and finance are apparent. The personal and human aspects of the day-to-day involvement with individual children – the six-year-old autistic twins, Sally's son David, the excluded boy in year 2, Sean, Dan, Rachel, and the boy with autism in Ruth's class – however, reveal and illuminate the lived and performed realities. Ironically, these accounts also reveal the one feature that all the stories we were told had in common and that feature too, is, in itself, ironic. This is because inclusion was always defined (presented, indeed performed, perhaps) in terms of attempts to include individual, excluded 'others' who would still, essentially, be seen as 'others', even when included, owing to some characteristic that was seen to make them different. This illustrates Armstrong's (2005) point that 'while social policy is dominated by the rhetoric of inclusion, the reality for many remains one of exclusion and the panacea of "inclusion" masks many sins'.

Maybe this form of discourse is inevitable and possibly our research approach invited accounts which revealed what MacLure describes as the oppositional 'binary structure of discursive realities' (MacLure, 2003, p. 9), which, she goes on to say is 'everywhere to be found in the discourses of education' (p. 11). 'Us' and 'them' pervade the language and discourses of policy, practice and performance as it relates to inclusion. Since people use the vocabularies available to them to make sense of and to describe their worlds (Wittgenstein, 1953) we should not, perhaps, be surprised to hear it loud and clear in the stories we were told, or to feel it, viscerally, in our performance of those stories. We could also gain a sense of the ways in which understandings of inclusion are not fixed and definite, but rather are 'becoming', developing and changing as they are articulated and lived, as Sally and Theresa's stories clearly illustrate.

Maybe inclusion will remain a chimera until we can speak about it and perform it using discourses which do not fundamentally differentiate or petrify. One thing is certain, and that is that we can't know what people think and feel about inclusion until we hear and begin to feel what they say. In our view, performance methodologies can facilitate awareness of this kind. Awareness which, we believe, is essential for the development of socially just pedagogies. This awareness, for ourselves and for others, is what we have been seeking through this work.

References

Armstrong, D. (2005) 'Voice, rituals and transitions: what is inclusive education really about?' Paper presented at the 'Inclusive and Supportive Education Congress', Glasgow, UK, 1–4 August 2005.

Avramidis, E., Bayliss, P. and Burden, R. (2002) 'Inclusion in action: an in-depth case study of an effective inclusive secondary school in the south-west of England', *International Journal of Inclusive Education*, 6(2), 143–163.

Azzopardi, A. (2005) 'Narratives of inclusion'. Unpublished EdD thesis, University of Sheffield.

Benjamin, S. (2002) *The micropolitics of inclusive education* (Buckingham, Open University Press).

Broadfoot, P. (2002) 'Editorial', *Comparative Education*, 38(1), 5–6.

Croll, P. and Moses, D. (2000) 'Ideologies and utopias: education professionals' views of inclusion', *European Journal of Special Needs Education*, 15(1), 1–12.

Giddens, A. (1984) *The constitution of society: outline of the theory of structuration* (Cambridge, Polity).

MacLure, M. (2003) *Discourse in educational and social research* (Maidenhead, Open University Press).

Madison, D. S. (1998) 'Performance, personal narratives, and the politics of possibility', in: S. Daly (Ed.) *The future of performance studies: visions and revisions* (Annandale, VA, National Communication Association), 276–286.

Oliver, M. (1990) *The politics of disablement* (London, Macmillan).

Oliver, M. (1996) *Understanding disability from theory to practice* (London, Macmillan).

Thomas, G. and Loxley, A. (2001) *Deconstructing special education and constructing education* (Buckingham, Open University Press).

Wittgenstein, L. (1953) *Philosophical investigations* (Oxford, Blackwell).

Wolcott, H. F. (2002) *Sneaky kid and its aftermath* (Oxford, Alta Mira, Rowman & Littlefield).

The voices of these practitioners reveal the many contradictions which arise from their work with children and young people. It also reveals the commitment they feel and the complexities they face in dealing with the lack of consistency in our understandings, systems and working practices. In exploring these contradictions we are examining those values and practices which serve to exclude children and young people and those which facilitate inclusion.

Chapter 20

Lessons from the 1 per cent

Children with labels of severe disabilities and their peers as architects of inclusive education

Judy K.C. Bentley

Judy Bentley describes some of the lessons to be learned from students who historically have been excluded from 'inclusive' education (the 1 per cent). She explores children's construction of their own inclusive education in academic and social contexts, revealing how Symbolic Inclusion and inclusive pedagogical practices are found to be instinctively and effectively utilized by disabled and non-disabled peers, despite the exclusionary models offered by special education support staff (paraprofessionals). These lessons in communication and being alert to other's interests have a resonance far beyond the classroom.

Introduction

On the kitchen table in the fourth-grade life skills classroom, a Betta fish named Red lives with a philodendron plant in a small vase half filled with water. Today Red's water ripples, as the fourth-graders dash around the room. They are making last minute preparations for a very special guest.

Annabelle, dressed in velvet and lace for the occasion, is a notorious hugger. Already today she has hugged three teachers and a researcher. Ethan, a creative writer and Special Olympics athlete, can weave all ten of the week's spelling words into one stunning sentence. Katy, when asked what languages she speaks besides English, replies: 'Magic, a little Spanish, and Sign.' Krystal can restore order to an unruly classroom with the skill of a veteran teacher. She eliminates off-task conversations with a stern glance, straightens pictures on the wall, and paces in front of her classmates' desks to observe their work. Sammy is a law-abiding, quietly competent child. But today he was reprimanded for running in the hall, and bursting into the classroom through the forbidden side entrance. Breathless, he asked: 'Where's Lynda?'

Now she is here – Lynda – their classmate who has been absent for nearly a month! Lynda has deep, brown eyes with eyelashes so long they cast shadows on her fair face. She resembles Snow White, but she is much more independent and wide awake. Lynda's long, dark curls are tied back with a purple ribbon. It matches the two purple casts that embrace her from ankles to hips. She is enthroned on a padded wheelchair that will keep her legs thrust stiffly out in front of her for about four weeks.

Lynda's mom lets go of the wheelchair and steps out of the way as the children surround her. They are hugging her, piling presents on her lap, signing her casts. She is smiling. With the skill of highly paid parking valets, Krystal and Sammy manoeuvre the wheelchair up close to the kitchen table. Red's water stays smooth as glass. The chair does not bump into anything! The adults seem spellbound. Is anyone (besides the researcher) holding her breath? The label 'medically fragile' is appropriate here. But the children have never heard it.

Sammy holds Lynda's hand while Krystal helps her eat a cookie. Lynda chokes on the bit of cookie, then recovers. Ten hands help Lynda open her presents. Annabelle explains the frenzy: 'We missed her long!' Later, when she visits her inclusive social studies class, the children will admire Lynda's beautiful painted toenails and ask her if she liked the cookie bouquet, balloons, and cards they sent her to celebrate her surgery. Lynda will be tired from her visit, but she will continue to smile.

Lynda has just had the surgery that her physical therapist and paraeducator were talking about last month, as if Lynda were not there. But Lynda was there; and she frowned and whined when she heard:

> They'll do a hamstring release and cut her heel tendon. She'll be in full leg casts. If they decide to correct the scoliosis at same time she'll be *in a full body cast for months.* After that, *with Rett's, they usually never walk again.*
>
> (added emphasis)

Lynda's family moved across the country to find this inclusive school for Lynda; and they are pleased with her placement. Even so, her mother wonders:

> What does Lynda think? Does she just give up – 'Well, this is the way it's gonna be. They're gonna talk about me like I'm just this *thing* for the rest of my life'. You know, I always wonder, what does she think?

Talking about Lynda this way is a form of 'Medical Othering', defining Lynda by her symptoms, and as if she were so diminished by her disability that she was mentally absent from the room. Lynda's peers consider her symptoms to be similar to their own medical adventures, as they indicate by 'Medical Sharing'. For example, in a presentation by Lynda's mother about Rett Syndrome, her classmates offered: 'I have Tourette's syndrome.' 'I had a seizure.' 'My dog had a heart attack.' Katy shared a trip to the hospital that 'sucked'.

> When I was like three, I taked my mother's pills. I thought they were candy and they were blue. And I couldn't speak. And guess what happened. I went to the hospital and I had to drink charcoal and then I spit up on my mom's shoulder.

These examples help to illustrate the continuum of exclusive and inclusive interactions with Lynda, a child who is labelled with severe disabilities. The following research explores the wisdom and competence of Lynda and her peers, as architects of inclusive education.

Background

While the academic, standards-based education movement was under construction in the 1980s, special educators were developing a 'functional' curriculum for children with labels of severe disabilities. A functional curriculum teaches access skills (communication and mobility) and life skills (daily living competencies), which neither promote nor require an understanding of general academic content (Browder et al., 2006). Galvanizing the paradigm of standards-based education reform, the *No Child Left Behind Act of 2001* held schools accountable for challenging standards of student achievement in reading and math, to be measured with rigorous, state-created, standardized tests. For students with labels of severe disabilities, states were allowed to develop alternative achievement standards. These standards were required to promote access to, and progress in the general curriculum, and reflect the highest possible achievement.

With the emphasis shifting to academic goals, for which the assessment of functional skills is not required by NCLB, twenty-first-century US educators struggle with new questions about inclusion. Can the omission of academic content for a designated group of students ever be justified? What is the proper balance between functional and academic curriculum content? To what extent are current state standards relevant to maximizing students' adult potential (Browder et al., 2006; Wehmeyer, 2006)? If these questions were asked for all children, the answers could contribute significantly to systemic education reform. But they can more easily slip into the negative context of 'problems' associated with educating the 1 per cent. Since the law does not specifically define the context where these students will access the general curriculum, the answers to these questions may result in expanded opportunities for inclusion, or strengthen the historic trend toward separate and unequal placements (Spooner *et al.*, 2006).

Decisions about them are made without them

[…] There is a need for educators, policy makers, and researchers to hear *from*, as well as *about*, children with labels of severe disabilities. What are the meanings and interactions of social and academic inclusion as they are constructed and experienced by children? What is the nature of the power, or lack of it, which children exert on their own learning environments? The purpose of this study was to explore children's construction of their own inclusive schooling. The research question was: What is the lived experience of a child labelled with severe disabilities, and her peers with and without disabilities, in an 'inclusive' school environment?

Methods

This study utilized symbolic interaction (Blumer, 1969) to explore children's constructions of inclusive education. Data were reported in the form of a case study (Miles and Huberman, 1994). Symbolic interaction operates on the premise that we shape our behaviour by the stimuli and objects we 'take into account' (Sandstrom *et al.*, 2003, p. 11), and how we define them. Symbolic interactionist research is considered 'from the position of the actor' (Blumer, 1969, p. 73), as individuals develop awareness of their own being by attending to and interacting with selected aspects of the environment (Mead, 1934). Symbols have meaning because group members use them in a consistent way. They make it possible to transfer mental states from one person to another. Our symbolic involvement in society is essential for the realization of human potential (Blumer, 1969; Sandstrom *et al.*, 2003). This assertion is compatible with the social model of disability (Oliver, 1996), which views disability as a socially constructed phenomenon.

While symbolic interaction acknowledges the influence of habit, and of social forces and constraints beyond individual control, symbolic interaction also grants us individual freedom and flexibility in our choice of actions. This flexibility gives us the power to give new meanings to things, and thereby reconstruct or transform society (Blumer, 1969; Sandstrom *et al.*, 2003).

Constructivist sampling

My sampling frame required the participation of a child with a label of severe disabilities, who was placed with non-disabled peers in both academic and social situations at school. The search for this relatively rare situation led me to a rural intermediate school with 474 students, serving grades four and five.

[…]

This study explored the lived experience of Lynda, a 12-year-old girl with Rett syndrome, in situations that presented the possibility of interaction with non-disabled peers. Lynda was included with general education peers in fifth-grade homeroom, science, physical education, music, art, lunch, and social studies. She and her peers with disabilities spent the remaining, approximately 20 per cent, of their day in a self-contained classroom for instruction in functional skills, and modified math and reading.

[…]

I was permitted to interview teachers and paraeducators who participated in inclusive education for Lynda and her peers with various disabilities, and observe her classes and homerooms. I was permitted to observe and speak with Lynda, interview her parents and her sister, and observe and interview Lynda's five special education classmates and 18 general education classmates who volunteered for Circle of Friends activities.

[…]

I spent 210 hours observing and interviewing children with and without disability labels, noting their attitudes and interactions with Lynda. I attended and observed Lynda's inclusive academic classes, life skills classes, and Circle of Friends activities. I sat near Lynda and took field notes. I observed interactions with teachers and paraeducators; but I did not assist them or comment on their interactions.

Symbolic inclusion: a social constructivist definition

My research agenda posits a socially constructed meaning of inclusion – Symbolic Inclusion – which transcends traditional, legal definitions. Symbolic Inclusion is defined as the accommodation, assimilation, appreciation, and engagement of one's interaction partner. Symbolic Inclusion can occur in any place, at any time, when individuals choose to become conscious of and pay attention to one another. Symbolic Exclusion occurs when individuals consciously refuse or habitually fail to accommodate, assimilate, appreciate, and engage one another. Symbolic

Inclusion can occur in a segregated classroom; and Symbolic Exclusion can occur in 'inclusive' educational contexts.

Symbolic communication as intentional behaviour

Lynda's peers used conventional verbal communication. Lynda's communication strategies were different. Lynda vocalized with variations in tone and volume, but she used no identifiable words. Her vocalizations produced no consistent patterns or sounds approximating phonetic syllables. Her behavioural communication repertoire included: characteristic clasping, pinching, and rubbing hand mannerisms of Rett Syndrome (Sigafoos *et al.*, 2000); eye gaze for about three to five seconds; smiling and frowning; and a few apparently purposeful body movements (swinging her feet in a kicking motion, moving her head and torso toward or away from a person or object). […] For the purpose of this study, gestures, vocalizations and other unconventional behaviours were defined as communication, if they appeared to the researcher and/or the communication partner to indicate intentionality.

Results

Though Lynda's school was defined by administrators, teachers, and her parents as inclusive, data analysis led me to deduce that participants were practising both Symbolic Exclusion and Symbolic Inclusion. Excluding interactions, which were practised mostly by paraprofessionals, diminished the universe of Lynda's social roles, and assigned negative meanings to her difference. Paraeducators removed Lynda physically from academic classes when she was most alert and vocal, spoke *for* her instead of *to* her, gave her infant's toys instead of instructional materials to keep her occupied in class, and fed her goldfish crackers to stifle her verbal communication. One paraeducator, assigned exclusively to Lynda, cooed to her in nonsense syllables, and usurped her attention with infantilizing interactions, when Lynda was more appropriately focused on a teacher or peer. Lynda's physical therapist spoke about Lynda as a collection of symptoms, pointing to and manipulating Lynda's body to illustrate her medical anomalies. Teachers who witnessed these interactions did not attempt to curtail them. Since Lynda was always accompanied by a paraeducator, these excluding interactions served as negative models for her peers.

[…] The excluding actions of adult professionals toward Lynda were especially significant in the context of a school in which inclusion was described as an overarching philosophy and practice. […] Yet within this context, which fell far short of authentic inclusion, Lynda's peers with and without disabilities clearly modelled Symbolic Inclusion. They accommodated, assimilated, appreciated, and engaged her as an interaction partner. They invited and expanded Lynda's presence in a variety of social roles, and assigned positive meanings to her differences. Lynda's peers showed an instinctive capacity to practice research-based strategies that have been identified as inclusive best practices. From a single case study by a single researcher, I offer the following inclusion strategies, conceived and practised by children, as 'lessons from the 1 per cent'.

Dynamic communication assessment

[…] Snell (2002) recommends dynamic assessment – building on existing vocalizations, gestures, and behaviours – to foster the growth of more complex communication. Dynamic assessment is appropriately conducted by: using familiar contexts for assessment, relying on information gathered over time and with people who know the learner, increasing communication output by manipulating the environment, and probing potential for learning rather than simply describing current performance.

Lynda's peers with and without disabilities took the initiative to assess and comprehend her unique communication strategies. They assessed her communication within the familiar contexts presented by the school environment. They relied on information gathered over time, and actively discussed what she might be thinking or trying to achieve. They explained to me that she had her own way of talking – 'Lynda's way'.

> Sometimes she'll rub her eyes; kinda like with the side of her hand. That means she's tired. And when she's like this – 'aaaaaah' – she's happy. That's her way of talking to people.

A boy who got to know Lynda from inclusive academic classes explained:

> You can tell when she's really happy. She'll be smiling and talking in her way. And when she's sad she'll get a frown, and sometimes be very quiet or sometimes be very loud. And sometimes, when she's just, I guess, just being Lynda – she'll kind of pick up something and start banging it on the table. She really likes noise … I think it's because if everybody else is making lots of noise, why not make some noise too? Sometimes when the class is really quiet she'll go 'Yeahhh!' I think she's saying that she wants to be a part of everything, and not be left out.

A clear example of manipulating the environment and probing potential for learning occurred in Lynda's inclusive general education social studies class. The teacher had the children count off by threes, with each group forming a political party. Each party was to choose a presidential candidate, design a symbol, write and deliver a campaign commercial, and coach their candidate for a debate. A paraeducator brought Lynda, in her wheelchair, over to her group. The presidential candidate spontaneously held out a list of jobs (campaign worker, press contact, etc.) and read them aloud. The children waited patiently for several minutes while Lynda willed her finger to point to a choice of assignments. 'She picked campaign worker', the candidate said. He used the same technique several days later, waiting for Lynda to put her finger on a list of topics she would like him to debate: 'We would have ideas written down, and she would keep a finger on it. We would sorta, like, check it with everyone.' Cause I think they were all good ideas.' (Lynda's candidate was elected president of the class.)

If Lynda were given choices of pictures, objects, or even a list whose content was verbally described by a communication partner in other situations, what would Lynda do? Her classmate's spontaneous probe could serve as a valuable model of dynamic assessment for adult practitioners.

The presidential candidate's spontaneous adaptation of the curriculum can also be viewed as an effective example of 'curriculum overlapping' (Giangreco, 2007, p. 36), in which a student like Lynda, who presumably has learning outcomes that are significantly different from those of her classmates, shares an activity (mock election), but may have learning goals of communication within the curriculum area (social studies).

Structured over-interpretation

[…] When utilizing structured over-interpretation, significant persons interpret behaviours that indicate interests, needs, and preferences as communicative strategies. Von Tetzcher (1997) notes that these strategies contribute to a 'responsive and predictable' environment (p. 33), and are useful for communication partners. Lynda's peers developed a set of strategies for consistently interpreting her communication behaviours – an instinctive and effective form of structured over-interpretation, which led to a deeper understanding of Lynda's expressive verbal and behavioural vocabulary (see Table 20.1).

[…]

Table 20.1 A communication signal inventory utilizing structured over-interpretation

Signal	What it means	How to respond
What Lynda does	What Lynda's communication partner thinks the signal means [Information provided by]	How partners should or could consistently react Frequently describe the signal immediately after it is performed. Comment perceived meaning. Interact with appropriate response. ('You're pulling your hair. That tells me you're sleepy. You can lie down now.')
Vocalizes	'I'm here!' (loud, with smile) [Mom, peers, participant observation] 'I'm participating!' (Lynda's volume and pitch matches volume and pitch of another speaker or group of speakers)	Greet Lynda; acknowledge her presence Adult partners need to find and assess alternative, consistent reactions to replace stuffing food in Lynda's mouth, covering her mouth with their hands, or removing her from class
Frowns and whines; cries with or without tears	'I hurt' [Mom, peers, participant observation] 'I have to go to the bathroom' [Paraeducators]	Peers should alert teacher or paraeducator Adults should figure out source of discomfort and respond accordingly Could a more consistent eating, drinking and bathroom schedule be implemented to avoid removal from class?
Pulls on her hair	'I'm sleepy' [Peers]	Adults should tell Lynda if/when she will be able to rest Peers should recognize that Lynda is sleepy (Lynda's peers indicated accurate interpretation of this signal)
Walks toward a person or object and stands in front of it	'I am interested in this person or object' [Mom, peers] 'I want to interact with this person or object'	Allow, observe, and assess walking communication Incorporate walking communication into instruction and social interaction
Makes eye contact for three to five seconds	'I am making purposeful eye contact with this person or object' [Participant observation, Mom, peers]	Interact with Lynda and/or the object of intent Be alert for, recognize, and capitalize on occasions of purposeful eye contact
Grasps and pulls a person or object toward herself, or reaches toward a person or object to grasp it	'I want to interact with this person or object' [Life skills teacher, Mom, peers, participant observation]	Provide opportunities to interact with the person or object
Pushes a person or object away, or turns their head away	'I don't want to interact with this person or object' [Participant observation]	Recognize protest behavior and do not force unwanted interaction with a person, food, drink, or object
Jokes (spills water, laughs at a person, interaction, activity or conversation)	'I understand this person or interaction and I think it's funny' 'Gotcha!' [Mom, peers, participant observation]	Recognize the complex cognition and receptive communication skills involved in humor, and provide opportunities for Lynda to use these skills

Ecological assessment

Ecological assessment [...] focuses on assessing the support needs of a person with cognitive impairment and severe disabilities in her current environment and culture (Schalock, 1999). Questions asked by Lynda's peers comprised a spontaneous ecological assessment of the skills she would need to succeed in her current and future environments, with an emphasis on communication and self-determination:

> Can she walk? Can she see? Can she write? Can she express her feelings? Can she cry? Can she hear people? Does she try to talk back? When something's bothering her, how can you tell? How do you know if she's mad? How's she gonna get married? How's she gonna drive a car? How's she gonna have a baby? How's she gonna earn money?
>
> The salience of the children's questions, and their observed skill in recognizing functional environmental needs, illustrates the value and applicability of peer interaction and understanding to assessment and curriculum development.

Partial participation

[...] Partial participation refers to being flexible about how children participate in environments where they do not have all of the skills the environment requires (Turnbull *et al.*, 2004). Inviting Lynda to participate in the mock election in social studies class is a clear example of partial participation initiated by her peers. Although she could not speak, and was not perceived as being able to read a list of topics for the presidential candidate to discuss, she could indicate her choice of topics by pointing to one, as a peer read them aloud. The presidential candidate let Lynda make the initial selections by pointing. Her choices were then approved by the rest of the committee through traditional, verbal discussion. Lynda's peers were creative and flexible in their ideas for including her in instruction by partial participation.

Transdisciplinary transition planning

Lynda's peers in life skills class troubled the discourse about her adult life ('How's she gonna earn money? How's she gonna drive a car? How's she gonna get married?'). Such probing questions would be appropriate for the process of transition planning, which is traditionally conducted by a child's special education transdisciplinary team of teachers, parents, and related service professionals (Hamill and Everington, 2002). [...] Lynda's peers were skilled at recognizing some valuable adult goals and objectives. Though adults may have seen them as overly optimistic, the goals children saw for Lynda are worth discussion, and traditionally ignored, when individuals with cognitive impairment are traditionally portrayed and treated as eternal infants (Barton, 2001; Wehmeyer, 2000).

Person-centred planning

[…] Children's instinctive interactions revealed complex understanding of Lynda's present and future needs. Lynda's peers showed they were capable of making a significant contribution to her communication, curriculum, instruction, and person-centred planning. Throughout the school year, the children noted Lynda's strengths. They considered her a friend, and saw her as a role model.

Recognizing Lynda as a friend and role model

Lynda's peers with and without disabilities described a friend as:

> someone you hang out with; someone loyal and trustworthy; someone you play with and have fun with; someone caring … and very sweet; someone whose house you go to; someone you like to be around; someone that likes you and is friendly to you; someone you help; someone you teach; someone who helps you; someone you eat lunch with; someone that you feel what they're feeling sometimes.

They found many of these qualities in Lynda, and participated in these activities with her. They said they would introduce her to sixth graders as 'my friend'.

Though most positive relationships between children with and without disabilities fall into the 'abled helper' category (Grenot-Scheyer *et al.*, 2001; Sapon-Shevin, 2007), Lynda's peers saw her as a helper and teacher as well.

> When I was really desperate in a test or something, Lynda would look over to me and smile, and I'd kind of perk back up again, and get that problem done and move on to the next one. She is a really sweet person. I just like her.

Three children said they learned not to judge a person by their outward appearance. A student identified as gifted learned 'not to judge people by just what they do in class'. He said Lynda taught him a new definition of talented: 'Even though [Lynda] can't walk by herself, or talk, that she's still one of the most talented people here. Since she's gone through all that.'

Re-imagining disability

Two children expressed re-imagined meanings of disability after spending time with Lynda. One of them described Lynda and the other life skills students as 'very gifted'. Another classmate said he enjoyed learning about Rett syndrome, because 'I never knew anybody like that. It's pretty cool, because it's a different person.'

One girl said knowing Lynda had helped her understand the difference between being popular and being happy:

> There's nothing wrong with being different. [Lynda]'s so much happier than, probably, the most popular girl in school, and she's not popular at all.

The same girl offered a thoughtful explanation of difference:

> People that's in a wheelchair, they can't go play kickball or anything like that. That doesn't mean that [Lynda] can't be a good friend, or that you can't hang out with her. You can always do something else. They're just like you, except in a different way.

When the Circle of Friends group was making gingerbread, several classmates admired and emulated Lynda's prowess in using a switch that ran the mixer. When, after many tries, she was able to hit the switch, a girl yelled: 'I can't believe she did it by herself! Tell her mom!' Another said: 'That's so cool! She pushed it by herself! If I was like Lynda, I would do that!' A boy added: 'That's awesome!' Another girl said: 'Pretend I'm a person that's like Lynda is', and depressed the switch herself. She flexed her arm and announced: 'See; I have small muscles like Lynda'. In this context, Lynda's disability was seen as a positive difference, and Lynda was seen as an able role model.

Discussion

Implications for practice: the importance of conscious intent

[…] Lynda's peers exercised the power to resist entrenched meanings and practices, and transform beliefs, in a nascent inclusive context that was less than ideal. They were given place and time, negative interaction models by paraprofessionals, and one brief explanation of Circle of Friends by Lynda's special education teacher that described 'volunteering'.

> At the beginning of the year I [describe] the programme: 'You're not gonna get paid. You're not gonna get a grade. You're gonna take your time out of recess or something. This is the programme we offer, to come and volunteer in our [self-contained life skills] room and to be a friend to our kids.'

Volunteering is a conscious and intentional act, which can transform access into interaction, and allow reflective choices. As children consciously volunteered to be a friend to Lynda they developed rich relationships, in which friendship, helping, and understanding were reciprocal, and not just one-way transactions.

Lynda's paraeducators were not volunteers; they were employees assigned to facilitate Lynda's inclusion. The juxtaposition of adults' stated beliefs that their school was 'doing inclusion right', and the excluding interactions observed, underscores the power and persistence of inclusion confusion and disability negatives. Lynda's inclusion providers were caught in the paradox, perhaps because they were given no opportunity to consciously and intentionally define, communicate, and critically reflect upon their individual and collective meanings of disability and inclusion. Symbolic Inclusion and Symbolic Exclusion may serve as useful tools to guide such reflection.

Changing paradigms involves all stakeholders

Inclusive, systemic education reform calls for reflective collaboration among all stakeholders: children, families, researchers, faculty and administrators in public schools and teacher preparation programmes. [...] Lynda's peers instinctively demonstrated a competence orientation (Smith, 2000, 2006), perceiving her as a whole, complex, maturing young woman. They recognized and interacted with her strengths, and demonstrated great skill in interpreting her unique communication. If Lynda's friends were enlisted to provide professional development for teachers and paraeducators, they might begin with the salient introduction Annabelle said she would give to sixth graders, when she and Lynda made their highly anticipated transition to intermediate school: 'This is my friend Lynda. She can't talk and you're going to get used to it.'

References

Barton, E. L. (2001) 'Textual practices of erasure: representations of disability and the founding of the United Way', in: J. C. Wilson and C. L. Wilson (Eds) *Embodied rhetorics: disability in language and culture* (Carbondale, IL, Southern Illinois University Press), 169–199.

Blumer, H. L. (1969) *Symbolic interactionism: perspective and method* (Englewood Cliffs, NJ, Prentice-Hall).

Browder, D. M., Spooner, F., Wakeman, S., Trela, K. and Baker, J. (2006) 'Aligning instruction with academic content standards: finding the link', *Research and Practice for Persons with Labels of Severe Disabilities*, 31, 309–321.

Giangreco, M. F. (2007) 'Extending inclusive opportunities', *Educational Leadership,* 64, 34–37.

Grenot-Scheyer, M., Fisher, M. and Staub, D. (2001) *At the end of the day: lessons learned in inclusive classrooms* (Baltimore, MD, Paul H. Brooks).

Hamill, L. and Everington, C. (2002) 'Establishing the context', in: L. Hamill and C. Everington (Eds) *Teaching students with moderate to severe disabilities: an applied approach for inclusive environments* (Upper Saddle River, NJ, Prentice-Hall), 1–24.

Mead, G. H. (1934) *Mind, self, & society from the standpoint of a social behaviorist* (Chicago, IL, University of Chicago Press).

Miles, M. B. and Huberman, M. (1994) *Qualitative data analysis: an expanded sourcebook* (Thousand Oaks, CA, Sage).

Oliver, M. J. (1996) *Understanding disability: from theory to practice* (New York, NY, St Martin's).

Sandstrom, K., Martin, D. D. and Fine, G. A. (2003) *Symbols, selves, and social reality: a symbolic approach to social psychology and sociology* (Los Angeles, CA, Roxbury).

Sapon-Shevin, M. (2007) *Widening the circle: the power of inclusive classrooms* (Boston, MA, Beacon).

Schalock, R. (1999) 'Adaptive behavior and its measurement: setting the future agenda', in: R. Schalock (Ed.) *Adaptive behavior and its measurement: implications for the field of mental retardation* (Washington, DC, American Association on Mental Retardation), 209–222.

Sigafoos, J., Woodyatt, G., Tucker, M., Roberts-Pennell, D. and Pettendreigh, N. (2000) 'Assessment of potential communicative acts in three individuals with Rett syndrome', *Journal of Developmental and Physical Disabilities*, 12, 203–216.

Smith, R. M. (2000) 'Mystery or typical teen? The social construction of academic engagement and disability', *Disability and Society*, 15, 911–924.

Smith, R. M. (2006) 'Classroom management texts: a study in the representation and misrepresentation of students with disabilities', *International Journal of Inclusive Education*, 10, 91–104.

Snell, M. E. (2002) 'Using dynamic assessment with learners who communicate nonsymbolically', *AAC: Augmentative and Alternative Communication*, 18, 163–176.

Spooner, F., Dymond, S. K., Smith, A. and Kennedy, C. H. (2006) 'What we know and need to know about accessing the general curriculum for students with significant cognitive disabilities', *Research and Practice for Persons with Labels of Severe Disabilities*, 31, 277–283.

Turnbull, R., Turnbull, A. P., Shank, M. and Smith, S. J. (2004) 'Ensuring progress in the general curriculum: universal design and inclusion', in: R. Turnbull, A. Turnbull, M. Shank and S. J. Smith (Eds) *Exceptional lives: special education in today's schools* (Upper Saddle River, NJ, Pearson Merrill Prentice-Hall), 43–76.

Von Tetzcher, S. (1997) 'Communication skills among females with Rett syndrome', *European Child and Adolescent Psychiatry*, 6, 33–39.

Wehmeyer, M. (2000) 'Riding the third wave: self-determination and self-advocacy in the 21st century', *Focus on Autism and Other Developmental Disabilities*, 15, 106–115.

Wehmeyer, M. (2006) 'Beyond access: ensuring progress in the general education curriculum for students with labels of severe disabilities', *Research and Practice for Persons with Labels of Severe Disabilities*, 31, 322–326.

At the heart of this chapter is the notion of trust. To develop an inclusive working environment we need to trust children and young people's capacities to support and understand each other. The challenge is to create the space for them to demonstrate these capacities within institutionalized systems and processes. If we rise to this challenge we will find that we learn a great deal about ourselves, our working lives, and the children and young people around us.

Part 5

Looking around us

A broader experience

Chapter 21

Children's 'social capital'

Implications for health and well-being

Virginia Morrow

This chapter describes a research project intended to probe the concept of 'social capital' in relation to the health and well-being of children and young people. Virginia Morrow finds that 'social capital' can be a useful tool for exploring social context and social processes; in so doing she also highlights the need for a right to participation, which becomes apparent by its absence. You may wonder, as you read these accounts, whether it is naïve of policy makers to focus upon young people's individual responsibilities without providing the right to collective resources that make it possible to meet those responsibilities.

Introduction

Specialists in health promotion and public health have become increasingly aware that the ways in which individuals relate to wider social networks and communities have important effects on health and well-being. One way to explore this has been to develop the concept of social capital. Social capital is seen as a community-level attribute, and consists of the existence of social and community networks; civic engagement; local identity and a sense of belonging and solidarity with other community members; and norms of trust and reciprocal help and support (Putnam, 1993). The premise is that levels of 'social capital' in a community have an important effect on people's well-being. Health behaviours and practices may superficially appear to be a private matter for the individual, but in reality health practices take place in a range of social arenas, which, for children,[1] are constrained by everyday contexts, which will vary from school institution, family, and peer group and neighbourhood. ... The research reported here attempted to explore how the

---

1 The paper follows the definition in the UN Convention on the Rights of the Child and refers to children and young people under the age of 18 as 'children'.

concept of social capital might relate to children's social lives, and the implications of this concept for their well-being and their health.

[…]

Methods

Research was carried out in two schools in 'Springtown'. Springtown is one of the 'New Towns' about 30 miles from London, and has continued to grow very rapidly. […] Children who attended schools in which research was carried out were drawn from wards of relatively low socio-economic status. At the time of the research, both schools had a roll of about 800, and both schools had a significant proportion of pupils from minority ethnic groups. […] The total number in the sample was 101, in two age bands, 12–13 year olds (Year 8s), and 14–15 year olds (Year 10s). The children were in mixed ability tutor groups, with the exception of the Year 10 class in School 1, which consisted of a mixed ability sociology class.

[….]

Research tools

[…] The whole class was asked to write, as freely as possible, open-ended answers to a series of questions, as follows:

- Who is important to you, and why? (=social network/social support data)
- What do you do outside school, who with and where? (=shared activities, opportunities for independence)
- Where do you live (general area), how long have you lived there and how do you feel about where you live? (=sense of belonging)
- What is a friend, and what are friends for? (=normative views of friendship)
- What do you want to do when you leave school, and do you already know someone doing this kind of thing, if yes, who? (=social networks)
- Where do you feel you belong? (School 2 only, and only if they chose to answer this question) (=sense of belonging)

Visual methods were also used. Individuals and/or groups of Year 10 students were asked to photograph places that are important to them (using disposable cameras) and then to describe why. […] Finally, group discussions, facilitated by the researcher, were used to explore young people's use of and perceptions about their neighbourhoods and town. […]

Findings

Social networks: friends and family

Friendship

This research reinforced the familiar perception that children often spend more time with their friends than they do with their families, especially as they get older. For example, as Veronica, age 15, put it: 'Why are my friends important? Because I spend nearly all of my time with them'. Daily activities were often structured around encounters with friends. Shannon, 13, described how, after school, she plays outside, goes to her friend's house 'or up the park with my sister. At the weekends I sometimes sleep over my friends'. Friends were central to many of the activities described outside school, and this was very marked among the older children in School 1, and both year groups in School 2. This may reflect the time of year that the research was carried out: data were collected in School 2 during the summer term, School 1 during the winter, so there were more opportunities for going out to play, and they were slightly older, mostly 13. On the other hand, it could reflect the fact that in West Ward, there are fewer parks and places to go out and much less of a 'street life' for children.

In many cases, how children felt about where they live seemed to depend on proximity to friends: as Maggie, 15, put it: 'I love my house and my area, because there are three parks near me, the town is a five minute walk away, the school is close and I can visit my friends without having to take a bus or walk miles. Most of my friends live in Hill Ward, or my area'. Not having friends living nearby was a problem, and this seemed to be more marked in School 1 which [...] was in a quiet, sprawling, suburban locality with few facilities for young people. It was also mostly girls who described this, which could reflect constraints on girls' mobility.

Longevity of friendship

Some children described having known their friends for a long time. For others, however, friendship networks were dynamic, not static or fixed, and some described falling out with friends. The downside of friendship was that when things went wrong, children could be quite badly hurt: despite school being a place for socialising and being with close friends, it was also a place where fights break out, and young people get physically and emotionally hurt.

On the whole, friends were central to many activities outside school, and were clearly very important as a source of emotional support. Yet friendship can operate in contradictory ways in terms of health behaviours. [...] Simon, 14, S1, described how 'During the night my friends and I go down [main road] and drink alcohol. Us teenagers don't go into any buildings, just walking on the street'. Zishan, 15, who regretted falling out with his friend, wrote 'I don't need friends because they pass their bad habits to you'.

'Being part of the group' was crucial and one discussion with Year 10s focused on peer pressure (one boy used this term and the others clearly related to it) and Amy explained what it meant:

> It's blending in with the rest of the group, if the rest of the group are wearing Nike trainers, you feel like you've gotta have Nike trainers, if the rest of the group are smoking, you feel like you've gotta smoke.

The groups and associations that matter to children appeared to consist of clear hierarchies: Amy described it thus:

> You get class peer groups, you get like first class, like they're all popular, and if like say a third class person walked past em, they'd be jeering. They're exactly the same age, they know them, but in the street ... you get some people who are so popular, everyone will be, often they're really horrible people as well, but everyone's like 'oh, yeah, let's join their gang', then you get these other people, that nobody seems to like, and they're really nice people, and they walk past the other people, and they're like jeering at them, they've done nothing wrong.

Dave said: 'that's back to clothes, and stuff, again, though, innit'. This could be seen as 'social capital' in the here-and-now: belonging to a particular 'class peer group' may have provided a sense of belonging that relates to well-being, but may also have set up habits that may be damaging for future health. As Amy said, 'you feel like you've gotta smoke'. [...]

Familial networks: parents

Parents, and especially mothers, were very important to both age groups. Virtually all the written comments the children made about their families (especially their mums) were positive, and this appeared to be regardless of family structure. Children were not asked a direct question about family structure but sometimes it was described in a matter-of-fact way:

> The most important people to me are my mother and my best mate. My mother because she always manages to cope with me and can manage to

look after me and my brother on her own, my dad got divorced from my mum 5/6 years ago. I still occasionally see him, but not all the time.

(Jody, age 14)

Boys again were less expansive but did convey the importance of parents: Harry, age 13, wrote: 'My parents are very important to me as if I did not have them I would not be able to survive. It's not just about money, because they care for me and will always stand by my side'. And Dave, age 14, wrote: 'My most important thing is my family'. Clearly, parents are important to young people' sense of well-being, not least because they are a source of emotional support just by 'being there'. However, in many cases, it was difficult to separate support provided by family members from that provided by friends in the children's responses.

Wider kin

Several children (15 from School 1 and 16 from School 2) mentioned wider kin (usually grandparents), and some described a good deal of regular contact. Shenna, age 12, described how:

> At weekends I do dancing at [a nearby secondary school, in Moss Hills] for 3 hours. Every other week on a Sunday I go to my dad's because my mum and dad are divorced. I go to my Nan's every Saturday ...

Family appeared to be the main source of close relationships and support for children of Pakistani-Kashmiri origin. This is not surprising, because the basic tenets of Islam emphasise the importance of family obligations and interdependence. For example, Sabrina, 13, S2, whose family is from Pakistan, wrote:

> The most important people in my life is my family. Although most of my family live in Pakistan, I still think they're really important to me. For example, I can't remember my gran or grandad, for 8 years I haven't seen them. They still write letters to me and send me nice things from there.

So for Pakistani-Kashmiri children, 'family' is clearly central, but the fact that so many white children maintain close ties with their family members, especially grandparents, contradicts the stereotypical that kin ties are no longer as central as they used to be as families have become more dispersed. [...] Family members do not need to live round the corner to be important.

On the whole, family relationships seem to give young people a context and a grounding for their lives in the sense of 'being there' in the background for them.

Disrupting social networks: moving house

Moving house obviously disrupts the social networks of parents and children, especially if it means a change of school. Mandy, age 14, described how she had moved house several times within the town. 'I'm really happy where I live now but I want to move to (West Ward) so I can be closer to school, my friends, and my boyfriend'.

Some children described having 'two homes' after their parents had divorced and this meant that they had two sets of friends, one in each place: Sonia, 14, described how she had lived in Moss Hills, but she has two sets of friends, because 'I also have a home in (outskirts of London), with my dad for nearly 6 years'. In stark contrast to the negative conclusions that research has often made about the effects of parental separation on children, this was not necessarily seen negatively by the children themselves.

Sense of belonging

Given the centrality of family and friendship that emerged so clearly from these data, it was not surprising that a sense of belonging appeared to derive from people and relationships, rather than place. In School 2, young people were asked to try to write about 'where do you feel you belong?' if they had time; 25 answered the question. None described themselves as a 'Springtonian'.

A number of elements of social life appeared to be sources of a sense of belonging, but home and family were the primary ones: e.g. one girl wrote: 'I feel most comfortable at home with my Mum and Dad because I can be myself and I don't feel like they are looking at me and judging me'. As Rock, 15, put it, 'I think I belong in a community where I am treated right and a place that is warm and friendly'. A sense of one's roots was also important to some.

One girl in School 1, when asked 'where do you feel you belong?', replied enthusiastically 'St Lucia!!', and others in School 2 mentioned the place they were born, or where their families had come from. However, as the account of the children's views on moving house shows, place and neighbourhood are strong influences on how or whether young people were able to access the relationships that are so important to their sense of belonging.

Experiences of town and neighbourhood

Differing perspectives

This section explores young people's perspectives on their town and neighbourhoods. There were differences in the accounts according to gender, ethnicity, and age. Girls tended to talk about fear of rapists though some boys mentioned this too, and it was possible that they were using this as a generic term for 'a threat'. In fact there had been a series of rapes and sexual assaults in the town while the research was taking place, so the threat was very real. Children from minority ethnic groups spoke of racism in their neighbourhoods. Younger children were more preoccupied with practical issues like traffic, and not having decent places to play in their localities, while older children were more likely to describe the need to go into the town for entertainment and to talk about the constraints of cost as a barrier to enjoying themselves.

Views of town

In School 1, in nearly all group discussions a local housing estate, Moss Hills, was seen as a problem. This estate, which borders on the West Ward where School 1 was located, had in fact experienced a week of riots three years previously. As a prompt, groups were shown a news cutting which described Springtown as a 'town ravaged by joblessness and heroin addiction', accompanied by a photo of the blocks of flats at Moss Hills. Some were well aware that the town had a negative image, but they distanced themselves from the description, e.g. Mark, 12, said ''cos that's not a part of where we live, that's Moss Hills, we're West Ward'. However, others were well aware of the bad reputation of the town as a whole. Natalie commented: 'I'll tell you something, Springtown will never have peace, and it's not fair'. In the same group, Robert said: 'you see, miss, it's not like everyone in Springtown is bad, it's just, like, groups of bad people start something up, and then everybody starts joining in, and then it gets in the papers and we have a bad name'.

Neighbourhood safety

There were a range of responses to questions about feeling safe in their neighbourhoods. This varied right down to the street level, so if they lived in a cul-de-sac in a suburban area, it was often seen as 'too quiet' and 'boring', and if they lived on a busy street, they often thought there was 'too much traffic'. Some older children were aware of advantages of living in a quiet area because they could get their homework done. One girl described her part of town as 'trampy'; this was a word other children in School 1 used too to mean 'not very nice, dirty'.

Children in both year groups in School 1 mentioned not feeling safe in local parks and on the streets:

> … like someone was assaulted down [in the local park], I mean, that makes you scared to go down there, and that was in broad daylight, so God knows what it's gonna be like at 10 o'clock at night … I live in like a secluded road, hardly anyone comes down my road, but there's nothing there, there's like a little park down the road, but someone was assaulted there, you're scared to go there. So if I was, like, 20, and I had two little kids, I'd have nowhere to take them in [this area], that was safe (Amy).

In School 2, Year 10s expressed a strong sense that if they were on their own territory, they were OK. […] In another group of Year 10s, the boys seemed to feel safe in their area, but the girls less so. One girl said 'Sometimes, there's trouble round our area'. […] On the other hand, sometimes neighbourhoods were seen positively. […] In conclusion, there was no clear consensus about their neighbourhoods: some felt quite positive, some felt quite negative, and some were ambivalent. Girls expressed more concern about safety than boys.

Neighbours

There were some negative accounts of neighbours in both schools, and particularly from younger children. One boy complained about his neighbour in the block of flats he lives in and described how his family were trying to move:

> I live on the top floor, right, … and the next door person got really drunk, and he's always having fights, with other people, and last time, he left blood all over the things and don't really like that, so we're still looking for a house …

In Hill Ward, neighbours seemed to be much more problematic, or 'moany', as the children tended to put it. Fred said about his area 'It's ok, apart from the neighbours, they're moany, say if you're playing in the front garden, yeah, and you make a bit of noise, they moan. They moan. So you can't do anything when they're there'. Noise from loud music, being sworn at, racial harassment, fighting, were all described. However, there was apparently no mechanism for young people to complain about their neighbours.

More exceptionally, children commented that their relationships with neighbours were good, but mostly this seemed to relate to how long they had lived next to each other, and some children reminisced fondly about close relationships to neighbours. Charles (who had lived in Hill Ward all his life) described how 'Our neighbours are friends, 'cos where I live, my granny lived there before, so the neighbours all know the whole family', while Shannon, 13, described how:

> We used to have an old lady called Violet, and a family, they had kids and we used to all play together … they got made redundant, had to move out … and then Violet moved out, to a special bungalow place so she didn't have to go up the stairs and that. And this bunch of students come in. Violet used to look out for us and everything, we used to help her out and everything. Now the music's thumping, they can't hear, when we've knocked on the door, they don't listen, like at 3 o'clock in the morning, trying to get to sleep … they don't care anymore.

This was in contrast to the example given above, where quiet, older neighbours meant that the neighbourhood was perceived as boring. The quality of young people's relationships with their neighbours seemed to be experienced differently by different individuals, rather than be generalised to the neighbourhood, though there were more complaints about 'moany' neighbours in Hill Ward.

Where relationships were perceived as good, children described a kind of familiarity that appeared to arise in settled neighbourhoods, where neighbours were well-known to each other over long periods of time. […]

Racial harassment and racism in the neighbourhood

Several children in both schools described explicit racism and racial harassment. One boy, whose family was originally from Bangladesh, described how he did not play outside his flats: 'if I've got nothing to do I play inside with my own computer, [not] outside [because] usually people are quite racist to me, because that's why I don't like my area that much'. The word children used to describe how racist attacks made them feel was 'angry'. However, fear of racial harassment may have implications for their overall psychological and emotional well-being.

Road traffic

Traffic was a major preoccupation for the Year 8 children in both schools. For example, Emma, age 12, said she didn't feel safe in her neighbourhood, 'because there's like boys coming along, and then there's people swearing at each other, and you've got like, people driving like maniacs'. Others complained of pollution; some complained about motorbikes joyriding or riding on pavements. [...] The practical constraints on young people's environments may have impinged on their social interactions. The responsibility of adults to drive safely, use their indicators, and keep to speed limits is rarely given much attention, yet individualised traffic safety messages emphasise the responsibility of children to learn to cross the road safely.

Noise

In Hill Ward, in particular, some children complained they could not sleep because of noise from cars, particularly from joy riders. In both schools, the noise from a police helicopter was frequently mentioned. School 2 was also affected by aircraft noise – often teachers, children (and researcher!) had to stop talking while the planes went over – though children reported that they were used to it. One 14-year-old girl wrote 'I live near Hill Ward. I have lived there for nearly five years. I like the area where I live, apart from the fact that the loud aeroplanes are a bother'.

'No ball games'

Both year groups in both schools talked about not having enough to do in terms of facilities. Most children described playing out with friends in local parks, especially boys. Very few children described involvement in organised voluntary activities (six boys, three in each school, mentioned being members of a formal sports team). There were no clear differences in out-of-school activities between the two sites.

In School 1, the local youth club was seen by older children as suitable for younger children, and a few of the younger children did use it, and said they liked it. Other girls commented about a youth club in their neighbourhood: 'it's boring, the same things happen all the time'. Some girls felt there was not enough for girls to do at the respective youth clubs: 'all they do is play football and basketball'. Or 'there's nothing for girls'.

In both schools, the cost of activities was frequently mentioned. The town centre was an attraction. Older children in School 1 said things like 'I like town better, there's much more action'. However, as they did not necessarily have much money, they were preoccupied by bus fare, which increased to an adult fare when they were 13 or 14 years old. One girl (School 2) said: 'the thing that annoys me is that the police always moan that we're on the streets, so they build places like the new clubs and stuff, but we have to pay to get into that'. Children in both sites were aware of the constant threat of closure of one of the main sources of employment in Springtown; one girl explained that 'my mum hasn't got a lot of money'; and Shannon (cited above) mentioned her neighbours moving because of redundancy.

In terms of local parks, younger children described how:

> There's a park where we live, we call it 'Motorway Field' because it's right by the motorway, and it's just covered in dog's muck, you just don't like to go there, people let their dogs go anywhere, so we like to play football there, but 'cos you don't know where the dog's muck is, you don't play because you don't want to get covered in it (Harry).

Several Year 8 children mentioned the lack of wild places to 'make dens'. One girl mentioned 'we used to have a den, in the woods there, and me and my friend found loads of like drugs and stuff, packets and things, so we took them to the police'. One girl photographed a tree, and described how: 'This is the best place to go when it's really hot. However, if you look carefully the grass is covered in rubbish so we avoid going there'.

In School 2, children in both years mentioned that they (and younger children) were not allowed to play football near their houses on patches of communal grass, and one girl photographed a sign that said 'No Ball Games'. She commented: 'this is a sign that is on a piece of greenery on my road. It stops children from playing typical games, but little children need somewhere to play ... they may not be allowed to go to the park, etc.'.

Mistrust

While there was some evidence of good relationships between children and their neighbours in the past, overall there was very little evidence of trust between different generations in neighbourhoods. This was especially evident in School 2, where there was a good deal of blaming neighbours, or being blamed by neighbours, for noise disturbance. Nor was there much evidence of trust in relationships young people had with those who worked in and frequented the town centre, where they were well aware of how they are perceived by the adults around them.

In School 2, in a discussion with Year 10s, one boy said press representation of young people was 'insulting' [...]

Participation in decision-making

School

[...] Many of the children [...] understood the logic of school councils, and thought they were a good idea, but felt that they did not always work in practice. This was because of problems of representation, the issues that were discussed, and a (perceived) reluctance on the part of teachers to take suggestions seriously.

The effects of school on children

The institution and experience of school appeared to have contradictory implications for children's well-being. In some ways, school was experienced positively by the children. As discussed above, schools form an important kind of 'community' for young people. [...] Positive accounts of teachers were more marked in School 2. For example, Rock included teachers in his list of people who are important to him: 'They are the only route to a good education'.

In contrast to the positive effects, the non-democratic nature of school, the content of school work, and the relationships between teachers and pupils, appeared not to enhance self-esteem for some children. In School 1, children spoke of how the teachers' 'favourites' were usually 'boffins' or 'brainboxes' and some of them seemed to express a sense that only one form of knowledge – i.e. academic knowledge – was valued. [...] As one 14-year-old boy put it: 'None of the teachers really build up our confidence or anything'. Other children complained that teachers 'put you down'; they 'don't really care'. One boy said 'I hate being told what grade the teachers expect of you, it's very high expectations'.

[...]

Community participation

Participation in community decision-making in both locations was extremely limited. In School 1, only one person felt they could go to their residents association and make suggestions about their local area (when he said this in the group discussion, someone whispered that 'ah, but that's a posh area'). If the council did come and ask about local facilities, they felt that their parents were consulted, not them. Amy said: 'they send like questionnaires to our parents but it's not our parents who want to go to the Youth Club, it's us. So they should ask us'. Among Year 10s in School 2 there was no sense of community participation, and one girl commented that she felt they should have a say in the community, 'because what happens does affect us as well as the adults and they don't seem to think about that when they're making decisions'.

[...]

Discussion

The social determinants of health and well-being in childhood

Many factors impinge on children's well-being, and to attempt to analyse these I adapted Dahlgren and Whitehead's (1991) 'onion ring' model to the themes raised (Figure 21.1).

The top two 'layers' of Dahlgren and Whitehead's model, personal behaviour and lifestyle, and psychosocial environment, are well recognised in research that links 'social capital' to health. However, a focus purely on social relationships and the psychosocial environment is in danger of missing the factors that also emerged as significant for the children that fall under the other headings in the onion model, such as the importance of the physical environment, of socio-economic context, public services, and public policy. The study highlighted how a range of practical, environmental, and economic constraints were experienced by this age group.

In conclusion the findings suggest that a broader approach to children's health and well-being is needed than one that is centred upon individual behaviour. For the children in the study, a clear dynamic existed between social life and environmental factors. An environmental justice perspective on health and well-being highlights the ethical and political questions of who gets what, why, and in what amounts (Bullard and Wright, 1993). Social and health promotion policies need to pay attention to children's quality of life (Casas, 1997), in the broadest sense, in the here and now, rather than be driven by a perspective that prioritises children as future citizens, in terms of human capital (Qvortrup, 1994). The focus on the 'here-and-now' of children's lives adopted in this study shows that these children were generally excluded from the social life of the community by virtue of their age. However, they also exist in the future, and activities they undertake now for whatever reason have implications for their future well-being.

[....]

While the children in this study did not use a language of rights, they seemed to be well aware that they were effectively denied a range of

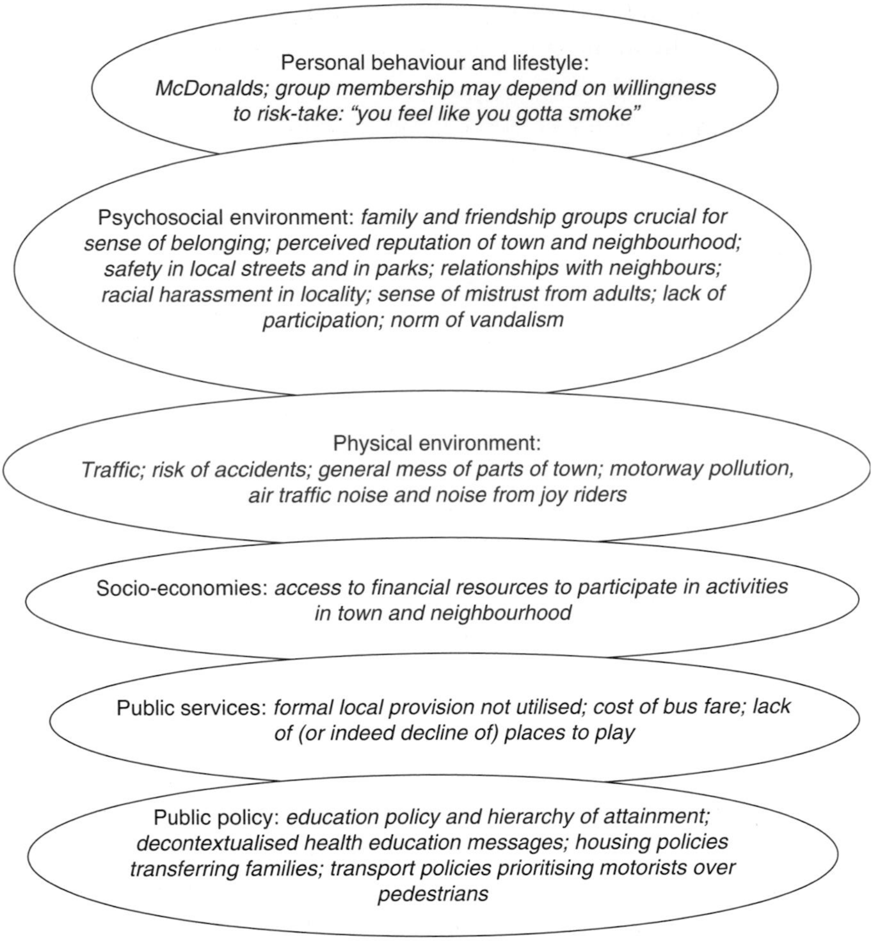

Personal behaviour and lifestyle:
McDonalds; group membership may depend on willingness to risk-take: "you feel like you gotta smoke"

Psychosocial environment: *family and friendship groups crucial for sense of belonging; perceived reputation of town and neighbourhood; safety in local streets and in parks; relationships with neighbours; racial harassment in locality; sense of mistrust from adults; lack of participation; norm of vandalism*

Physical environment:
Traffic; risk of accidents; general mess of parts of town; motorway pollution, air traffic noise and noise from joy riders

Socio-economies: *access to financial resources to participate in activities in town and neighbourhood*

Public services: *formal local provision not utilised; cost of bus fare; lack of (or indeed decline of) places to play*

Public policy: *education policy and hierarchy of attainment; decontextualised health education messages; housing policies transferring families; transport policies prioritising motorists over pedestrians*

Figure 21.1 The social determinants of health: from children's accounts of their everyday lives.

Source: Adapted from Dahlgren and Whitehead (1991).

participatory rights that adults take for granted. This awareness may become more problematic as they get older, and was likely to limit their sense of self-efficacy. They were not as rebellious and disaffected as dominant imagery depicts them to be. They had a strong sense that they needed their educational qualifications, and that school was important, and at the same time, they would like to have had access to safe local streets and neighbourhood spaces, but they were well aware that they were neglected. Many of their experiences seemed likely to have an impact on their well-being.

[...] Asking questions about social capital focuses on one specific element of individuals' or neighbourhood quality of life. There is a danger that in doing so, broader questions of social justice are overlooked. The wider responsibilities of central and local government to ensure a good quality of life for children in environmental terms – whether in their institutions or neighbourhoods – also need to be addressed.

References

Bullard, R.D. and Wright, B.H. (1993) "Environmental justice for all: community perspectives on health and research needs', *Toxicology and Industrial Health*, Vol. 9 No. 5, pp. 821–41.

Casas, F. (1997) Children's rights and children's quality of life: conceptual and practical issues', *Social Indicators Research*, Vol. 42, pp. 283–298.

Dahlgren, G. and Whitehead, M. (1991) *'Policies and Strategies to Promote Social Equity in Health'*, Institute for Futures Studies, Stockholm.

Putnam, R.D. (1993) *Making Democracy Work. Civic Traditions in Modern Italy*. Princeton University Press, Princeton, NJ.

Qvortrup, J. (1994) "Preface', in Qvortrup, J., Bardy, M., Sgritta, G. and Wintersberger, H. (Eds) *Childhood Matters: Social Theory, Practice and Politics*, Avebury/European Centre, Vienna.

Virginia Morrow suggests in the paper which this chapter is adapted from that a focus upon rights is a valuable way of addressing health inequalities and quality-of-life issues for this age group. Her research reveals how the views of children and young people need to be closer to the centre of so many social processes from which they are currently marginalised.

Chapter 22

Taking looked after children's views into account on a day-to-day level

The perceptions and experiences of children and social workers

Children in Scotland

This chapter draws upon a much longer report looking at the participation of looked after and accommodated children in decision-making concerning their care. The research study was undertaken in two Scottish local authorities, involving nine looked after children, four social workers, two reviewing officers and two children's rights officers. Here we focus upon the children's views of talking to social workers and upon social workers' views on how to encourage young people to talk and balance their best interests and wishes. The challenges faced by these children and young people, and the adults involved in their lives, will be familiar well beyond the confines of social work.

[…]

Children's perceptions and experiences

The children interviewed for the research were asked whether they thought their social workers knew how they felt about things, how their social workers found this out from them, and what this is like for them. They were also asked how the social worker responded when they (the children) expressed their feelings and views.

The experience of communicating feelings and views to social workers

Most of the children felt that their social workers knew how they were feeling about things. […] Two main factors affected the children's experience of talking to their social workers about how they were feeling, and how able they felt to do this. These were:

- **The topic:** several children described the topic as key to their experience of talking to their social workers about their feelings. They found it much easier to talk about positive feelings or more prosaic issues than about negative feelings or emotive issues.
- **The nature and quality of their relationship with the social worker:** namely, the time and quality of attention that the social worker gave them, and the extent to which their feelings and views were being responded to.

Regular, individual attention from the social worker was valued, for example:

> Interviewer: How does [your social worker] know how you're feeling about things?
>
> 11-year-old-child: Well, she always comes to see me. She always comes to visit me. And makes sure that … she knows how I'm feeling.

For some children, doing enjoyable things with the social worker was an important part of feeling that they had the social worker's full attention and that they were valued. One had enjoyed being taken to the beach and was already looking forward to the next outing, whilst another enjoyed being taken out to lunch.

Unsurprisingly, where a child liked their social worker and felt that he or she genuinely cared, it was much easier to talk about feelings. For example:

> Interviewer: So how does [your social worker] know how you're feeling about things?
>
> 12-year-old child: 'Cause I like my social worker and when she comes up, well, I just think she's a really nice social worker. 'Cause she's genuine and I feel I can be relaxed with her, and genuine, as well. And she's just – a friend, as well. Like, if I had a friend like that I would talk to them about things.

Conversely, where contact with the social worker was uncertain, or where the child did not feel that the social worker valued his or her feelings, the children found it more difficult to talk to him or her. Some children had issues they wanted to talk about with their social workers, but reported that they hadn't seen the social worker for a while and were not sure exactly when they would see her. Another found his social worker unapproachable, feeling that she was not paying attention when he spoke to her, and was sometimes grumpy and dismissive of his feelings. He also did not trust that what he said to her would remain confidential. He was the only child to raise concerns about confidentiality in this context.

[…] Another key factor in the willingness of the children to talk to the social worker about how they were feeling was the extent to which their views were being taken into account, whether by the social worker or in a general sense. […] Some children described their social workers as sorting things out or supporting them with difficulties, and this gave them confidence that the social worker would respond to any issues they raised. Conversely, another child was angry that his wishes regarding contact with his father were not being fulfilled and saw little point in discussing his feelings with his social worker since the social worker was already well aware of his views about contact. He did not direct his anger towards, and did not appear to blame, his social worker, but this issue eclipsed all others in terms of its importance to him and he therefore felt there was little to talk about with the social worker.

As might be expected, high quality relationships, in which children found it easiest to talk to the social worker and found him or her responsive to their feelings and views, tended to be characterised by a combination of the closely related features outlined above – regular, individual attention, liking the social worker and feeling him or her to be caring and responsive. Conversely, talking about feelings was found to be most difficult where the relationship was lacking in these qualities.

The experience of social workers' response to feelings and views

Most of the children had a sense of how the social worker responded to their feelings and views, but two found it difficult to say. This difference did not seem to be age-related – rather it seemed that these children did not have a strong sense of themselves as having feelings and views that might call for a response. They did have things to say to the social worker, but they did not express, and did not appear to have, specific hopes or expectations about how the social worker would respond to them. The impression of the interviewer was that they would not express feelings and views unless this was prompted, and given careful attention, by the social worker.

As explained previously, one child said that he did not normally talk to his social worker about his feelings and views. Amongst those children who *were* willing to talk to their social workers about their feelings and views, a range of factors impacted on their experiences of the social worker's response. These were:

- the extent of opportunities to talk to the social worker
- the extent to which the child's wishes were fulfilled
- the social worker's handling of the situation
- the issues at stake
- the relationship with the social worker.

Some situations were difficult for the children by their very nature, but the findings from the interviews indicate that there was scope within inherently difficult situations for the social worker to respond to children's feelings and views in a way that could impact positively or negatively on the child's experience.

Children gave examples of a range of responses that they had found helpful. Some of these related to situations in which it was not possible to fix a problem easily, or to respond to feelings and views in a straightforward way, and where the social worker's response had mitigated its effects on them. For example, one child was glad that, after his mother had missed their contact session, his social worker had passed on information to her about how he and his sister were getting on. Another child had been seriously ill with anorexia and had not initially wanted to be admitted to hospital, despite the risk to her health. Although her social worker had been instrumental in ensuring she was admitted, and this child believed her opinions had not been as valued then as they now were, she appreciated that during this time her social worker still had regular sessions with her and talked to her. The quality of her relationship with the social worker was very good and this was a key factor in her sense that the social worker responded positively to her feelings and views.

Other responses that the children had found helpful were:

- Explaining and/or reassuring: for example, one child had found a sibling's behaviour difficult and his social worker had explained why this might be happening and reassured him that it was likely to be temporary.
- Passing on information or concerns to relevant others: for example, some children said that their social workers fed in their views at Looked After Children (LAC) Review meetings. Another said that her social worker tells the nurses at the day unit she attends when she is unhappy about aspects of her care there.
- Fixing or helping with difficulties or requests: for example, one child valued the help she received from her social worker with managing difficult emotions. Another said that her social worker would be responsive to arranging more contact with her grandmother if she (the child) asked for this.

As explained above, two children had issues they wanted to talk about with their social workers but reported that they hadn't seen the social worker for a while and were not sure exactly when they would see her. Another 11-year-old child found it difficult to remember what he had said to his social worker because of the length of time since her last visit. Two of these children did not express unhappiness about this, and these were the same children who appeared to have very limited expectations concerning the social worker's response to their feelings and views. The other found it problematic, saying that it was difficult to talk to her social worker "when she's, like, busy or that, and I really want to talk to her." She described an occasion when a foster carer had telephoned the social worker on her behalf and been told that the social worker might be available in the afternoon – however, when she (the child) had called back in the afternoon, the social worker had not been there. It seemed that she had found this difficult.

For some children, issues inherent to the situation – their conflicting feelings, their distress at being removed from home – contributed to the experience of aspects of the social worker's response as negative. One child had told his social worker that he wanted to get on better with his parents, and he said that the social worker's response to this had been to remove him from home and place him with foster carers. He believed that this had helped to achieve this wish and made things much better. On the other hand, he wanted to go home to be with his parents, and this was upsetting for him. Inevitably, therefore, he had mixed feelings about the social worker's response to his feelings and views.

In the case of another child, however, his distress about not being allowed to see a parent was compounded by the way in which the social worker had handled the situation. He experienced the social worker as dismissive of his feelings and had gained the impression from her that he was partly responsible for the situation:

> I just says that … I didn't want to go into foster care and that I wanted to go and live with my dad. She just says, well, she just says that you've got to – you've got to just – behave more, and that it's not up to her, and I've got to bring it up at one of the meetings. (Ten-year-old child)

As can be seen from some of these examples, the social worker's response to the children's feelings and views occurred in the context of the relationship with the social worker. Where the social worker's response was experienced as most helpful, the relationship was a positive one, characterised by regular, individual attention, liking the social worker, and feeling him or her to be caring and willing to respond to feelings and views. Where it was experienced as least helpful, the relationship was experienced as the opposite.

Social workers' perceptions and experiences

Social workers' views about consulting children aged eight to 12 and the methods used

[...] All the social workers interviewed expressed strong commitment to the principle of consulting children about their care. They believed that it was important to find a way to consult children that was appropriate to their age and understanding[....] All reported that they asked questions and talked to the child about how things are and how the child was feeling. Some emphasised that the way in which this was done was important: one said that talking in the context of doing fun things such as playing or artwork helpfully took the focus away from the child; she found that children experienced this as less threatening than being asked a series of questions. Some found play, including role play, useful for finding out children's feelings and views and one used conversations generated by story books (about animals leaving their mother to go to a different family, for example), as well as life story work, and specific work on aspects of the child's past, to elicit feelings and views.

However, another social worker felt that using particular tools to consult children had the potential to put pressure on them, in a situation in which they were already subject to a considerable degree of (perhaps unwanted) attention from a range of adults. He said that children often "build a wall around their emotions" and he found that a subtle approach to finding out feelings and views was required; he believed a good relationship between the child and the social worker, and a situation in which the child felt comfortable, was essential:

> Getting alongside them in their own environment and their own interests, and then not asking questions for some time, and you can get the odd little gem [about how they feel] thrown in on a random car journey at some point in the future … you could get one significant sentence … in a two or three hour contact. It's not subterfuge … but I think it's a point at which you have a bond.

Another social worker also found that children talked to her in the car.

When asked how she found out children's feelings and views, one social worker described asking questions about how children were feeling about things to try to help them understand the situation and the reasons for decisions such as being removed from home: "How did you feel about that then?", "Are you still feeling like that now?" … rounding it up at the end.

She acknowledged that this could be at odds with eliciting their feelings and views:

> Usually the children end up agreeing … I've got to be careful about that because it's easy to railroad children.

This illustrates the challenges for social workers of handling a situation in which it is not possible to fulfil children's views. […] It suggests that it is important for social workers to be clear whether the purpose of their questions is to help to *explain* a difficult situation to a child with *reference* to the child's feelings and views, or to elicit the child's feelings and views about the situation (even where the child's wishes cannot necessarily be fulfilled).

[…]

How social workers judge the weight to be given to children's views

In explaining how they judge how much weight to give to children's views, the social workers referred to a range of considerations. One simply said that her approach was to try to fulfil a child's wishes unless these were not in the child's best interests, and unsurprisingly, this was a key consideration for all the social workers. One placed emphasis on assessing the child's level of understanding of the situation, while for another a primary consideration was establishing the veracity of what the child said. The other social worker referred to all of these considerations: assessing whether it is in a child's best interests to fulfil his or her wishes, assessing the child's level of understanding of the situations, and being able to verify what a child has said.

Where social workers referred to verifying a child's views, they said they used their knowledge of the child and the situation. One referred to using sources of information such as the child's behaviour, or other adults involved in the child's life, to try to establish the truth of what was being said.

Key reasons given by social workers for *not* fulfilling a child's views were:

- Fulfilling their views would put them at risk. This concerned issues such as contact and whether the child could return home.

- The child's wishes were unrealistic – one social worker gave examples of a child wanting a horse, or wanting to buy his mother a house.
- A lack of appropriate resources – some social workers referred to a lack of foster carers which meant that there was little scope to respond to children's wishes concerning foster carers and which generated uncertainty and insecurity for them. […] One social worker also saw a lack of resources as preventing the fulfilment of a child's wish to change social worker or to change his or her school or guidance teacher.

[…]

Views and best interests as one and the same?

In some examples given by social workers there were indications that, when it came to establishing a child's views by observing his or her behaviour, no clear distinction was being made between the child's views and the child's best interests. These examples concerned young children whose observed needs were defined as their views. One social worker said that the success of this depended on how able the children were to react to situations – this is more difficult where children have become withdrawn as a result of their experiences.

This "blurring" of the definitions of children's view and best interests, as interpreted by the social worker, is a reflection of the fact that the two are closely linked. However, the fact that while a child's views and best interests may coincide, they may also differ, suggests that eliciting feelings and views may be helped if social workers make distinctions between:

- The directly expressed view of the child and the social worker's interpretation of the child's view based on observation
- The social worker's interpretation of the child's view and the social worker's judgement of what is in the child's best interests.

This would seem to be particularly salient in the case of younger children and those with additional needs, where particular skills are required to consult effectively and where observation may play a greater role in discerning feelings and best interests. The balance between the use of direct and indirect methods to obtain children's feelings and views, and whether this balance is appropriate to the child, is also a relevant consideration here.

[…]

At the heart of this chapter is the need to build successful, trusting relationships between children and young people and adults. Frequently this requires giving up some of our power within a relationship and finding ways to share our experiences without dominating the other. But how do we achieve this when we are working within systems and structures that are premised upon hierarchical responsibilities and externally defined targets; and when failings are judged so harshly by powerful others?

Chapter 23

Aversive disablism

Subtle prejudice toward disabled people

Mark Deal

Mark Deal highlights how blatant forms of prejudice towards a range of different groupings appears to be disappearing in the UK. More subtle forms of prejudice are still much in evidence however, not only in those who have learned to hide their more extreme views. This subtle prejudice is also hidden within many who consider themselves to be open minded and supportive of the idea of equality for all. This chapter helps us to consider how our behaviours, however well meaning, can act in prejudicial ways. Its focus is primarily upon disabled people, but its lessons can equally apply to a whole range of individuals in our communities and within our own lives.

Introduction

In 2005 the UK Government stated its vision for disabled people in Britain whereby:

> By 2025 disabled people … should have full opportunities and choices to improve their quality of life, and will be respected and included as equal members of society.
>
> (Prime Minister's Strategy Unit, 2005, p. 44)

As a disabled person myself, such a vision is heartening; however, the gap between intent and reality can be wide. As a disabled person from birth and a wheelchair user for over 20 years I have experienced improved access to public buildings, better service on the railway network, greater protection under the law (Disability Discrimination Acts 1995 and 2005) and so on. But, as Martin Luther King said, 'Judicial decrees may not change the heart, but they can restrain the heartless' (cited in Law Society, 1992). In other words, behaviour towards people who are discriminated against can be modified, but the attitude towards such people may still remain prejudiced.

Not all forms of prejudice and discriminatory behaviour, however, are blatant and therefore easily identifiable, as subtle forms of prejudice also exist. Therefore, any attempt to tackle prejudice towards disabled people must not only focus on overtly discriminatory behaviour but also recognize subtle forms of prejudice, which can be equally damaging. In order to develop the debate relating to subtle prejudice towards disabled people this paper will utilize a term that is developed from modern or aversive racism (Gaertner and Dovidio, 2000) that I have called aversive disablism.

Prejudice toward disabled people

[…] At first sight it would appear attitudes towards disabled people in the UK are improving (Bromley and Curtice, 2003, pp. 41–45; Department for Work and Pensions, 2003) and therefore the prejudice faced is in decline. […]

However, it is possible that people have learnt acceptable behaviours and verbal expressions towards disabled people, thus exhibiting non-prejudicial behaviours, but at the same time holding prejudicial feelings and beliefs. Many of these subtle forms of prejudice may not even be recognized by the holder or others as being negative, but may still have a significant impact upon the lives of disabled people as more blatant forms.

In order to explore this contention further I propose to extrapolate ideas from aversive racism theory in order to present the concept of aversive disablism.

Aversive disablism

[…] Disablism has been defined as 'discriminatory, oppressive or abusive behaviour arising from the belief that disabled people are inferior to others' (Miller *et al.*, 2004, p. 9). This definition, whilst emphasizing overt forms of prejudice towards disabled people, argues that the behaviour stems from the beliefs held about the attitude object (in this instance, the attitude object being disabled people). However, it is my contention that much of the prejudice faced by disabled people is in fact subtle in nature, therefore, by relating the definition of disablism to aversive racism theory, subtle forms of prejudice can be incorporated into a framework of prejudice.

Meertens and Pettigrew (1997), in their research into racism throughout Europe, raised the important distinction between 'blatant' and 'subtle' prejudice. […]

Subtle racists reject crude expressions of prejudice, but nevertheless still view minority groups as 'a people apart' (Meertens and Pettigrew, 1997).

[…] Aversive racists recognize that racism is bad, but do not recognize they themselves are prejudiced; likewise, aversive racism is 'often unintentional' (Dovidio *et al.*, 2000, p. 137). An aversive racist may, therefore, vote for a political party at a General Election that holds values that reflect equality and diversity and yet would choose a school for their child that is attended predominantly by white children and does not reflect the ethnic mix in their local community.

[…]

Gaertner and Dovidio (2000) argued that aversive racists hold ambivalent attitudes towards black people that are 'rooted in the tension between feelings and values' (p. 13). These authors continued: 'These negative feelings do not reflect open hostility or hate; instead, the feelings involve discomfort, uneasiness, disgust, and sometimes fear' (p. 14), which means 'aversive racism theory focuses on the conflict between an individual's negative feelings and his or her personal self-image of being fair and nonprejudiced' (p. 4).

Thus, relating this to disabled people, the feelings listed by Gaertner and Dovidio are likely to cause the attitude holder to avoid contact with the attitude recipient. Support for well-meaning social policies that reduce the possibility of meaningful interactions between disabled people and others are therefore likely to be supported by aversive disablists, for instance: supporting segregated schooling due to the belief that it can offer a higher quality education to disabled children, rather than mainstream education with appropriate backing within the school; the continuation of Day Centres, rather than providing the same services and support within an integrated environment; the use of residential care homes rather than community-based housing schemes; supported/sheltered businesses rather than job coaching schemes […] assisting disabled people to work in integrated work environments.

[…]

Subtle prejudice or a matter of opinion?

Aversive racists, Gaertner and Dovidio (2000, p. 29) argued, are not anti-black, but pro-white. Likewise, aversive disablists may not be anti-disabled, but rather pronon-disabled. […] Such in-group favouritism has important implications for disabled people if they do not identify as a disabled person. Non-identifiers, whilst believing they hold liberal attitudes towards disabled people, may support behaviour and social policy that excludes other disabled people. This argument links with what Soder (1990) associated with 'common sense knowledge' when he commented that people do not want 'disabilities' [meaning impairment] and 'we don't envy those who are disabled', arguing that this is a reflection of an ambivalent attitude towards disability. However, this ambivalence can, Soder noted, 'evoke strong feelings of sympathy and altruism'. It is such 'sympathy and altruism', whilst well-meaning, that can lead to paternalistic approaches to social policy that in turn may be viewed as being aversive disablist. Bauman (1993, p. 11), whilst making no explicit reference to disabled people, in his exploration of postmodernist ethics argued:

> virtually every moral impulse, if acted upon in full, leads to immoral consequences (most characteristically, the impulse to care for the Other, when taken to its extreme, leads to the annihilation of the autonomy of the Other, to domination and oppression).

The fight against such 'domination and oppression' was central to the civil rights movement in the US, which made significant strides in tackling racism in the 1960s. However, critical race theory (CRT) emerged in the mid 1970s when Bell and Freeman expressed concern over the slow pace of racial reform since the 1960s and how progress had begun to stall (see Delgardo and Stefancic, 2000, p. xvi). Importantly, in relation to the argument being presented in this paper, the premise underpinning CRT is that elite whites will only tolerate or encourage racial advances when such advances also promote white self-interest (p. xvii). This premise may have a degree of resonance in relation to the progress made for disability rights in the UK. For instance, the expansion of direct payments since 1996 under the Community Care (Direct Payments) Act, whereby a disabled person is given cash payments by the Local Authority to pay for his/her agreed care needs (Department of Health, 2005), may have less to do with the laudable claim that it is delivering the promise of greater choice and control and more to do with reducing the tax burden. […]

In such instances it can be argued a win–win situation is evident and, therefore, what is perhaps more important is when the advances do not appear to promote non-disabled self-interest. Hence, there is the potential for conflict between the rights of disabled people and the self-interest of the non-disabled population. For instance, builders and building control officers have been reported as seeing Part M Building Regulations as 'a half hearted and tokenistic regulation' in relation to housing design (Imrie, 2006, p. 8). The objective of Part M is to ensure all new privately constructed dwellings in the UK are 'visitable', permitting ease of access for disabled people. However, to be 'visitable' is a far cry from being habitable by a person who uses, for example, a wheelchair. However, to make new housing throughout the UK truly accessible would be extremely costly and was therefore resisted by the building industry and consumers alike. However, the paucity of truly accessible housing throughout the UK (Office of Population, Censuses and Surveys, 2001) not only restricts the location some disabled people live in, but also restricts the ability to take up employment opportunities that may necessitate moving home. Hence, what appears on one level to be a subtle form of prejudice may in reality add significantly to the social exclusion of some groups of disabled people.

This is not to argue that the building industry is inherently disablist, but, as Young (1990, pp. 41–42) noted, 'The conscious actions of many individuals daily contribute to maintaining and reproducing oppression, but those people are usually simply doing their jobs or living their lives and do not understand themselves as agents of oppression'.

[…]

Does subtle prejudice really matter?

It would be easy to be dismissive of subtle forms of prejudice in the light of the atrocities that have befallen disabled people in the past, for instance the eugenics policies of the twentieth century. […] However, as disabled people become more integrated into society, if we are to be valued as equal citizens it is vital equity is evident is all aspects of life, therefore, subtle prejudice in the form of aversive disablism must be confronted. […]

Psycho-emotional effect of impairment

Subtle forms of prejudice towards disabled people should not be seen exclusively as attitudes of non-disabled people toward disabled people. People who have recently acquired an impairment are likely to hold pre-impairment attitudes towards disability and thus the disabled self (Morris, 1989), which are predominantly negative. Such attitudes are likely to influence the individual's psychological well-being, for as Johnson *et al.* (2000) found when investigating how people respond to discovering they are members of a group to which they hold negative stereotype attitudes, 'a newly acquired identity in the minority group was not enough to attenuate the previously formed negative stereotypes'. Such beliefs can create subtle forms of self-oppression. […] Subtle forms of prejudice can make disabled people feel as devalued or insecure as more blatant forms, for instance, being consistently overlooked for promotion in employment situations.

Employment and subtle prejudice

[…] Blatant forms of direct discrimination in the context of refusing to employ a disabled person as a consequence of their impairment, and therefore breaching UK law under the Disability Discrimination Act (1995), may be declining (albeit very slowly), but subtle forms of prejudice still persist.

[…] Whilst any employer will argue that the recruitment of staff must be based on a sound business case, this does not explain the discriminatory practice experienced in the workplace by disabled people. Structural factors can lead to inequality, such as fewer opportunities for training and development being available for disabled people in the workplace. Such factors will inevitably lead to lower skill and knowledge levels than their non-disabled counterparts, which in turn will lead to fewer opportunities for promotion and a greater risk of redundancy. Aversive disablism may have an influence whereby an employer, through good intentions, could decide not to put a disabled employee under additional pressure by exposing them to a new function or requiring them to attend a stressful training event, but doing so inadvertently limits career development and thus places the employee in a more vulnerable position with respect to his/her career. Therefore, by putting in place mechanisms to support the disabled employee that may be additional to those for other employees, which under the Disability Discrimination Act (1995) would be termed a 'reasonable adjustment', the disabled person can develop their career in line with other staff. However, such support must be carefully managed, for instance a well-intentioned use of an internet training course for a person with restricted mobility as an alternative to attending a training course perhaps located at an inconvenient location is likely to deny the disabled employee the opportunity to network with other colleagues on the course and so once again places the disabled person at a disadvantage and may make them feel more isolated.

[…]

Allies of disabled people

Subtle forms of prejudice may be more difficult to combat than blatant forms, especially when they arise from people who one would expect to be allies. Stephen Ladyman (minister with responsibility for disability policy in the UK Department of Health until April 2005) recognized that people who would have been expected to have liberal (with a small 'l') attitudes towards people with learning disabilities actually hold 'almost Victorian attitudes about what can and cannot be achieved' (Holman, 2004). In other words, advocates of liberal policies such as the implementation of direct payments (whereby disabled people receive money direct from the local authority in order to employ their own care staff) may be reluctant to encourage the use of this service by people with learning disabilities (Commission for Social Care Inspection, 2004). Aversive disablists may believe direct payments are overly difficult to administer, with residential care or care services provided through an agency or social services being a 'safer' option. Hence, it could be argued that by holding stereotyped beliefs towards people with learning disabilities these people may be exhibiting aversive disablist attitudes through a form of indirect discrimination. Unintentionally, aversive disablist beliefs could in this instance be placing some disabled people in a position whereby their rights of choice and control are denied. The importance of understanding the impact of subtle prejudice on the lives of disabled people by allies from other minority groups will become increasingly important in the UK with the creation of a single equalities commission, and this specific issue will therefore be discussed next.

Commission for Equality and Human Rights

[…] In the creation of this commission subtle forms of prejudice must be identified in order to ensure all minority groups are treated with equity. […] This merger may well create opportunities for collaborative working and the forming of strategic allegiances. […] However, unless each minority group within the Commission is conversant with the complexities of the discrimination faced by each other group they may, albeit inadvertently, support policy decisions that are aversive disablist in nature.

[…] Any assumption that minority groups are automatic allies, despite holding similar agendas, must be viewed with caution. People facing multiple discrimination can attest that simply belonging to a minority group does not automatically make someone aware of the needs of other minority groups, nor even hold accepting attitudes toward those other groups. Begum (1994) recalled how, as a child from the black and minority ethnic community attending a 'special needs' school, she received racial taunts from the white disabled children, and Appleby (1994) found how disabled lesbians were often regarded by non-disabled lesbians as asexual at the same time as encountering homophobic attitudes from within the disabled community. In addition, Wolbring (2001) cited gay activist Stein who, whilst defending the right of homosexual babies to be born, views the use of genetic technology to prevent the birth of babies with 'serious disorders' as acceptable, on the grounds that it will reduce suffering. […]

Aversive disablism has inevitably focused on attitudes toward disability, viewing the person's impairment as his/her main identity marker. However, it is important to recognize that we all carry multiple identities and whether one's sex, sexual orientation, race, social class, etc. is regarded as the principal identity marker depends on the perspective of the individual themselves or the observer towards the individual. Gordon and Rosenblum (2001) contended, however, that:

> Whites do not worry about becoming black; men don't worry about becoming women. Disability, however, is always a potential status and in that it is perhaps closest to sexual orientation, whether the latter is considered a choice or biologically determined.

Tregaskis (2004) recognized the difficulty in disentangling multiple identities, for prejudice towards an individual or even group may be for a number of reasons. For instance, Tregaskis considered the hostility she originally faced when initiating research in a leisure centre may have been because she is female, white, dressed formally, a disabled person or, of course, any combination thereof. In addition, it may even have been because she was accompanied by a black male.

Therefore, aversive disablism may need to be viewed simultaneously with aversive racism, aversive sexism, etc. Whether it is truly possible to disentangle the motivation for prejudice towards people facing multiple oppression is questionable. Such an argument can also be extended to people living with multiple impairments, which, when placed in the context of a hierarchy of impairment whereby people with different impairments are viewed as more accepted by society than others […] aversive disablism may have a greater affect depending on the impairment.

Conclusion

It is vital that ways of interpreting attitudes towards disabled people are further developed in order to identify subtle forms of prejudice, otherwise subtle forms of discriminatory practice will become even more entrenched and will be left unchallenged. Aversive disablism, therefore, requires further development in order to capture these subtle forms of prejudice, even from amongst those who purport to hold positive attitudes towards disabled people. Disabled people must be at the heart of this process, making clear what is regarded as a positive attitude toward disability, even if this debate is at times confrontational.

The Labour Government Cabinet Office report on ethnic minorities and the labour market (Prime Minister's Strategy Unit, 2003, p. 101) recognized that 'overt forms of discrimination have become less frequently observed, while covert, indirect forms of discrimination have been more widely recognised', in other words subtle forms of racism are being identified, whereas blatant forms of discrimination are now less prevalent. As a consequence, this administration recognizes that a multifaceted strategy is required to deal with racial discrimination, including new legislation. This 'multifaceted' approach includes not only effective enforcement of legislation, but also regulatory mechanisms, information and guidance, encouragement to members of the BME community to take advantage of opportunities and strategic timetables with measurable objectives.

What may now be required in order to tackle aversive disablism is a multifaceted strategy, as proposed for combating race discrimination in the UK. Attitude change strategies targeting non-disabled people need to take account of subtle forms of prejudice, highlighting the implications of not tackling them. The principal techniques used in the attempts to modify attitudes towards disabled people tend to be: (a) direct or indirect contact with or exposure to disabled persons; (b) information about disabilities; (c) persuasive messages; (d) analysis of the dynamics of prejudice; (e) disability simulations; (f) group discussions (Donaldson, 1980). Failure to incorporate subtle forms of prejudice into attitude change strategies may result in only blatant forms of discriminatory behaviour being challenged, leaving insidious subtle prejudice undermining the lives of disabled people. The identification of unintentional discriminatory practice will play an important part as part of this strategy, which may even come from allies of disabled people. Hence, the 'negative feelings' towards disabled people that are in conflict with the individual belief of being 'fair', as suggested above in terms of aversive disablism, need to be identified in all groups of people, including disabled people.

It has been argued in this article that attitudes towards disabled people in their blatant form may be improving, but more subtle forms of discrimination still exist. Well-intentioned services or even social policies may in reality create forms of oppression towards disabled people. Whilst we may not choose to be a disabled person, it can equally be argued that many of us do not choose not to be disabled either, we simply are who we are. What we must not be is ambivalent about the discrimination and prejudice we face as a consequence of who we are. Likewise, we must challenge prejudice, whether it is subtle or blatant, or the UK vision of disabled people being equal members of society by 2025 will remain just that – a vision.

References

Appleby, Y. (1994) 'Out in the margins', *Disability & Society*, 9(1), 19–32.

Bauman, Z. (1993) *Postmodern ethics* (Oxford, Blackwell).

Begum, N. (1994) 'Snow White', in: L. Keith (Ed.) *Mustn't grumble* (London, The Women's Press).

Bromley, C. and Curtice, J. (2003) *Attitudes to discrimination in Scotland* (Edinburgh, UK, Scottish Executive).

Commission for Social Care Inspection (CSCI) (2004) *Direct payments: what are the barriers?* (London, CSCI).

Delgardo, R. and Stefancic, J. (2000) 'Introduction', in: R. Delgardo and J. Stefancic (Eds) *Critical Race Theory: The Cutting Edge* (2nd edn) (Philadelphia, PA, Temple University Press).

Department of Health (2005) *Independence, well-being and choice* (Norwich, UK, The Stationery Office).

Department for Work and Pensions (DWP) (2003) 'Diversity in disability: exploring the interactions between disability, ethnicity, age, gender and sexuality', Research Report Series no. 188 (London, Department for Work and Pensions). Available online at: www.dwp.gov.uk/asd/asd5/ rports
2003-2004/rrep188.asp (accessed 9 January 2004).

Donaldson, J. (1980) 'Changing attitudes toward handicapped persons: a review and analysis of research', *Exceptional Children*, 46(7), 504–514.

Dovidio, J. F., Kawakami, K. and Gaertner, S. L. (2000) 'Reducing contemporary prejudice: combating explicit and implicit bias at the individual and intergroup level', in: S. Oskamp (Ed.) *Reducing prejudice and discrimination* (London, Lawrence Erlbaum Associates).

Gaertner, S. L. and Dovidio, J. F. (2000) *Reducing intergroup bias: the common ingroup identity model* (Hove, UK, Psychology Press).

Gordon, B. O. and Rosenblum, K. E. (2001) 'Bringing disability into the sociological frame: a comparison of disability with race, sex, and sexual orientation statuses', 16(1), 5–19.

Holman, A. (2004) 'In conversation: Stephen Ladyman', *British Journal of Learning Disabilities*, 32, 113–114.

Imrie, R. (2006) *Accessible housing: quality, disability and design* (London, Routledge).

Johnson, C., Schaller, M. and Mullen, B. (2000) 'Social categorization and stereotyping: "you mean I'm one of 'them'?"', *British Journal of Social Psychology*, 39(1), 1–25.

Law Society (1992) *Disability, discrimination and employment law: a report of the Law Society's Employment Law Committee* (London, The Law Society).

Meertens, R. W. and Pettigrew, T. F. (1997) 'Is subtle prejudice really prejudice?', *Public Opinion Quarterly*, 61(1), 54–71.

Miller, P., Parker, S. and Gillinson, S. (2004) *Disablism: how to tackle the last prejudice* (London, Demos).

Morris, J. (1989) *Able lives: women's experience of paralysis* (London, The Women's Press).

Office of Population, Censuses and Surveys (2001) *The 2001 census of Great Britain general report* (London, HMSO).

Prime Minister's Strategy Unit (2003) *Ethnic minorities and the labour market* (London, Cabinet Office).

Prime Minister's Strategy Unit (2005) *Improving the life chances of disabled people* (London, Cabinet Office).

Soder, M. (1990) 'Prejudice or ambivalence? Attitudes toward persons with disabilities', *Disability, Handicap and Society*, 5(3), 227–241.

Tregaskis, C. (2004) *Constructions of disability: researching the interface between disabled and nondisabled people* (London, Routledge).

Wolbring, G. (2001) 'Where do we draw the line? Surviving eugenics in a technological world', in: M. Priestley (Ed.) *Disability and the life course: global perspectives* (Cambridge, Cambridge University Press).

Young, I. M. (1990) *Justice and the politics of difference* (Princeton, NJ, Princeton University Press).

This chapter poses a serious challenge to all readers. What are the prejudices you carry within you? They may not be obvious. What are your unquestioned assumptions about those you consider to be like yourself and those you consider to be 'other'?

Chapter 24

A collective model of difference

Jonathan Rix and Kieron Sheehy

> At times you may be unsure of where this final chapter is taking you, but that is part of its purpose. It is attempting to get you to think about how our collective notions of what is normal are at the heart of our collective notions of what is different. We all carry with us expectations about appropriate behaviours, practices, ways of looking and being, which we apply to the contexts in which we find ourselves. Disrupting those expectations is a key requirement if we wish to break down barriers to equality, participation and inclusion. Hopefully, by the end of this chapter you will have some useful tools to help you disrupt your own thinking.

We come to this together

Everything we do and everything we say is in the context of other people. Every thought that we have is a social construct finding an individual representation within ourselves.

> *I'm driving a car; the sunlight is coming through from behind me, and I can see it lighting up the trees.*

These words may create a very clear picture in your head. It can only create a picture however if we share an understanding of the words that I have used. Together we are part of a community that understands a language we have termed English. At a basic level this demonstrates the social construction of the ideas that we hold. But these words also rely upon the distribution of knowledge and understanding of ideas. In reading this you are relying upon vast historical and cultural knowledge and working practices, as well as upon the individuals who hold the necessary capabilities to publish this book – whether that be the builders of printing machines, computers, typesetters or the people who made the digital voice recorder that I'm talking into.

Now, of course, these ideas that I'm expressing are based on a multitude of readings, on a life embedded within a myriad of views and encounters. They are ideas and knowledge interpreted by myself – the author – for you to interpret. It is in the moment of recording this that new phrases and ideas come into existence; a new part of the collective knowledge of humanity.

Where you are?

But hold on a minute. Let's go back to the term 'author'. What is an author? Into your mind will have sprung an understanding or a series of understandings of what is meant by the term; but is one of those: *a person driving a Volkswagen Polo on the M25 at 5.38 in the morning, who just looked up at a Church tower between Junction 7 and Junction 8 and flipped the indicator whilst dictating onto an Olympus digital voice recorder?*

There are many questions we could ask to come to an understanding of your definition of this word 'author'. Its meaning and its use, of course, is different for different people, and serves a different function in a different context. It creates an identity that can be used as a resource in negotiating social interactions. *'I'm an author'* could invoke a sense of pity for someone with unrealistic ambitions or it could be a source of immense pride. It is a label that can gain you access to certain organisations or interviews or job roles. It can intimidate, carrying an implication of an access to knowledge that others may feel they lack. It is a term to be used at the right moment in a full understanding that it generates a myriad of different responses dependent upon the time and place, the context in which it is used.

Labels are like this, all labels are socially constructed and represent dispersed socially constructed knowledge, ideas and values.

Woman – Man – Boy – Girl – Cow – Dog

Each of these words suitably translated into a myriad of languages represent different things to different people all around the world.

- A dog is dinner in one place but an emotional companion in another.

> - A girl holds a very different meaning where women are seen to be the responsibility of men, and where their struggle for equality is acknowledged in law.
> - A cow is sacred here ... but an insult there.
>
> And these differences and meanings are debated and discussed, written about in poetry, films, academia, chat shows, soap operas, on buses, trains, between families, friends and colleagues. They are always in flux. You may feel that you have caught it, but they are always on the move, across time and space.
>
> > After all, I am not an author to my youngest child.

Who we listen to

The person who has most time to look at words, to watch them, to identify the concepts, ideas and actions surrounding them, the discussions and thoughts that people are having about them, becomes deemed to be the expert. Expert: another term which carries with it values, assumptions and connotations. A highly complex construct used frequently as if it was simple and self-evidently understood.

Now because we are expert authors on the use of labels we understand the subtleties and nuances, the tensions and contradictions inherent in the application of the term 'expert' to ourselves and to other people. We appreciate that expertise is purely a conjunction of circumstances that has meant that we can claim – and in some way prove our claim – to have access to knowledge and funds of knowledge to which others do not have access.

Given our status as expert authors we are now allowed to present our views on paper, and the publisher will invest money in the hope that our expert author status combined with their status as academic publishers, and the status of those other authors connected with this publication, will mean that this book is bought by those people who are either interested or need to be interested, or need to pretend to be interested in this subject area defined by curriculum and by expert authors across historical time. Maybe our ideas are significant enough to pass into the collective fund of knowledge of other author experts, or policy experts, or aspirational experts.

Importantly, by becoming experts we have ring-fenced our knowledge. We are not experts in football or French language learning or dog-rearing or dog cooking. Our job descriptions entitle us to talk about and be listened to in regard to, for example how people are labelled, and their subsequent engagement within the formal and informal learning process.

How far will you travel with us?

If we were qualified as medical doctors would you expect us to be writing this chapter? What if this chapter was entitled *'The functional relationship between spasticity and sensory development in children identified as having cerebral palsy'*? Would we seem to be the ones slightly out of our area of expertise without appropriate access to knowledge and funds of knowledge?

To validate our participation as medical experts we would have to use the language and the ideas of that predefined or apparently defined area of knowledge, the correct discourse. We would – according to our era – be able to list and name key aspects of the aetiology of cerebral palsy. We would use very specific terms and ideas that allow us to think medically, which have been used by a small number of people who had created and defined their field of expertise called 'cerebral palsy' across the years.

But now let us go back to the start of this chapter. When you started reading did you see yourself in a car with the first author, did you imagine this article being dictated into a machine; did this clash with an unthought-of image in your head of a person writing in a room? What happened when you realised the author was not sitting where he should be? Did you feel that we might be cheating you? And have you noticed a lack of academic references as you have read this? Might we actually not be experts?

You can't be absolutely sure, can you?

So herein lies the first conundrum; for those who do not have full access to the discourse of an area of knowledge, a label can only produce assumptions, ideas and beliefs which are both based upon and undermined by their lack of access to these funds of knowledge, and a conviction that someone must know what it means. But how do those people who don't know what it means know that we who claim to know do actually know? And how do you know we are right? Reputation? Trust? The reassurances of our peers?

History, of course, teaches us that this trust in the expert view is frequently misplaced. It also teaches us that the expert view is generally contradictory. The ineducability of idiots; the innate superiority of white Anglo-Saxon males; global warming; what to do about narcotics; the list goes on and on and on – through religion, politics, economics, healthcare, education, academia – wherever expertise exists there is the tendency towards disagreement and disappointment. Expertise is context specific and time and place dependent. The expert is an authority on very little; the closer they wish to get to certainty the narrower their view has to be. As a consequence, unless perhaps they are focused upon singular acts of cause and effect, they can never be aware of all eventualities; there is always something that was not considered, particularly from beyond their domain of expertise. This is not the same as saying they cannot be very skilled human beings who can make remarkable things happen or provide profound insights. Experts can be authorities on an issue. They can be more aware than others of competing arguments or detailed processes. But their expertise is only ever comparative; it is only ever relative to the ignorance of those people around them. You will have tried to explain to people something about which you know a great deal and seen the look of amazement or fascination, confusion or weariness, interest or ambivalence creep across their face. You know what it is like to have your expertise run headlong into a lack of shared understanding.

The way things are?

In 2000, Maureen Gillman, Bob Heyman and John Swain wrote a paper which outlined the way an identification of learning difficulties comes to define the lived experience of people, how they are viewed by others and themselves. They highlighted how a general belief in the expert medical perspective means that people accept diagnosis as a truth. The dominant expert discourse of the day comes to be seen by the majority as the natural way of things. So how does this work? Well let's see how such a category might arise.

In 2009 the UK government funded NOFAS-UK – an organisation with the strapline: *Protecting children and families by fighting the leading known cause of mental retardation and birth defects* – to run a research project entitled, 'Facing The Challenge and Shaping The Future For Primary and Secondary Age Students With Foetal Alcohol Spectrum Disorders' (Fas-Ed Project). Professor Barry Carpenter, a senior academic who is also a parent of a child with learning difficulties, led the project. The press release (NOFAS, 2009) had a paragraph about how prevalent the disorders are, then a paragraph on possible medical, physical and behaviour outcomes. It then stated:

> Children with FASD will present with a unique set of needs that can make it difficult for many teachers to know how best to support them. In the UK, little is known about FASD and the approaches that may be helpful in educating children affected, and there is currently no government guidance on this. (p. 1)

The statement went on to describe this as an 'emerging area of Special Educational Needs (SEN)', and included two aims:

- to enable educators to support the learning needs of children affected and construct personalised learning pathways that are relevant and pertinent to their learning profile;
- to develop a framework of information sources and teaching and learning strategies.

Within this NOFAS project we can see the development of an 'emerging' category (1-in-100) which needs to be responded to as an individual problem, requiring individual learning strategies based upon a Foetal Alcohol Spectrum learning profile. This repeats a pattern which has gone on since medical practitioners first took charge of 'dividing practices' (Foucault, 1982, p.208) and reaped the financial and professional advantages. For example, Attention Deficit Hyperactivity Disorder similarly involves teachers and physicians working together to identify and control those who step outside the norm. As Thomas E. Brown, PhD explains in his book *Attention Deficit Disorder – The unfocused mind in children and adults*:

> Sometimes an effective treatment for a disorder is discovered by accident, before there is a full understanding of what is being treated or why the treatment works. An effective treatment for ADD syndrome was accidentally discovered in 1937 by Charles Bradley, a Rhode Island physician who was seeking a medication to alleviate severe post-spinal-tap headaches in behavior disordered children he was studying. The amphetamine compound he tried was not helpful for the headaches, but teachers reported dramatic, though short-lived, improvement in the children's learning, motivation, and behavior while they were on the medication. Gradually the treatment gained wider use for hyperactive children with disruptive behaviour problems.
>
> (Brown, 2005, p xix)

So which came first? The drug, the diagnosis, the symptoms or the cure? It is worth noting that in the low doses these drugs are given, the same effect of increased focus and docility would be in evident in anyone, not just children with the ADHD/ADD label (Baughman and Hovey, 2006). Why then are just some children given it? The focus of our attention is of course based upon where we are encouraged to look. This also means we are frequently looking in the wrong place. As any good magician will tell you that is how sleight of hand works.

A good example of finding what we look for may well be autism. There are lots of schools that specialise in this category of students; there is an All Party Parliamentary Group on Autism; there are people in many parts of the world researching autism. These teachers, policy makers and researchers need to identify specific policies, practices and research which justifies their expert status. A key source of funding for researchers is genetics. In 2009, *New Scientist* (Geddes, 2009) reported Professor Simon Baron-Cohen as saying that there were now 133 genes linked to autism spectrum disorders:

> The challenge for future research will be to establish which aspects of autism they can explain, how many of these genes are necessary and sufficient to cause autism, and how they may interact with environmental factors. (p. 11)

In other words we have looked at some of the approximately 25,000 genes identified in the human genome and discovered that so far just over 0.5% can be seen to be to some degree associated with some cases of people identified as having autism spectrum conditions but we don't really know what their significance is nor how they are linked to numerous socially constructed variables and the vagaries of nature.

In the examples above we mention the academics and organisations, who, like the authors of this chapter, have a vested interest in people buying into their view of the world. Their reputations, identities and livelihood to some degree depend upon it. This is not to say that these people do not know a lot; nor is it to say that they are not genuinely convinced by their findings and ways of working. But speculation is at the heart of their certainty, yet this speculation is often not at the heart of those who listen to their words. Foetal Alcohol Spectrum Disorders, Attention Deficit Hyperactivity Disorder and Autism Spectrum Disorders are unquestionable truths for many people around the world, be they labelled themselves or parents, siblings, practitioners or a less interested public. We buy into this expert view as we use these labels in our everyday way; wherever they have come from and whichever profession has sought out and defined the category. As Laurence Kirmayer (2001) noted when talking about depression and anxiety: How depression and anxiety present:

> is a function not only of patient ethnocultural backgrounds, but of the structure of the healthcare system they find themselves in and the diagnostic categories and concepts they encounter in the mass media and in dialogue with family, friends and clinicians. (p. 27)

Or would Laurence Kirmayer just say that because he is Professor and Director, Division of Social and Transcultural Psychiatry, Department of Psychiatry, McGill University and Editor-in-Chief of Transcultural Psychiatry?

Does one thing have to lead to another?

Now you may have spotted a mistake, depending upon how you understand some key terms in this article. At the start of the last section we cited research which said that an identification of learning difficulties comes to define the lived experience of people and how they are viewed by others and themselves. Individuals with Foetal Alcohol Spectrum Disorders, Attention Deficit Hyperactivity Disorder, and Autism Spectrum Disorders would not all fall into the category of people with learning difficulties. People experiencing challenges to their mental health would almost certainly not.

Well ... probably not ... maybe ...

It all depends on what we mean by the label.

The authors use the term people with learning difficulties to label people who are identified as having differences in relation to thinking, remembering and communicating. These individuals are commonly sorted into a whole raft of label subgroups which change across the years (Rix, 2006). In using the term 'people with learning difficulties' this chapter adopts the language advocated by self-advocates such as Simons (1992) and self-advocacy groups such as People First (1992, 2006). They request that labelled individuals are recognised as people before anything else, and that we use the term 'learning difficulties' to remind others that they can learn for the whole of their lives like everyone else. Within UK legislation, however, this group of individuals would come under the broad label of 'learning disabilities'. So let's go back to the mistake; Foetal Alcohol Spectrum Disorders, Attention Deficit Hyperactivity Disorder, and Autism Spectrum Disorders would not necessarily fall into the category of people with learning difficulties who are regarded as having learning disabilities in legislation; however, they would all have learning difficulties in the sense in which it is applied within the education field because they would experience difficulties in an aspect of learning. But this explanation only holds true at the time of writing, within the UK. In the United States, for example, only a small number of these individuals would have learning disabilities because this label is applied to those categorised as having dyslexia, dyspraxia and dyscalcula and none would officially have learning difficulties because the term is not formally recognised.

Our intention is to underline the confusion which exists around the identities and constructs which create and are created by labels. Meanings can often have particular purposes, but unless we have expertise within a discourse we may have an understanding of a word and its politics but be unaware of the purposes it serves for another group. We are unlikely to appreciate the connectedness and history underpinning and promoting the concept. We take it at face value that a word defines a reality, whereas it can shape reality, giving power to those who have control over how the word is used and defined. Consider Table 24.1 which outlines some of the issues which surround the use of labels. As you read through consider the

Table 24.1 Some significant issues for labels of difference (based upon Rix, 2006, 2007)

- We all group and label ourselves and others. It is how we position ourselves in social structures.
- There are tangible patterns of difference which people are drawn to.
- There are numerous social, psychological and historical reasons why certain characteristics and behaviours became categorised.
- Different cultures respond in different ways to different labels and characteristics.
- Terms have political and historical connotations of which many people are unaware.
- People respond to labels as if they are an empirical actuality which can be responded to using proven methodology.
- A label is a tool for communication, organisation and contemplation.

- A label is a generalised term which creates a specific identity.
- Labels mask the variability of labelled people.
- Labels call up stereotypes and carry with them expectations of behaviour.
- Labels frame and frequently limit our expectations of an individual.
- Individual achievements are frequently seen as being because of or despite the label.
- A label can be an excuse for poor behaviour and limit moral responsibility.
- We oversimplify an individual, limiting recognition of complex lives, identities and relationships.
- Labels inherently carry the notion of socially constructed norms.

- A label is frequently a marker of oppression.
- The labelled aspect of an individual is frequently a devalued characteristic.
- Reactions to labelled characteristics cause tensions with an individual's wider identity.
- Negative reactions to a label are a learned response.
- A label facilitates and justifies assessment of individuals within a range of professional discourses and making decisions on another person's behalf.
- Labelled individuals are frequently sidelined in discussion about the label and its application.

- Labels encourage us to see the individual as the problem or the solution.
- Labels do not focus on the kind of support we provide people.
- Labelling individuals encourages us to downplay the centrality of social collaboration.

Table 24.1 Cont'd

- Some individuals engage with labels because they see a benefit, others because the labels are forced on them; some are unaware they are being labelled.
- Labels can provide access to limited social resources.
- Labels can be a route to self-determination and self-awareness.

- People have different personal understandings of what a label means.
- People often have an ambivalence to labels they do not understand or have experience of.
- People tend to define a person by the formal label rather the many other identities which may be of more personal significance.
- There are many formal and informal labels which are used to define different groups.
- Different terms draw responses from people that are more or less positive.
- The meaning of labels and attitudes towards them change over time.

- Changing labels drives change which drives changing labels – a chicken and egg process?
- Changing labels can be seen as irrelevant, confusing, ineffectual, political correctness, misguided.
- Debates about language use are common, with labels as a site of disagreement and confrontation.
- People have favoured terms which many do not give up easily.
- When we change a label we re-engage people in debate about its purpose, form and function.
- Labels can (and should) be contested.
- Labels can confront values and assumptions that underpin our current thinking and actions.

contradictions, the positive and negative possibilities, the continua of responses involved in the classification of diversity and difference. Nothing is clear cut, as much as we might like to think it is or could be.

What should you choose to use?

An alternative to traditional deficit labels are labels of opportunity which 'clearly position the barriers faced by individuals within the social structures around them, not within the individuals themselves' (Rix, 2007: 28). For example Down syndrome is not a useful term in the majority of contexts in which a person with that label finds themselves. The first author suggests it would be more helpful to practitioners if his son (who has the Down syndrome label) was described as a 'person supported by signing and visual communication' (Rix, 2007: 26). How though can such an approach be appropriate for all labelled individuals and in all contexts? Which of the myriad of social structures would you focus upon if we were talking about an asylum seeker or a woman or a racist? And who chooses the label, who can apply it, and where and when? Some labels can prove to be very sticky and powerful. And which aspect of an individual do we label?

Consider this example: at the start of puberty, the first author had sexual explorations with a number of other boys his age. For many years since his sexual interest has been with women. So what is he? Is he bisexual? Is he heterosexual with his first sexual experiences dismissed as early acts of discovery? Was he homosexual at the point when it happened? Does it matter? Has this sticky label affected how you read this chapter? For the first author the label is immaterial. What is important to him is what he learned from the experience about himself and other people. Perhaps we need to see labels in this manner. What is it that is important to that person at a specific time, in a specific context? So the asylum seeker might be a person looking for a room to live in; the woman might be a person who wants the same chance of promotion as her husband; and the racist might be a person in need of a sense of community. These are labels which we can do something about and something with.

And does this mean that you could never use the labels which already exist? Why shouldn't you? If they are useful to that labelled person in that moment and is not diminishing them. If, perhaps, that is what they wish. The key element is the addition of a moral dimension; a consideration of the impact of our terms and thoughts. So when we focus on symptoms or the desire to stream children or our determination to set up a youth club for girls only, we have to consider whose best interests this division on the basis of identified differences serves. Is this just a matter of propping up the values, practices and roles which currently dominate – the preconstituted objects and social subjects of preconstituted reality (Fairclough, 1992) – which are creating and have been created by their own historical predominance? Or are we challenging the inequalities of the status quo?

And of course we still need to contest what we mean by the terms we use. We need to acknowledge the contradictions that are evident from Table 24.1. Suggesting we should just celebrate all differences has the potential to deny us our own rights and needs. Below, in Figure 24.1, we use a perspective lens[1] within a collective model of difference in an attempt to capture this approach to thinking about and labelling difference. The perspective lens is there to remind us that the meanings we attach to people and situations are dependent upon our individual understandings based upon our individual experiences creating and created within the collective context. It is a tool for discussion and reflection. The first four views through the perspective lens

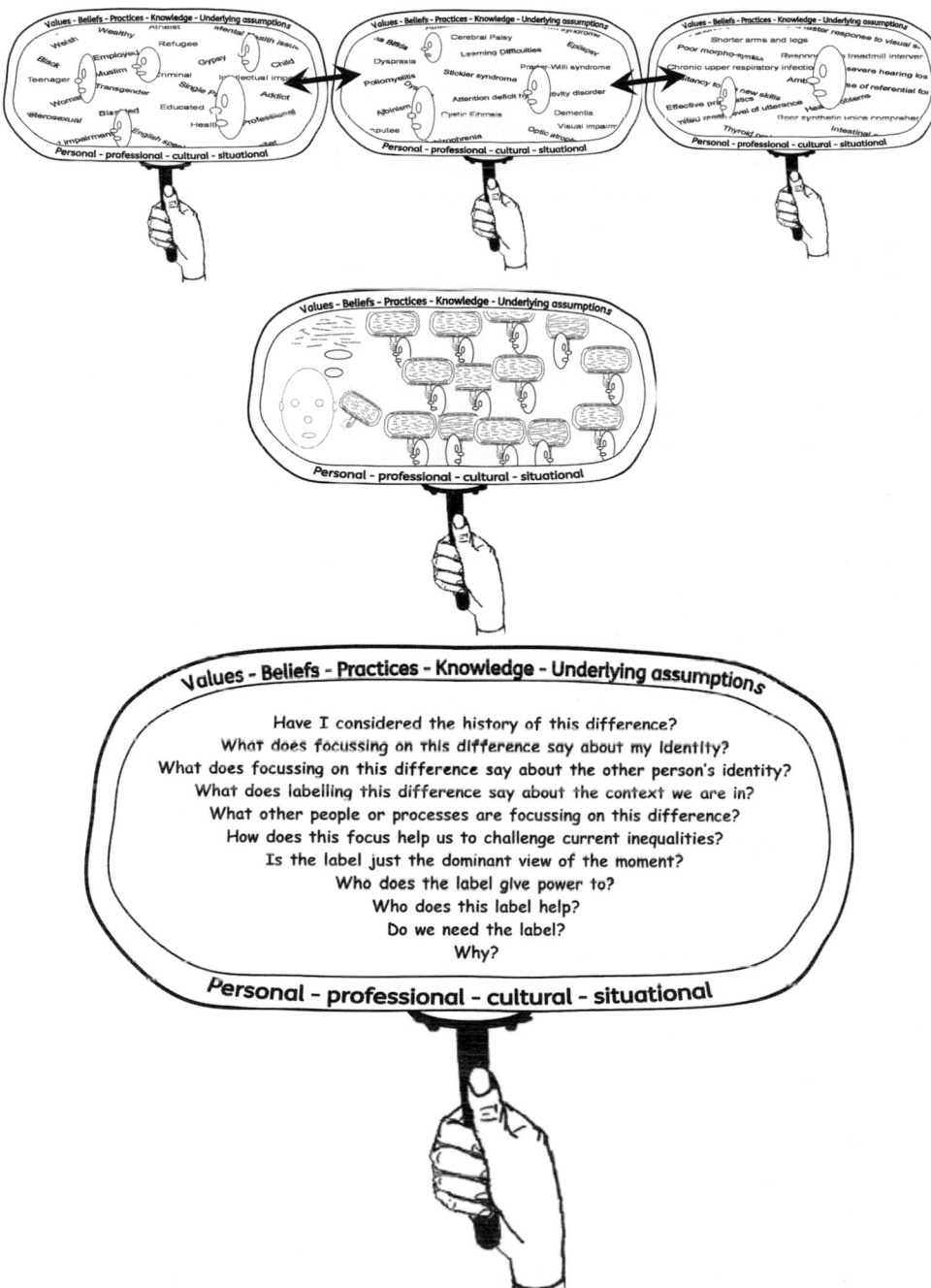

Figure 24.1 A collective model of difference? – Our labels lead to other labels.

are intended to help consider the ongoing process in which we are all involved, in which labels call up stereotypes and further labels to define an individual or groups of individuals. The questions contained with the final lens are laid out in a linear manner, but do not have to be answered in a linear manner. They require us to question our understanding of the historical context of a label, the impact its use has upon identity and power within relationships, and whether this label at this moment in this context is of value and to whom. The final Why? can be applied to all the previous questions, but it is most closely linked the penultimate question – Do we need the label?

This collective model of difference is a question. It challenges you to consider the meanings you apply to yourself and others based on your life embedded within a myriad of views and encounters. You are after all an expert when it comes to the terms you use and where this leads you to. Recognising difference and negotiating its meaning is our collective expertise.

Note

1 The perspective lens is developed from the analytic lens, a research tool described by Rogoff (2003).

References

Baughman, F. and Hovey, C. (2006) *The ADHD Fraud: How Psychiatry Makes "patients" of Normal Children*, Trafford Publishing.

Brown, T. (2005) *Attention Deficit Disorder. The unfocused mind in children and adults*, Newhaven, CT: Yale University Press.

Fairclough, N. (1992) *Discourse and Social Change*, Cambridge, Polity

Foucault, M. (1982) 'The subject and power', *Critical Inquiry*, Vol. 8, No. 4 (Summer), pp. 777–795.

Geddes, L. (2009) 'Gene variant found in 65% of autism cases', *New Scientist*, 28 April, accessed from http://www.newscientist.com/article/dn17041-gene-variant-found-in-65-of-autism-cases.html (accessed on 26 January 2010).

Gillman, M., Heyman, B. and Swain, J. (2000) 'What's in a name? The implications of diagnosis for people with learning difficulties and their family carers', *Disability & Society*, Vol. 15, No. 3 pp. 389–409.

Kirmayer, L. (2001) 'Cultural Variations in the Clinical Presentation of Depression and Anxiety: Implications for Diagnosis and Treatment', *The Journal of Clinical Psychiatry*, 62, 13, 22–28.

NOFAS-UK (2009) 'Facing The Challenge And Shaping The Future For Primary And Secondary Age Students With Foetal Alcohol Spectrum Disorders (Fas-Ed Project)'. From www.nofas-uk.org/PDF/FAS-eD-press-release.doc (accessed on 29 October 2009).

People First (1992) Letter to *Mencap News*, May.

People First (2006) Current Website (2006) Available from: Http://Www.Peoplefirst.Org. Uk/Whoarewe.Html (accessed on 9 June 2009).

Rix, J. (2006) 'Does it matter what <u>we</u> call <u>them</u>? Labelling people on the basis of notions o f intellect', *Ethical Space: The International Journal of Communication Ethics*, 3, 4, 22–28.

Rix, J. (2007) 'Labels of opportunity – A Response to Carson and Rowley', *Ethical Space*, 4, 3, 25–27.

Rogoff, B. (2003) *The Cultural Nature of Child Development*, New York, Oxford University Press.

Simons, K., 1992. *Sticking Up For Yourself: self-advocacy and people with learning difficulties*, York, Joseph Rowntree Foundation.

You may wish to apply the perspective lens to the world around you; perhaps to the first label you come across? Where you start your quest will help you identify your own underlying assumptions and values. And if we wish people to understand and respond to the perspectives of others, then we need to begin by understanding and responding to our own. After all, we are all in this together.

Index